CW01658867

Paying the Price

Paul
Best wishes.

Paying the Price

ROY MASON

Lord Mason of Barnsley

ROBERT HALE · LONDON

© *Roy Mason 1999*
First published in Great Britain 1999

ISBN 0 7090 6368 7

Robert Hale Limited
Clerkenwell House
Clerkenwell Green
London EC1R 0HT

The right of Roy Mason to be identified as author of this work has been asserted by him in accordance with the Copyright, Designs and Patents Act 1988.

2 4 6 8 10 9 7 5 3 1

Typeset in 10/13 Classical Garamond by
Derek Doyle & Associates, Mold.
Printed in Great Britain by
St Edmundsbury Press Ltd, Bury St Edmunds
and bound by
WBC Book Manufacturers Limited, Bridgend

for Marjorie

Contents

Foreword

I am privileged to write the foreword to this spirited and well told story by Roy Mason of his life from pit village to Minister of the Crown. Privileged because he is a miner from mining stock – words which conjure up for my generation a vision of proud men and indomitable women for whom drudgery and hardship were daily companions, with danger and death always close at hand.

From the day Roy Mason was born, his life was dominated by the pit. In his village every man worked at the pit; he walked three miles to school and the pit was there facing the school gates; he started work as a fitter's mate when he was fourteen and on the very first day was taken down the pit to a deep underground tunnel, two feet two inches high, three feet six inches wide and a hundred yards long,* in which men lay sideways hacking out the coal amid dust, fumes and water.

'That was the day my childhood ended,' he says, but already at that early age the pit had begun to shape his character and his beliefs. A pit village was a close community, each dependent on the other and always fiercely protective against the rest of the world.

The picture of the man emerges, steeped in the hardship of life, raging at injustice, ready to challenge authority, bold yet insecure, resourceful, giving no quarter to his enemies, unswerving in his loyalties. It proved a powerful combination when the youthful miner arrived at Westminster. You were never in doubt where you stood with Roy Mason.

When I invited him to become Secretary of State for Northern Ireland, that pot had already boiled over. The previous Government had published several sets of proposals one after another in their attempts to create a new order that would settle the two communities. On every occasion when one side might have been ready to begin talking, the other side would damn the proposals. The next time round the protagonists

* For the present generation, the working tunnel was 66 cm high by 106 cm wide.

would be reversed. And so the frustrating cycle continued. The security situation was dreadful; shootings and killings increasing every year.

I could think of no new proposal that would satisfy both sides. We would need to wait for a favourable opportunity before we made a new start, and meanwhile the deteriorating situation required us to root out the violence and its perpetrators. It was a tough assignment that Roy undertook, but he coupled with it a search for new economic investment that would create new jobs. As this book shows, the experience was an ordeal that left lasting scars and has cast a shadow over his life ever since, although it has never once checked his resolve.

I have always admired the determination with which Roy Mason has shrugged off adversity, conquered circumstance, and worked for the betterment of his fellows. I hope this book will be widely read, especially by that splendid army of new young recruits to the Labour Party to whom all this is history. They will surely realize why the triumphs and failures of the Labour Party in which we grew up will always be an inescapable part of our generation.

James Callaghan
June 1999

Acknowledgements

Many people helped in the preparation of these memoirs and I am grateful to them all. In particular, I must thank the Research Department at the House of Lords, Barnsley Metropolitan Borough Library and my old departments in Whitehall. Staff in all those places responded to my enquiries with unfailing courtesy and efficiency, making my task very much more manageable than it would otherwise have been. If any errors have crept into the narrative, the fault is mine, not theirs.

In particular I owe a special debt of gratitude to Michael Toner, without whose editorial help and encouragement this book could not have been written.

Preface: Targeted for Assassination

I spent most of that morning in 1979 on the unhappiest job any Secretary of State for Northern Ireland has to do: writing personal letters of condolence to the relatives of the dead. After nearly three years in the Province, maybe I should have grown used to it. I never did. Alone in my office at Stormont Castle, I would sit with pen and a notepad trying to find words which might have some meaning for people whose loved ones had been murdered by the Provisional IRA. So many killings, every one of them leaving behind a family sunk in misery. I'm not sure that it's possible to compose a message which can make much sense of that. Every single handwritten letter I finished left me with feelings of inadequacy, anger and sadness.

At least on this occasion I could look forward to going home. At the end of every week, I would take the HS125 plane from Aldergrove Airport, Belfast, to Finningley RAF station, near my constituency in Barnsley. For me, it was a necessary routine; it gave me the chance to spend some time with my wife Marjorie, in relatively normal surroundings. It made the pressures of the job more bearable.

This time, though, the trip promised to be somewhat out of the ordinary. The Prime Minister, Jim Callaghan, had just called a general election and it was pretty clear to all of us that the government had a desperate fight on its hands. The country had been suffering months of industrial disruption in what became known as the winter of discontent, with trade union militancy at such a pitch that even hospitals were picketed. In one notorious case, corpses were left unburied – because of a strike by gravediggers – and had to be stored in warehouses. Not surprisingly, the voters were in an unforgiving mood. I was under no illusions about my own future. In all likelihood, Margaret Thatcher and the Tories would shortly be in power. As I boarded that plane at Aldergrove, I couldn't help wondering what it would be like to go into opposition once more. Frustrating, probably. I believed I had achieved some success in Northern Ireland, not least in reducing the level of terrorist violence; but the letters I had just been writing were a depressing reminder of how much there was still left to do.

As usual, my protection team flew with me. Nowadays, the job of looking after ministerial security in Northern Ireland is handled by the Royal Ulster Constabulary, but back in 1979 it was the responsibility of Scotland Yard. I didn't pay much attention to them; the presence of armed officers was just a routine precaution then. I couldn't know how suddenly that routine was about to change.

As we came in to land at Finningley, I was surprised to see police lined up on the tarmac, all with flashing lights. Uniformed men stood by with flak jackets, carbines, sub-machine guns. I had no idea what was going on, but obviously my Scotland Yard people did. So as I stepped out onto the tarmac with Inspector Pat Thomas, a good man, always courteous and highly experienced. One instinctively had faith in his judgment. Naturally I asked him what was happening.

It seemed I'd have to wait for an explanation. 'Better not to talk here, Secretary of State,' he said. 'We'd better get you back home first.' He was quite firm about it. I was urged into the car and we set off straight away, two police vehicles in front, a third following as back-up, the whole motorcade travelling at speed through villages I'd known a lifetime, past pubs and pitheads and the houses of friends. Of course I was wondering all the while what the problem was, but it was clear that nobody was going to talk. Not then. I just had to contain my curiosity as best I could.

There were policemen everywhere when we arrived home, including an officer carrying a pump-gun outside my front door. I'd come across plenty of scenes like that in Northern Ireland. Never before in Barnsley. 'If you don't mind, I'd like to come in and talk to you,' said Inspector Thomas.

Now over the years, no protection officer had ever crossed my threshold. My home was the only place my wife and I had together, the only place we could enjoy anything like a normal life away from the pressure. But one look at Pat's face persuaded me not to argue.

We sat at the dining-room table, face to face, and he brought out a slip of paper. He told me to read it, 'just to make sure you understand some of the requests we shall be making of you'. And there it was, a printed intelligence report from over the water, from one of our agents, revealing that my house had been subject to reconnaissance and surveillance by the activists in the IRA. Clearly a local team of 'sleepers' had been activated to provide information about the property. They knew about the size of the house, the colour of the stone, the dimensions of the large gable end, the shape of the garden, even the cut and thickness of the privet hedge. It was all there. The significance was only too obvious. Every word on that piece of paper was useful knowledge to a potential gunman or bomber. The IRA intended to take me out during the election campaign.

Well, that sobered me up of course, as it would anybody. I couldn't ignore the threat. The death of poor Airey Neave was still fresh in my mind. He had been one of the Conservative Party's most robust thinkers on Northern Ireland matters and was a close, valued friend of Margaret Thatcher. He had been blown up in his own vehicle as he drove out of the underground car park at the Commons. Clearly I was next on the list. I found myself listening hard to any suggestion Inspector Thomas cared to make.

His first piece of advice was on how to protect myself from gunfire. For all anybody knew, the Provisionals might already have a skilled marksman in the vicinity, just waiting for his opportunity. Therefore I should never go anywhere without wearing a lightweight American bulletproof vest under my shirt. I was assured that it would be virtually unnoticeable; and despite its apparent flimsiness, it would stop most things. I was relieved to hear it.

The precautions did not end there. Two specially armoured cars were being sent up from London and I was told to use them whenever I went out on the campaign trail. Apparently, they were capable of withstanding gun attacks, so I could travel safely round the constituency I had represented for more than twenty-five years. I suppose there was comfort in that, of a sort.

And so began the strangest stint of electioneering I've ever done. There were police officers all around my house, equipped with flak-jackets, binoculars and what seemed to be pump-action shotguns. Nearby roofs were commandeered for round-the-clock surveillance. The wooden hut in the garden was being heavily reinforced to provide a headquarters for the security team. It seemed that the bandit-country of South Armagh had suddenly been transplanted to peaceful Barnsley.

Normal campaigning was out of the question. I couldn't do any canvassing or go walkabout through the town centre or even drop into a local pub for a lunchtime pint. Instead, I'd be hustled into my armoured vehicle every morning, while my protectors kept a keen lookout for anything untoward. We would race off to one of the nearby villages, where I'd be given ten minutes to deliver a short speech. Then it would be back into the car and off to the next venue for another swift blast on the loudspeaker. Nobody knew we were coming. My daily schedule was kept a closely-guarded secret. In fact nobody but my agent Trevor Lindley had the slightest idea where I would be or what I'd be doing. My friends and political supporters must have thought it all very odd. They probably thought it odder still that whenever I popped up so unexpectedly, I was invariably accompanied by tough-looking men who didn't seem remotely interested in Labour Party policy.

But it couldn't last. Barnsley folk don't miss much. Within a couple of days, the whole town was aware that something was amiss. My protectors were growing more anxious too. Somehow they had discovered that the IRA hit-squad was definitely nearby. Precisely what that meant, I never discovered. Somewhere in Yorkshire? In the next street? Round the next corner? Anyway, I wasn't entirely surprised to receive a message from the security service: perhaps the Secretary of State would consider leaving the election campaign; best if he returned to Northern Ireland and what's more allowed himself to be seen publicly on the streets.

Now this may seem a bizarre way of going on. It sounded as if I was being asked to jump straight from the frying pan into the fire. But I was assured that there was method in it. The IRA would know at once that its quarry had gone.The killers would be left kicking their heels, with no target for their attentions. I can't pretend I was happy to leave my constituency at such a time, but I had taken the decision to heed whatever my professional advisers had to say.

So I did as they asked. I packed up and went back to the Province, still surrounded by my minders. But it seemed we had underestimated the venom of the terrorists. My wife Madge had stayed behind in Barnsley, since we assumed at the time that she would not be a target. But the day after I left, she too was informed that she was at risk. The message was that if the IRA couldn't get me, they would probably try to kill her instead. So she flew across to join me.

Even that wasn't the end of it. The security service was convinced that the would-be assassins would not give up easily. If their human targets weren't available, they might well attack our family pet, if only to show that they could strike at will. It meant that Oscar, our much-loved Dalmatian, could be in danger too. So my wife arranged for him to be taken to a different location.

On my first evening back in the Province, I was in Stormont Castle when Jim Callaghan telephoned from Downing Street. Only he and the Home Secretary knew about the situation. He asked if I was all right and I said I was. Did I need any assistance? I told him I needed nothing at all.

'Well,' he said. 'If ever you do, let me know. I can run the show from Number Ten.'

'No,' I said. 'I'll carry on.' I appreciated his kindness. There would have been no reproach from him if had chosen to bat out my time fly-fishing in some remote glen. But I'd had enough of looking over my shoulder. The terrorists might have prevented me running a normal election campaign. I wasn't going to let them stop me doing my job as a minister.

I didn't know then that the threat was just beginning. Or that for years to come, my wife and I would have to be protected round the clock, at home and abroad, in the longest and most intense security operation ever mounted on behalf of a British politician. It wasn't until Labour lost the election and I was out of office that I began fully to appreciate how passionately the IRA wanted me dead. In the words of one Provo godfather, I was the minister who 'kicked the shit' out of the terrorists. Their desire for vengeance is implacable. My family and I have been living with the consequences for more than twenty years.

Illustrations

Illustration Credits

W.F. Gothard: 4. Roy J. Sabine: 7, 11. National Coal Board: 12. Press Association: 14, 24. Ministry of Defence: 19.

1 Beginnings

Like everyone else in our village, I always woke to a fierce rattle at the window. Each morning at 4.30, the official knocker-up would make his way along our street, rousting out the miners for the shift ahead. He had a long pole with a ridged bobbin at one end, which he would drag across the panes of bedroom after bedroom, house after house, with enough force and commotion to stir the dead. Another beginning. Another day. Soon the lampman would come to turn off the gas on the street lights outside. By then the men would be ready, all along our row. I would hear the slamming of doors, a few muttered greetings, the crash of clogs and boots on hard tarmac. Sometimes I'd creep out of bed to watch; my earliest childhood memory is of a dour army of men trudging in the thin light of dawn towards the waiting pithead. The human tide seemed to fill the street, for minutes on end. I think I knew even then that one day I would be making that regular journey.

Coal was the centre of our universe. My father was a miner. My relatives and neighbours were miners. All my friends came from mining families. Until well into adulthood I lived in the shadow of pit headgear and workings. My horizons were bounded by muckstacks which smoked and smouldered and cast a pall of dust and sulphurous filth over the brightest day. I took it all for granted then. Not until much later did I appreciate how heartbreaking it must have been for Mam to try and keep the house clean in such conditions. We had no bathroom in those early days, no flush lavatories. We had to make do with a dry closet, a midden at the end of the back yard, which the men from the council used to clear out every week.

But my parents, Joseph and Mary Mason, probably considered themselves fortunate to have any kind of roof over their heads at all. They had no money when they married. My Dad had walked from Staffordshire to Yorkshire in search of work; my Mam's family were all Yorkshire miners with little to spare. Young working-class couples then couldn't even dream of buying their own home. The best they could hope for was that one day, if lucky, they might be offered a council house. Until that happened, they simply had to take lodgings wherever they could find them.

Even Dad and Mam's married name wasn't quite their own. My Dad's real name was – or should have been – Joseph Smith. His father had left home to fight for Queen and country in the Boer War, leaving his girlfriend pregnant. Her name was Catherine Mason and when my dad was born he was registered in her name. The story had a happy ending though. My grandfather returned from the war in one piece and eventually wed his Catherine. But although they always intended changing my Dad's name from Mason to Smith, they somehow never got round to it. Hence Roy Mason.

I can't say I'm sorry about the omission. Though I served in the House of Commons for thirty-four years, I never came across another MP with my name. My mail never went astray. In ten years as a member of the Lords I've never come across another Mason either. I think I've been lucky: but for chance, I might have been swamped in a whole tide of Smiths.

At any event, with no money, few prospects and a bit of a family skeleton in the cupboard, my parents didn't have an easy start. My earliest years were all spent in other people's houses. I was born in Royston, a large village just outside Barnsley, on 18 April 1924. Mam and Dad were then lodging with people called the Shiltons, at 1 Jubilee Terrace. Shortly afterwards they moved to other digs in Carlton, the village which was to dominate my life until the day I left to go to Westminster. We lived at first in Long Row, a seemingly endless stretch of houses – ninety in all – with a working men's club at one end and a group of twelve stone, semi-detached properties at the other. The poky little houses in the Row, with their earth closets and endless draughts, were all occupied by miners. The respectable stone buildings were for pit deputies and overseers. So it was that I had my first, barely understood, lesson in the realities of money and class. I must have been about five.

Still, it was then that my parents had their first (perhaps their only) stroke of good fortune. After years of scraping by as lodgers – including a period living with my grandparents, the Smiths – they were offered a council house at last. And it wasn't any old council house either, but a property on a spanking new estate, with a patch of garden at the front and another at the back. There were no fewer than three bedrooms and, best of all, we had a bathroom for the first time. I was to live at 3 Manor Street, Carlton, until after I was married, nearly twenty years later.

For my father, it must have seemed the last word in luxury. Like every other miner I knew, his back and his chest, his arms and his legs, were pitted with blue scars, small wounds inflicted by the flying chips of coal as he hacked with his pick at the seams undergound. The slightest cut would fill immediately with black dust, grit which would work its way under the skin and tattoo the flesh. There were no pithead baths in those days, no means for men to clean themselves but for a small metal tub in front of the fire at home. So every miner's body was indelibly marked; you couldn't have put a pinhead on an inch of my father's body without encountering a scar. At least now he would be able to wash himself in relative comfort.

Not that our new house didn't have its drawbacks. Regularly, we'd have to cope with an invasion of crickets from the nearby quarry and muckstack, swarms of the grisly creatures, crawling and chirruping over every surface, scrabbling into clothes and cupboards and crevices, driving us all to distraction. It was a bit of a sport to go after them with rolled-up newspapers, shoes, bare hands; we'd spend hours at it, wiping the things out in battalions. But we never managed to get rid of them all.

By now it was the late Twenties and the country was in deep recession. The boilers and furnaces of industrial Britain stood cold and unused. Of every twenty men in the Barnsley district at that time, eleven were unemployed. Coal was no longer in demand, except in the home; and with unemployment rising by the month, fewer and fewer ordinary people could afford to keep themselves warm. The private coalowners were feeling the pinch too, though I doubt if any miner felt a shred of sympathy for them. They were the class enemy, people who had always kept wages as low as they could, people who pocketed large profits in the good times and thought nothing of closing pits as soon as the going got rough. Like every other mining village in the land, Carlton suffered.

Dad worked, when he got the chance, at Monckton Colliery, near Royston. Like most local miners, he did three days' work for three days' pay. The rest of his meagre income was made up by the dole. It was enough to live on. Just. With the arrival of my younger sister Edna, two years my junior, there were now four mouths to feed in our household. We'd exist on toast and jam, dumplings for the main meal – always at 2.30, the end of the morning shift – boiled and mashed potatoes, filling foods. Clothes were invariably old hand-me-downs. In the evenings, the whole family would sit round the clipping-rug frame and help to make a bit of floor-covering from old rags and remnants.

Sometimes the daily grind took a miserable turn for the worse. We would be told that the mine owner intended to open the pit for a fourth day's working. This was grim news, because anyone getting more than three days' pay lost his dole. The extra money from the pit didn't begin to compensate; though my Dad and the other miners would be working additional hours, their weekly income would fall noticeably. They all knew it would mean more hardship – and sometimes hunger – for their families.

There was one obvious solution. Somehow the men had to prevent the pit working that extra day. The whole village knew what had to be done. I remember dozens of shift-workers sitting anxiously on their doorsteps, waiting. Hoping. Suddenly, the pit-siren would blow, and they would all smile and relax and start chatting to each other. The signal told them that they would not be needed after all. They could still claim their two days' dole. It meant they would be all right for another week.

What had happened, from one point of view, was nothing less than a form of industrial sabotage. Or to look at it another way, a classic example of working-class co-operation. When the siren blared, it signalled that the pit had been 'flushed'; that is, flushed of men. Somewhere deep underground, well out of sight of the pit deputies, a miner would have deliberately staged an incident: a prop would snap, a fall of rocks might be engineered, or perhaps a line of tubs would be sent careering out of control along the tracks. Anything would do, so long as the mine could be temporarily crippled. Of course it would have to be evacuated. The safety-teams would have to be sent in then. There would be no fourth day's working. The dole on which most of the village relied would be guaranteed for another week. I doubt if a single miner took any satisfaction in damaging his working environment; but everyone knew it was necessary, in order to live.

At home, hardship was something we almost took for granted. I can never remember a time when there was enough money for clothes or furniture or anything but the most basic food. Even a coal fire was a luxury. We'd get free supplies when Dad was in work; when he was unemployed, we'd have to cadge the odd bucketful from neighbours, a favour we would of course repay when we could. We all stuck together because we knew no other way. It was how we survived.

But the strain was always there. Dad was on the committee of the Carlton Main Working Men's Club and often wanted to take himself off to the bar during the week. The trouble was, he never had any money and couldn't bear the thought of scrounging off others – especially as his mates were no better off. Since my mam controlled the purse-strings, he'd plead with her for the price of a beer, just fourpence halfpenny in old money. But those few coppers were too precious to be thrown away on a moment's pleasure. I can remember Mam shaking her head in refusal, Dad's raised voice, quarrels erupting out of nowhere. Usually, they would end in Mam crying, Dad sulking. But the pennies would stay in her purse. There would be money for food the next day, possibly a bit of pork dripping to go with it. Perhaps that made such moments of misery worthwhile, but there were many of them. Too many. I don't suppose my parents ever had much joy in their lives, or ever understood real happiness. The grinding business of everyday existence sucked them dry. The whole of my Mam's time on earth was marked by drudgery and worry and poverty until she died of cancer, worn out at the age of forty-six. My Dad outlived her by years, crippled by industrial injury, often in pain, with little comfort or satisfaction to ease him.

Yet for all that, I didn't have an unhappy childhood. Though we had few material possessions, my sister Edna and I grew up knowing that Mam and Dad cared for us – even if the way they showed it probably wouldn't be approved by some of our modern experts in child rearing. From a very early age, I knew that I had to obey the rules. Or else. For example, I was never allowed to play out late at night. A time for homecoming was given and it had to be observed. If I forgot, or attempted to try it on, Mam would be waiting behind the front door, armed with Dad's pit-belt. She'd use it on me too – and very painful it would be. But what I feared most of all was a backhander from Dad. He had hands like shovels; one clout would skittle me across the room. I don't think it ever did me any harm, but it certainly taught me what was what.

Sometimes there were treats. The only time my parents ever went out together was on Sunday nights, when they would go to the club. Mam always looked forward to it, spending an age getting herself ready and paying special attention to her teeth. Years of poor diet and neglect had left them stained and mottled, so she would try to bleach them back to an attractive whiteness. It never really worked, but I think the attempt made her feel better. Edna and I would always watch these preparations with keen anticipation. My parents seldom returned from the club without a chocolate biscuit for each of us, which they'd give us on the Monday morning. It was the greatest pleasure of the week slowly to peel off the wrapper and take that first, delicious mouthful.

Though we could never afford a family holiday – in fact I never had a holiday at all, except under canvas, until after I was married – the Club did arrange an annual day's outing to the seaside for all the youngsters of the locality. There would be buses lined up throughout the village, excited children in their hundreds, all clearly labelled with their names and addresses, parents milling and fussing around, Club officials with lists; it always seemed to take forever before we could set off for Blackpool, Scarborough or Skegness. It was the one day in all the year that any of us ventured outside the village, the only day we would glimpse the sea. Of course we would talk about it for weeks afterwards.

Little by little, the wider world was beginning to make itself felt. In an attempt to make their money stretch just a little further, my parents took in a lodger, Tom Stevenson. Tom was a quiet man, a bachelor and a loner, with no friends or family. He was a non-drinker, a non-smoker and never seemed to spend a penny on clothes, so although he was on the dole he actually managed to put a pound or two aside. Out of his modest savings, he managed to build a crystal radio set. It made quite an impact on the family. For the first time, there was music in the house, dance bands broadcasting from London. The sound must have been atrociously thin and tinny, but to us it seemed a miracle. There was the news too, solemnly read to us by someone who sounded at least as grand as a mine owner.

By this time I was going to Carlton Spring Lane School, run by the fearsome Miss Crackel. She was a lady who seemed to me as ancient as Methuselah, but was probably only in her thirties. Nearly all my schoolmates came from poverty-stricken families, mostly dressed, as I was, in old hand-me-downs or togs bought at the jumble sale. There was a boot fund at the school; when pupils outgrew their shoes and had no younger brothers or sisters to inherit them, they'd be put into the common pool for others to use. It was a question of self-help and common sense among poor people who needed to make every penny count. None of us considered it in the least strange. After all, the soup kitchen would make periodic visits to the village, and we children thought it perfectly normal to queue up for a bowl of something that was always hot and sometimes quite tasty.

At Spring Lane we very quickly learned about the hierarchy. There were the teachers first of all, figures possessed of a terrifying authority who knew everything there was to know. Then there was Miss Crackel, even more remote, who could curdle any one of us with a mere glance. Beyond her stood the grand picture of the King; and at the top of the whole awesome pile we had the image of God, a Being who recorded all our faults in his book of judgment and never missed a thing.

Appropriately enough, our days began with prayers in the school hall, the lesson always read by Miss Crackel in tones which suggested that she had just brought the tablets down from Mount Sinai. Afterwards we would troop off to class, where we'd sit in neat rows chanting the alphabet and our multiplication tables. Seven times seven is forty-nine; nine times nine is eighty-one. Rote learning, maybe, but it worked. I seem to remember that all my classmates could read by the time we left Miss Crackel's care; and to this day I can rattle out the answer to seven times eight without having to think about it.

But a time of decision was approaching for all of us. At the age of nine, we transferred to the top school – also in Carlton – where for the next two years we'd be prepared for the exam which could make or break us: the dreaded County Minor Scholarship. Those of us who overcame that hurdle could go on to the big school in Barnsley, where they taught exotic subjects like French, and where it was possible to dream of becoming a bank clerk or a civil servant, someone who wore a collar and tie to work. But to fail . . .? It hardly bore thinking about.

I wanted to pass, desperately. Somehow I sensed that a whole world of opportunity was out there, just waiting for me to grasp. As the day of the exam approached, I began to pray, harder than I'd even prayed before. I convinced myself that, with a bit of a helping hand from the Almighty, I would succeed. It was a bitter disappointment – one of the worst of my life – when I failed. I knew then that I'd have to leave school at fourteen as I knew the truth of what all my Dad's friends kept telling me: 'There's nowt for thee, lad. Only pit!'

And that was the trouble. I didn't want to go down the pit. My dad didn't want me to either. Precious few miners urge their sons to follow them underground. Yet looking back, I'm pretty sure that my parents nevertheless felt a guilty sense of relief over my result. Had I passed, they would never have been able to afford to kit me out with school uniform, or pay my daily bus fare to Barnsley. They must have been dreading the moment they had to tell me. At least now that was one worry out of the way.

So it was that even before I set foot in the senior school, a little way up the village, my future was decided. In three years' time I would become a miner, like my dad and his dad before him. Since the Old Carlton Pit (later Wharncliffe Woodmore 1, 2 and 3 pits) was just across the road from my new school, it wasn't a prospect I could ever forget.

For a while, though, I could still enjoy what was left of my childhood. Since I had a good singing voice, I joined the choir at Carlton Church and spent many a pleasant Sunday at devotions. We began with a confirmation service at 8.30 in the morning (at which I was later confirmed), followed by the eucharist at 10.30 and Bible practice at 2.30. Then it was back in the choir for the final service of the day, at 6.30. I loved dressing up in my cassock and surplice; in fact they were far and away the best clothes I ever wore. I loved the hymns – and still do.

I was twelve years old when the ultimate tragedy struck my village. It began in the small hours of Thursday 6 August 1936, with a long, low rumble, a sound like the mutter of distant thunder; only it wasn't thunder. Nothing so innocent. Even as I rushed to the window to see what was happening, the street outside was filled with people, women in shawls, men still buttoning up their working togs, all of them with strained, frightened faces, all of them rushing to the pithead. They knew what had happened: the worst thing possible. The old Carlton Pit had blown up at 3.15 a.m., with fifty-eight men on the night-shift still underground.

There was no question of staying indoors. My dad and mam were out of the house instantly and I followed behind with Edna tagging along. We were only children, but we knew where we had to be. There was chaos round the pithead, a harsh glare of lights, crowds milling in despair, women crying, men numb with shock. I think every miner there knew how bad it was. For hours we watched and waited, desperate for news from below. Ambulances came, mine-safety teams, union representatives, management officials. By dawn, hope was giving way to fear. Rumours swept through the crowd whenever a body was brought to the surface. 'Who is it? Who is it? Who?' Wives and relatives pushed themselves forward, frantic for news of their husbands., brothers and sons. Pit deputies would twitch the blankets covering the dead. 'This is Bill,' they'd say and some poor woman would collapse in grief. 'This is Johnny. This is Dave. This is . . .' We could only listen helplessly as name after name was announced.

As my school was so near, it was used as an emergency mortuary, the bodies laid out with whatever reverence could be managed in the school hall and in classrooms where evidence of the last lesson was still scrawled on the blackboard. There were whole lines of them, men I knew, neighbours, friends, the fathers of schoolmates. It could so easily have been my own dad lying there.

There were no survivors from that awful night. Only one man was brought up still alive, but he died of his injuries soon afterwards. A single, devastating gas explosion had torn the heart out of our village. To this day, there are families in Carlton who well remember the misery of losing a loved one in that disaster. My close friend lost his father, Wesley Hall.

The event shocked the whole country. The King sent a personal message of sympathy to the bereaved. But in those pre-war days of private enterprise, little practical help was offered by the pit owners. Most of the assistance came from the miners themselves. They set up a disaster fund and gave until it hurt.

I will never forget George and Beryl Formby, two of the very biggest stars of the variety circuit, coming to the Alhambra Theatre in Barnsley to give their services free in aid of the stricken families. There were many, many private acts of generosity like that. But few of them came from the miners' employers.

Slowly, over weeks and months, Carlton struggled back to something which seemed like normality. Children returned to school. The pit reopened. Everyday life began reasserting itself. But there was always something missing; and all those newly dug graves were a constant reminder of what we had lost.

I no longer spent my weekdays in the shadow of the Old Carlton pit. Shortly after the disaster, my school was condemned and I was transferred to Royston Secondary, about 3 miles from my home. I walked there and back every day, rain or shine, usually in the company of my mates. For the first time, I was being taught exclusively by male teachers, but it made no difference to my rather indifferent standards of academic attainment. Though I enjoyed school, I can't pretend that I worked especially hard. After all, there wasn't much point. I knew what the future held.

Now and again my lack of attention would land me in trouble. The art master was one John Willie Davey, more than 6ft tall and fierce with it; when he told us to sit and listen, he meant it. Unfortunately, I wasn't the least bit interested in what he had to say and spent my time at the back of the class daydreaming, whispering to my friends and generally wasting my time. Sadly for me, he caught me at it. He ordered me to the front, told me to bend over, and gave me ten sharp whacks with a paint palette.

For some reason, this struck me as seriously unfair. I stamped back to my desk, kicking a chair over on the way. A bad mistake. John Willie ordered me out again, bent me over and gave me another ten wallops.

Steaming at the injustice of it all, I went home and told my Dad. Normally, this was something I would never do, since there was a high risk of getting another clout for my trouble. This time, though, he seemed to take my side. He put on his coat and strode off to have it out with my teacher. I stayed behind, eagerly awaiting the outcome.

Eventually Dad returned, in a subdued frame of mind. He'd had second thoughts about the incident, he said. My teacher was right to punish me after all. I looked at Dad, all 5 ft 7 in. of him. I thought of John Willie's hulking, 6 ft 2 in. frame. It began to dawn on me that size might have something to do with it.

But I was far too busy to dwell on such setbacks. By now I had joined the Scouts, the 34th Methodists in Royston, and threw myself enthusiastically into a whole range of new activities. For the first time, I was actually beginning to achieve things: proficiency badges, gold cords, a bushman's thong and entrance into the Scout Craft Shield competition. I became a patrol leader and eventually I made it to the dizzy height of First Class King's Scout, an award presented to me during the war by the Mayor of Barnsley, Councillor George Mason (no relation).

Best of all, I managed to get access to a tent and learned how to camp in the open air. On Friday evenings I'd head off by myself into the countryside, hiking miles through fields and woodland, sleeping under canvas and not returning home until Sunday night. I'm still not sure whether it was the solitude I enjoyed, or just the break from routine; but those little trips added up to the only holidays I'd ever known.

I left school in the summer of 1938, more or less literate, moderately numerate and without a prospect in the world. I was fourteen years old. On the other side of the North Sea, Hitler was ranting and strutting and threatening all Europe; at home there was talk of war and belated preparations for the ordeal to come. The coal industry was picking up at last, with both pits in my village offering employment – most of the time – for the more than 2,000 experienced miners on their doorstep. But there was no work for an unskilled lad straight out of the classroom. My first experience of the adult world was to trail off to the benefits office in Carlton and sign on the dole. It wasn't worth much. In those days, a 16-year-old unemployed lad would receive just 6s a week; so at 14, I'd have been getting even less, probably no more than 5s.

I felt lost. It didn't matter that there were dozens of other boys in my position. It seemed I'd been judged by the grown-up world and found wanting. Though I gave the dole money to my Mam, I couldn't help seeing myself as a useless mouth in the community, frittering my time away, making no useful contribution. I'd play kick-can along the street with the other jobless lads or go for long walks, looking for birds' nests on the way. In those days, it wasn't thought a sin to rob a thrush of her eggs. Sometimes, when it was hot, I'd swim in the canal, known locally as the cut. In the evenings, a crowd of us would hang around under the corner streetlamp, idling the hours away, fighting occasionally, as youngsters do, spinning out the tedious hours. It never occurred to us to cause any real trouble or to damage our neighbours' property; we'd never have got away with it even if we'd tried.

The nearest form of what you might call proper entertainment was in the village of Cudworth, about 3 miles away. The Rock Cinema was a wonderful place, with silent films and a pianist banging away industriously below the screen. Every week when I got my Saturday penny – which had to last seven days – I'd walk there, anticipating the treat to come. It cost ½d to get in. Alternatively, you could pay for admission by handing over two clean, empty jamjars. But I didn't have those very often. My other halfpenny went on a small bag of what we called spice, usually broken bits of liquorice allsorts. Bliss. The show was always worthwhile, with a main film – usually a western – followed by a serial guaranteed to bring me back the following week. Invariably, each episode ended with the hero hanging over a cliff or tied securely to the rail tracks. Could he possibly manage to avoid the drop? Would he escape before the approaching train cut him in two? It was always a relief to discover that somehow he'd managed to scramble free. With one bound.

My other glimmer of light in those frustrating months came from my closest schoolmate, Roy Mansfield. He was the son of a pit under-manager, the closest thing to nobility known in a mining village. Roy's dad had the power to hire and fire, which meant that he was both respected and feared. A nod from him ensured that a family could live in some security. A frown guaranteed trouble. But I always found him a friendly, approachable man. I was often invited to the Mansfield house, a large, detached stone bulilding in the village, where everything was more gracious and spacious than anything I knew at home. The family were great musicians. Of an evening, they'd gather round the piano; a violin would be produced, then a mandolin. We'd sing ballads, love-songs, traditional airs, everything from 'Greensleeves' to bits of Gilbert and Sullivan. It was wonderful – all the more so because of my choral training.

Better still, they had that rarest of luxuries, a car. Thanks to my friendship with Roy, I'd occasionally be invited to go for a spin. Now and again, I was even lucky enough to be taken to the Ritz Cinema in Barnsley, where we'd sit in the circle to enjoy the cartoons. But for me, the real magic was what came before the programme; I'd stare open-mouthed as the mighty Wurlitzer organ rose from the orchestra pit with Trevor Willets at the keyboard and the latest tunes at his fingertips. It was a glimpse of another world.

Roy knew how frustrated and unhappy I felt as my weeks of involuntary idleness extended to months. He had been taken on the moment he left school and was now gainfully employed in the pit as an apprentice electrician. It couldn't have been easy for him to have a friend who was just kicking his heels. So one day he came up to me, an excited look on his face. He told me to go and see his dad. I knew this could be my chance at last; and so it proved. Old Mr Mansfield offered me a job as a fitter's mate underground. It was, of course, just about the lowest position in the pit. My duties would basically be to carry the fitter's toolbag and do as I was told. But that didn't matter, any more than it mattered that I'd got the job through a bit of friendship. I finally had some kind of a future.

My dad was ambivalent. He was a proud man and he still didn't want me to go undergound. Mam, I think, was reluctant to lose her little boy – I was still only fourteen – to the dangerous world of work. But they desperately needed the extra money my job would bring. And there was nothing, absolutely nothing, in the village which offered alternative employment.

At least I was to be given a flying start, as the under-manager's protégé. When I turned up for my first shift, nervous as a kitten, I discovered that the pit overman, Ken Lee, had been given special instructions to look after me. He presented me with an official's spotlight and a deputy's yardstick, which had been cut down to size to suit me. I've never been the tallest of men; when I was fourteen, I suppose I must have been all of 5 ft 2 in.

With those small ceremonies completed, I was shown into the pitcage, still clutching my gear. I had no real idea what to expect. Suddenly the cage began to drop, faster and faster, a terrifying rate of descent which left my stomach desperately trying to catch up. Down and down we plunged into the darkness. Two thousand feet. Then I staggered as the cage jerked to an abrupt halt.

I discovered then that it can be a godsend to be small. We stepped out at the bottom of the shaft into a chamber not much more than 5 ft 6 in. high. In front of us stretched the tunnel to the coalface, low and narrow, full of clamour and activity and the screech of tubs on rails. Apprehensively, I followed as Ken Lee led the way, trying not to imagine the crushing burden of rock which lay above us. Deeper and deeper we went, sometimes bent double, heading always towards the noise ahead, squeezing past miners and pitprops and secondary tunnels which had long been exhausted. It was difficult to believe that men had actually dug coal in such cramped conditions; difficult, that is, until we reached the coalface, the Beamshaw Seam, 1 ft 10 in. of coal, 4 in. of clod, total height 2 ft 2 in. A bedlam. The noise was overwhelming, thickening the air, pounding through the bones. I was on my belly, crawling through, coughing in the swirling dust. Men were ahead of me and around me, lying on their sides, contorted, black with muck, stripped to their underpants, cutting and hacking with picks, sweating, tearing out the coal and clod.

So this was to be my future: squeezed with so many others into a tunnel 2 ft 2 in. high, 3 ft 6 in. wide and 100 yd long. The story was that even the mice were bow-legged in this place.

For the rest of the shift I followed Ken Lee through all the other workings, trying as best I could to make sense of it all. I don't think I succeeded. It was beginning to dawn on me that the pit was a terrifying place and I understood at last why Dad had been so reluctant for me to follow him underground. Still, at least I'd been given my introduction to the pit. Next day I would have to begin work in earnest.

And that proved an even more sobering experience. I was introduced to my new 'gaffer' the next morning, just as I emerged from the cage at the bottom of the pit shaft. His name was Joe Newman, a rough, tough Geordie, hard as nails and brusque with it. I learned just how brusque at the end of my shift, as I was approaching the shaft ready to go to the surface. Suddenly Joe grabbed me, hauling me out of the way. A stretcher party rushed past, urgently making for the cage. The blanket-covered figure on the stretcher lay very still.

'There y'are, lad,' growled Joe. 'First casualty. Feet first means they're dead.'

I watched too shocked to speak as the cage shot up towards the surface, carrying the remains of another dead miner. I think that was the moment my childhood ended.

2 A Working Life

I would stumble out of bed at 4.45 a.m., splash a little cold water on my face – I was still too young to be shaving regularly – and grab a quick cup of tea. No time for breakfast, when I had to be at the pithead for 5.15. I'd hurry along the lane with my fellow miners, sometimes sniffing the sweet aroma of pipe tobacco in the still morning air. I seldom noticed the muckstacks which lined the route, but sometimes a skylark would swoop low over the lines of trudging men before soaring our of sight. I would stare after the little creature, envying her freedom to fly in the sun.

Working underground was hard, dirty and dangerous; working as Joe Newman's lad made matters worse. I was intimidated by him from the start, shrinking from his barks of dissatisfaction. Occasionally, when I made a mistake or lagged behind, he'd threaten me with a raised hammer. He never used it on me, but I didn't doubt that he was capable of it. Only when I developed a basic competence underground, long months later, did we settle into anything that could be called a partnership. But it was strictly for underground. We never got together on the surface and never became friends.

Meanwhile I carried his tools and picked up what I could of the fitter's trade. Little by little, I began to learn how to do the simple jobs: laying compressed air pipes in the tunnels, cleaning and polishing the compressors, oiling the coal-cutting machines. By now the nation was at war, struggling to survive the onslaught of Adolf Hitler; but my world was more than 2,000 ft below, crouched in darkness, wrestling with equipment I barely understood.

We always had a brief break at 9.30, twenty minutes for our 'snap', which in my case was usually a bottle of water with four slices of bread and lard. Now and again there would be pork dripping instead, but that was a rare luxury. To preserve my food, I had to tie my paper-wrapped sandwiches and hang them from an overhead girder. Otherwise the mice would have had them. There were whole armies of these vermin down the mine; if you turned out your lamp and sat in the pitch blackness you could hear them scrabbling and scuttling all around. Originally, they had come below in the feed given to the pit-ponies; now they were breeding and roaming all over the place.

I never got used to the squalor underground; like every other miner, I just learned to live with it. I worked in filth, ate in filth and was filthy myself from the moment I started a shift until after I finished. There were no lavatories, of course; men just squatted where they could, in any convenient corner. The smell was part of everyday experience, like the dust, noise and darkness.

And always there was the unending battle for survival. At the face, men fought each other for access to the tubs which took the coal to the pit shaft. Their wages depended on how many they filled; if there were no tubs, they would receive only the basic minimum pay. It wasn't nearly enough for a decent living. So they threatened each other, shouting and shoving, sometimes punching, to gain access to those precious tubs. It was a rotten system, imposed by the pit-owners in search of what they no doubt thought of as efficiency; they called it piece-work, but it set man against man and stripped honest workers of their last shreds of dignity.

Not that anybody in charge gave a damn for what the miners felt. Every morning at the pit bottom, we had what I can only describe as a human cattle market, where men with no regular jobs would simply stand, hoping desperately to be given a temporary stint on the coalface or in the stalls – other working units – if a regular employee had failed to turn up. The pit deputy in charge would size these 'casuals' up like an auctioneer, selecting the ones he favoured. The leftovers were condemned to do the most menial, lowest-paid jobs in the pit, which meant they would hardly be paid enough to keep body and soul together. Such was the power of the deputy.

Injuries in those days of private enterprise grabbing and getting were commonplace. The most dangerous practice then was piece-work, where a man got paid for what he did. It meant that safety was all too often pushed to one side in the drive to get the job done. Men would cut corners, take chances, anything to earn a few extra shillings. For example, a coal-cutting machine would always have a water-spray fitted to it to kill the dust while the men were working. One of my many jobs, once I learned the fitter's trade, was to go and repair these sprays. The miners were in the habit of breaking them off. They didn't care about the dust they were breathing; they just didn't want to be kneeling or lying in water while they worked. They were quite prepared to risk their health in the long term in order to be comfortable in the short term. It was a crazy attitude, but one actively encouraged by the way the pits were run.

Perhaps it's not surprising that pit safety became something of an obsession. I'd seen the tragedy of what happened at the Old Carlton mine. I'd seen a dead man carried out on my second day underground. I was stretchered out myself on no fewer than three occasions, damned lucky to be alive.

While still in my teens, I managed to master most of the machines which cut the coal and kept the mine alive: the conveyors, the compressors, the big Jeffrey Diamond coalcutters and the tupping machines which – despite their suggestive name – did nothing more exciting than separate the coal from the rock and clod.

So on this unforgettable shift, I went to maintain a machine driving one of the tunnels. It was still operating, roaring and grinding in the dust and near darkness as I crawled towards it. The two colliers working it grinned and waved me on. A routine moment, until everything changed. I saw the sudden change of expression on my mates' faces. One of them shouted: 'Look out! Look out!' I was backing away, frantic to get out, not quite understanding. Then I knew. The roof was groaning and bucking, coming in. Great rocks crushed down, unstoppable. I lost sight of the others as I turned and wriggled to reach safety. I was on my feet, stumbling. Then a vast slab crashed on its end, toppled and slammed into me. I was laid out, helpless, unable to move. All the lamps were out. My section of the pit was in complete darkness. The dust was choking. Obviously more rocks were about to fall. I knew my colleagues were buried somewhere nearby. I could hear groans. I screamed for help, trying to pull myself free. Impossible. There were lights in the distance, bobbing towards me. They seemed to take an age. But at last my fellow miners were around me, grunting and heaving to move the rock which had me trapped. Others started tearing at the rubble covering my mates.

We were rushed out on stretchers, all three of us. One of the others went feet first. Dead. His name was Laverick, and I think it was his timely shout which saved my life. His mate was still alive, but badly injured, his bones crushed and broken.

Once on the surface, we were given a quick check in the first-aid room and then taken to the old Beckett Hospital in Barnsley. Poor Laverick went to the mortuary, we two survivors to casualty. They were well used to industrial injuries there; in fact they were often grossly overworked by the sheer number of men pouring in with injuries suffered in all the pits of the locality.

In the event, I was found to be suffering from nothing worse than bruises and shock. I was discharged there and then, returning to work next day. No miner could afford to do otherwise.

My second accident was even more terrifying. I was repairing a coalcutting machine in a side-tunnel, a cul-de sac with no means of escape if anything went wrong. I was working by myself; it's possible to feel very alone underground. Suddenly I heard a crack. I turned. The pit props were bending and snapping, the roof beginning to crumble. I didn't wait another second. I was crawling and scrambling towards the tailgate, 10 yards away, when the roof collapsed. I was panicking as rocks crashed on my back and legs and all around me, heaving them out of the way when I could, desperate not to be trapped. It's true what they say about your life flashing before your eyes at such moments: I thought of Mam and Dad, my sister and home. In that awful moment I was convinced I'd never see them again. But I was still capable of movement, still wriggling. I reached the entrance as the roof roared down behind me, tons of crushing rock that would have snuffed me out like a candle. I lay there shaking. Praying. Thanking God for my escape.

So once again I was taken by ambulance to the Beckett. Once again I'd got away with it, suffering nothing but shock and bruises. And of course I was back underground next morning.

As indeed I was after my third accident. I was repairing another machine which was fitted with a large metal key. I must have struck the thing with a careless hammer, because it suddenly flew out, whacking me across the head and knocking me out. But this time I didn't have to go to the hospital. The boys in the first-aid room on the surface took one look at me and decided that I had only been concussed. Nothing to worry about. They assured me I'd be as right as rain after a good night's sleep; and so it proved. But I could have had a hairline fracture and nobody would have been much the wiser.

Yet in my first few uncertain months underground, such dangers were far in the future. My concern then was just to get through each day without upsetting Joe Newman or letting my family down.

Now that Mam had another breadwinner in the house, she was trying so hard to please. When I got home after a shift, covered in grime and my pit togs stiff with dust, she'd always have a hot meal waiting. I'd take off my outer clothes before I walked in the back door, banging them against the wall to shake off the worst of the muck, then have a quick rinse of the hands before getting down to a plateful of dumplings and gravy. As soon as I'd finished eating, I would stretch out on the clipping rug in front of the coal fire and fall fast asleep. I don't think I've ever felt so tired. But I was earning, which was something to be proud of. The pay at the end of my first week was 19s 4d – less 6d. Dad insisted that I went straight to the union box, paid my tanner and joined the National Union of Miners. So I became a fully paid-up member at the age of fourteen, and I've never regretted it.

I was learning all the time, not just about the way the pit operated but about my new working colleagues. What struck me from the very beginning was that almost every miner wanted to escape. Somehow. Anyhow. They didn't like spending their lives underground, shut off from the sun and the wind, hated the rotten working conditions and the power of the distant coalowners. Who could blame them? So they'd fill in their football-pool coupons week after week, dreaming of that elusive treble chance. Some bet on the horses as well, others on the dogs. They must have known they were wasting their hard-earned money; but few of them could see any other way of breaking free. One stroke of luck might transform their lives.

I very soon came to share in that hope for something different, though I was pretty sure the answer didn't lie with Littlewoods, Vernons or the local bookies' runner. There had to be a better way of making something of my life.

And then, quite suddenly, my small ambitions hardly mattered any longer. On Sunday 3 September 1939, I was down the pit maintaining a compressor when the word came down: 'We're at war.' Within minutes, the details of Neville Chamberlain's broadcast spread throughout the workings. The whole nation was plunged into the crisis it had desperately sought to avoid and for which it was still unprepared.

Like thousands of others, I couldn't wait to get into uniform. Though too young to fight, I was eligible to join the cadet force; before the year was out I had signed up with the Air Training Corps in nearby Royston, spending my nights after work in square-bashing, rifle drill, aircraft recognition and the (very) basic principles of flight. As in my activities with the Scouts, I tried my hardest to master every skill I could. By the time of the fall of France, in 1940, I'd been made up to cadet flight sergeant. Sometimes of an evening I'd take my squad at the quick march through the school yards at Royston Secondary Modern School, where the lasses of the Girls' Corps would be playing netball. They'd squeal in mock outrage as we crashed through their game, but I think they were all delighted to see the cadets. Certainly my lads enjoyed the attention, puffing out their chests and doing their about-turns as smartly as Guardsmen.

I had eyes only for one of the girls. Her name was Marjorie Sowden and she lived on a nearby railway estate. Though we'd known each other for some time, gradually becoming friendlier, the relationship wasn't entirely straightforward. Her father was an engine-driver. Mine was a collier. The feuds between railwaymen and miners were well known in those days. I think a few eyebrows were raised when I started going out with Madge; but as far as we were concerned, our relationship was helping to bridge the gap. It was to prove a long and enduring courtship.

By now the pits were going full blast to meet the demands of war.

Thousands of Bevin Boys were being conscripted – young men ordered to work underground. I was no longer the most junior and insignificant employee at the mine, but well on my way to becoming a skilled fitter. I was beginning to feel more confident underground, more aware of the earning opportunities. So it was with the best of intentions that I encouraged Dad to leave Monckton pit and come and join me at the New Carlton, where there were jobs going begging at the coalface and the money was better.

It was a bad mistake. Dad was older than the other men on the face and from the start found it difficult to match their strength. The stint was 10 yd of coal-getting a day – approximately ten tons – and the miners had to crouch on hands and knees, cutting and shovelling in a seam just 2 ft 2 in. high. It was backbreaking, exhausting work, demanding reserves of stamina Dad just didn't have. At the end of most shifts, he'd find himself way behind the others. But his stint had to be cleared before he could go home. He would work on, up to an hour or more, determined to reach his quota no matter what. At the end of it all, he'd drag himself off, almost too tired to put one foot in front of the other. But for the first time I could remember, he was earning a decent wage. That mattered to him more than anything.

Meanwhile, I was counting the days until I was old enough to join up. The war was going badly. Most of Europe was now under Hitler's heel. Panzers were thrusting towards Moscow. U-boats were prowling the Atlantic, leaving scores of sunken ships and thousands of dead seamen in their wake. Whether through youthful patriotism or a desperation not to be left out of a turning-point in history, I wanted to fight. Mining, of course, was a reserved occupation then, but I was convinced I could talk my way through. So shortly after my eighteenth birthday, I presented myself at the Barnsley recruiting office to volunteer for the RAF. I was genuinely surprised to be turned down.

But I wouldn't give in. At Barnsley they were obviously primed to keep a lookout for miners trying it on. Perhaps in distant Sheffield they wouldn't be so alert. I made the trip into the big city, rehearsing what I would say, hoping not to be tripped up. Some hope. The recruiting officer must have known exactly what I was the moment I walked through his door. It only took him a couple of pointed questions to confirm the truth. I was turned down again and had to endure a ticking-off for wasting everybody's time. I would never serve with the RAF in time of war. It was the most bitter disappointment of my life. I feel it still.

There was nothing for it now but to make the best of my work underground. I'd already been going to evening classes to earn my pit deputy's ticket and after a year of study passed the exam. In theory, it meant I was now qualified for middle management, but I was pretty certain I would never be offered such a post. It didn't really matter; I had another plan. I suspected that after the war, the coal owners would go back to their bad old ways, closing down pits willy-nilly and throwing countless miners on to the dole. But safety men would still be needed to keep the pits ticking over. A man with a deputy's ticket could always be sure of finding work. My qualification, in fact, was nothing less than an insurance policy.

There was another advantage too. Miners were allowed to elect their own safety experts, men who regularly checked every nook and cranny of the pit. Once I had my deputy's ticket I was qualified to be an inspector, representing my fellow workers in a way which really mattered to them.

Meanwhile there were other activities to fill my days. Madge had gone off to join the Land Army, where she learned to plough, drive a tractor and milk cows in the cause of the war effort. I'd spend hours scribbling letters to her, describing in exhaustive detail the gossip of the pit, how I was getting on since joining the local Labour Party ward and my plans to take a qualification in mechanical engineering at Barnsley Technical College. Hardly the most romantic correspondence, but we both knew how we felt; it could be difficult to set out emotions on paper in those constrained times.

But in one area at least, I was beginning to venture into more glamorous territory. As the war dragged wearisomely on, with more and more men called away to fight, there developed a chronic shortage of musical talent. Anyone who could hold a tune or play an instrument – however indifferently – would automatically be in great demand. So it was that almost by accident and without any great pretensions to talent I found myself playing drums with the Elite Dance Band – and being applauded for it too. We may not have been the greatest group ever to hit Yorkshire, but we could get an audience to its feet for anything from a jitterbug to a slow waltz. On Saturday nights we would play at the Royston British Legion Club or at local school halls; and in an area starved of live entertainment we usually drew an appreciative crowd. It was then I discovered a strange law of economics. In four hours of enjoyable drumming, I could earn more than in an eight-hour shift underground. But the money wasn't all that mattered. On her weekends home, Madge would sit below the stage and after we'd played our last number – usually 'Who's Taking You Home Tonight?' – she would help me carry my drum kit home. That was always the best bit of the evening.

Then came a series of events which marked me indelibly and set me on the long road which would end, so many years later, in tribal hatred, armed police outside my front door and the constant threat of assassination.

3 A Union Man

The war in Europe was at last grinding to a close. In the West, British troops had crossed the Rhine. In the East, the Red Army was racing towards Berlin. At Wharncliffe Woodmoor pit in Carlton, another miner was caught in a fall of rock, lying crushed and terribly injured under the weight of clod and stone. It was an ordinary occurrence, one of the routine risks of work underground. It didn't rate so much as a single paragraph in the local paper. In fact no fewer than 5,400 men were killed in the mines during the war.

It wasn't routine to me. It was my Dad they carried out of the mine that day, all cut and broken and more dead than alive. They brought him home, perhaps in the hope that familiar surroundings would help his recovery. It didn't work. He lay in pain for days, then developed rheumatic fever. He burned with it, struggled for breath, clung on by a thread.

But for Mam, I think he would have died. She stayed with him day and night, nursing him, cleaning him, bathing him in oils to stop the bones protruding through his skin. She was only a small woman and frail, already tired from a lifetime's drudgery, but she kept at it to the edge of exhaustion. At last Dad began to rally. He started taking food, sat up in bed and even managed to take a few slow, limping steps.

The effort proved too much for Mam. As Dad improved, she weakened. The doctor had to be called again. Cancer was diagnosed. She took to the bed my dad had just vacated and sank rapidly. Nursing sessions were arranged, but it was no use. She continued to deteriorate in agonies. The doctor could only prescribe pain-killing drugs and not very effective ones at that. We could only watch helplessly. We had no National Health Service, no hospital treatment, no access to a consultant or to higher medical expertise. I was the breadwinner now, in a house with a crippled Dad and a dying Mam. I raged inside at the injustice which had brought my family to this; but for all my strength, youth and working skills there wasn't a thing I could do about it. Not then.

Mam died in 1944. We buried her in Carlton Cemetery. She was forty-six years old, and had she lived in happier circumstances would probably have survived for decades.

Perhaps it was the shock which persuaded Madge and me to wed without any further delay. We'd been courting, after all, virtually since the war began; now we'd learned, in the cruellest way possible, that time is the most precious of all commodities. We married in 1945 at Royston Anglican Church. It was, without doubt, the best and wisest decision of my life. Afterwards we honeymooned in Blackpool; though the town wasn't nearly as boisterous, bustling or crowded as before the war, I don't think we really noticed. It was the first proper holiday either of us had ever known.

We returned as man and wife to my old house at 3 Manor Street, now seeming very different with Mam no longer there. Dad had been fitted with a special boot because one of his legs had been shortened in the accident; he managed to get around only with the aid of two walking sticks. My sister Edna was working at the local Co-op; it was pretty clear that the money I was earning would be more than welcome.

By now I was a skilled fitter, one of the men responsible for keeping the coalface machinery working at full blast to ensure that production didn't fall. Often I'd be called out at dead of night to sort out some problem underground. The windows of our house in Manor Street would rattle as the messenger from the pit rousted me out of bed. I'd crawl to the door, still half asleep.

'What's up?' I'd mumble.

'Cutting machine on 2 Face Beemshaw Seam's broken down.'

'Oh, aye. What is it, d'you think?'

'Clutch slipping,' he'd say. Or maybe it would be a broken chain, a new pall spring wanted, any one of a dozen possibilities. Whatever it was, I would tell the messenger to go to the fitting shop and pick up whatever spares and materials were needed and within minutes I'd be on my way, picking my way up the road in the darkness, intent only on effecting the repair and getting the machines moving and cutting again. Important work. The machines had to operate. Coal had to be cut. Men's wages were at stake. If I didn't do the job properly there would be lost shifts and lost pay. So I slaved without thinking twice about it, often on my own in some remote part of the mine, squeezing along on my side and more often than not up to my elbows in thick oil. The conditions were intolerable, yet as fitters we tolerated them. The colliers had it just as bad; but we knew they depended on us. This was our life and our livelihood. In spite of the fights I had witnessed when I first went underground, we miners stuck together over the isues which really mattered, in the kind of camaraderie I've never found before or since.

There was a buzz in the air then. Our world was going to change. We could feel it in our bones. With victory in Europe we believed we were on the threshold of a new age. Certainly nobody dreamed that we could ever go back to the miseries of the hungry Thirties, when pits could be closed and men discarded on a coalowner's whim. We'd not endured a war for that. So when Labour's overwhelming general election triumph was declared, miners and their families danced in the streets. Neighbours embraced publicly for sheer joy. Some broke down in tears. We were in power at last, all the working people of Britain, miners and factory hands, railwaymen and shipwrights, the men and women who had always made the wealth and never enjoyed it. Now was our moment. Now. Never was there a gladder or more confident morning.

At home, things weren't going quite so well. There was a certain tension in the house – inevitably, perhaps, with Edna and Madge competing in the kitchen. Anyway, we began to think of moving on. When our first daughter, Susan, was born – a moment of supreme happiness in our lives – we left on amicable terms and went into lodgings with a charming old couple, Mr and Mrs Frank Tyler, on the same estate. It meant we could be in constant touch with Dad and Edna, without living in each other's pockets.

It was around this time that I started smoking a pipe, a lifelong pleasure to which I still cling, in spite of fashion and the frowns of the health-conscious. I had never taken to cigarettes, which I thought unsatisfying and expensive; but a pipe was something else. Whenever I came across a proper smoker, I saw contentment and peace of mind; and so it proved for me. In fifty years of puffing, I've discovered that a pipe can smooth the edges of every difficulty.

Meanwhile I was swept up in the optimism of the new age. I was well into my mechanical engineering course at the local mining college, studying one full day a week and three evenings. It was difficult, challenging stuff, but I was confident of passing my final examination the following year. I was becoming more active in the Carlton ward Labour Party too, full of excitement at the possibilities being opened up by the Attlee government. I can still remember my emotions when the mines were nationalized in 1947. I was at my pithead as the plaque was unveiled and felt close to breaking down. The pit was ours. Ours! I thought of Dad with his ruined body and the poor man whose shouted warning once saved my life; I thought of the bodies laid out in my school when the Old Carlton pit blew up; I thought of the private coalowners, distant men who never knew us, never came near us and in my view never gave a damn. The wheel had turned with a vengeance and we were the owners now. We all thought there would be better conditions, better pay, greater safety. We had visions then.

Of course nationalization wasn't a magic wand. The work underground was still hard and dangerous. Pits still closed when they became exhausted or unprofitable. And the National Coal Board still had to grapple with the kind of economic difficulties which had confronted the private owners. But we miners felt better all the same – and with good reason. Working conditions improved markedly almost from the beginning. Training was introduced for newcomers before ever they went down to the coalface. A ban was introduced on young boys going underground before they were sixteen. We had a national safety scheme at last, with proper standards at every colliery. And for the first time, pithead baths became a standard facility. No longer would men have to walk home, stiff with grime after their shift, to knock the dust off themselves outside their front doors before scrubbing themselves in tin baths before the hearth.

Those new pithead facilities at last restored a bit of dignity to the miners' working lives – though not all of them saw it that way. Some of the older men hated the thought of being seen naked, especially by younger workmates with more athletic bodies. Still, such reservations couldn't dampen the general enthusiasm for the new way of doing things.

However, life has an unhappy habit of kicking you in the teeth when you least expect it, and it wasn't long before I discovered a worm in the apple. As part of the nationalization deal, the Minister of Power, Hugh Gaitskell, had agreed that miners should receive six days' pay for every five worked, a measure intended to help combat absenteeism. Naturally that bonus shift was greeted with delight in every mining community; it meant that at last the men who worked underground would receive a decent wage for what they did. But there was a horrible – and for me unacceptable – flaw.

The trouble as far as I was concerned was that nobody had thought the deal through. It didn't cover students like me who were attending day school at a quite considerable financial sacrifice. Not only would I continue to lose money every time I took time off to attend my mechanical engineering course; I wouldn't qualify for the bonus shift either, since I hadn't put in a full working week underground.

This was serious. In spite of my fitter's skills, I wasn't earning much. My day at the miners' college was a hardship. That bonus shift would have made all the difference. But I would never get it unless I gave up my studies.

I found it impossible to believe that a government to which I was so passionately committed ever intended such a consequence. It was so obviously a mistake, brought about by ignorance. And it probably wouldn't be rapidly corrected, because so few people were affected; for example,

I was the only miner at my pit caught in this particular trap. But that was poor consolation. I wasted no time before rushing off to the next meeting of my local NUM branch, which was held at the Sportsman's Inn on Wakefield Road. There I buttonholed members of the local committee, especially Percy Seaman, the Secretary, and Tommy Degnan, delegate to the Yorkshire Miners' Council. I left them in no doubt that I wanted something to be done.

Two weeks went by. I attended the next branch meeting, expecting to hear some promising news. Instead I found that nobody had lifted a finger for me, or for the handful of other miners who were in a similar situation.

It was clear that if I wanted anything done, I would have to do it myself. I went to see Horace Holmes, then the Member of Parliament for Hemsworth, who by fortunate chance happened to be Parliamentary Private Secretary to the man who really mattered, the Minister for Fuel and Power, Hugh Gaitskell. I was probably rather too vehement in telling him my tale, but he listened sympathetically. Seven weeks later, the ministry announced that it was amending its bonus shift agreement to include day students. But it was too late for me. I'd never been sure that my appeal would be successful. I couldn't bear to think of Madge going through hardship and scrimping while I studied without pay. So I had abandoned my engineering course after three years and given up all hope of passing the exam which would have opened so many opportunities for us.

I was bitterly disappointed. Disappointed because my ambitions had been thwarted. Disappointed with a government which shouldn't have made such an elementary error in the first place. And especially disappointed with my union committee for what I considered its ineffectiveness: it hadn't managed to solve my problem in two whole weeks. Of course it was naïve of me. Possibly a bit bumptious too. But I thought working miners deserved better.

So it was that at the age of twenty-three I put myself forward to stand for union office as one of the committee members for my pit. I dare say I was motivated more by frustration and anger than anything else, but they can be a formidable combination in any election. I was determined to win. When I went undergound for my daily stint – and I had access to every part of the pit – I'd take a piece of chalk with me and scrawl VOTE MASON on the girders and roof supports in all the roadways. Maybe it was a little pushy; but I was canvassing. And I topped the poll.

I was now an elected representative. Twice a month, on Sunday mornings, I had to attend committee meetings at the Sportsman's Inn. For me, they were always enjoyable, satisfying occasions. I had to report on all kinds of problems involving safety in the pit, complaints from miners, questions over wages, water money, dust, bonuses and all the rest. Whenever I was underground, I'd be stopped in the main roadways or the tailgates by fellow workers who wanted something raised in committee; with something like 1,500 men in the pit, it meant a lot of work and responsibility. I have to say I loved it. So much so that when my two years as a committee member were coming to an end I began to think of taking on even more, and becoming the NUM delegate for the pit.

It was a daunting prospect. As a delegate, I'd have to attend the Yorkshire Miners' Council once a month, arguing on behalf of my pit in front of a hundred seasoned union representatives from every mine in the county. This wasn't some gathering in the back room of a local pub. The Council met in the much grander surroundings of the main chamber in the Miners' Hall in Barnsley, home then to some of the biggest names in the Labour movement. The things discussed there didn't just concern local issues, but matters of national importance. What I was aiming for was without question the most important union job in the pit.

The problem was that we already had a delegate, and a pretty good one too. Tommy Degnan was an old campaigner, a dyed-in-the-wool Communist but straight as an arrow with his members. Though he hadn't managed to help when I'd complained about the unfairness of bonus shifts, he was a good trades unionist. In theory, he should have had no trouble seeing off a challenge from a young whippersnapper.

But by this time I had a bit of form. I had not only been very active on the pit committee, but had been getting myself known elsewhere. I was finding my feet in the local Labour Party and on top of that had joined the National Council of Labour Colleges, where I became a voluntary lecturer. It was probably a bit of a cheek standing against him, since I really didn't know all that much about anything, other than maintaining underground machinery. But I was willing to get up on my hind legs and I would regularly tramp round in the evenings to school halls, village halls, Labour Party ward meetings, anywhere I could find an audience and always with material I'd carefully mugged up. One of my themes – a rather unpopular one – was to call for German rearmament; I thought it essential for the nations of Europe to come together, particularly as the threat from the Soviet Union seemed to be growing ever more serious. Eventually, of course, that threat and the way to meet it inspired the great division which split the party from top to bottom; but in those days the chasm between Left and Right was only a cloud on the horizon. I doubt if my rather unfashionable views did me much harm in the party or the union.

Tommy Degnan obviously didn't think so either. Since I'd done so well in the committee elections two years previously, he must have sensed that he was in trouble. So rather than fight and risk losing, he stood down as delegate and put himself up as pit secretary instead. In the event, we both won and became quite a formidable negotiating team. I learned a lot from Tommy.

So I was now in the senior league. Pit delegate to the Yorkshire Miners' Council. Of course I was nervous at the challenge, but I was determined to make a sucess of it. From the outside, it might have looked like cockiness, but it really wasn't. I tried to appear self-secure and confident because I'm smaller that most and have always felt it. I'd give the impression of being ebullient and knowledgeable, but it was all a bit of a cloak. Inside I'd worry about everything I was doing and saying. What if I made some terrible blunder? Had I misread the situation? Might I be letting down the lads? Such questions mattered because my new role wasn't just to make speeches in the Miners' Hall. Often I'd have to lead delegations to see Gordon Jackson, the manager of the colliery or Jack Sykes, his deputy. I'd argue for better deals on water money, paid when men had to work in the stuff sometimes up to their knees, yardage payments, the amount a miner got for hewing 10 yd of coal, holidays with pay, a whole host of other matters. Any one of them could stop a mine and leave families in the village struggling to pay their bills.

This was the sharp end of industrial relations; quite an experience for a young man of twenty-five who wasn't nearly as sure of himself as he appeared. When there was a dispute with the management, miners would gather at the pithead, reluctant to go underground until they got some reassurances. I would stand on an upturned tub, appealing to my members not to do anything rash. Pick two or three men, I'd urge them. I'll take them as a delegation to see the boss and we'll sort things out. Meantime, get down the pit or we won't be able to negotiate at all. I would always be watching for the inevitable troublemakers, the one or two foolhardy young men – they were invariably young – who might very ostentatiously empty their water bottles and slouch away home. That would be the start of it. After such a demonstration, the others would stream away too, all on their way back to their houses, 'ragged up' as they called it. So we would have another one-day strike over an issue which could and should have been settled in half an hour's hard bargaining.

In spite of such frustrations, I found myself revelling in my new role. I was beginning to learn how to make a difference. There's something tremendously satisfying in winning an argument on behalf of your workmates and coming out at the end with improved conditions, better pay or higher bonuses. But as always, I was thinking ahead, even in the midst of my union activities. What would happen if economic circumstances changed and there was no longer such a demand for coal? How would I fare if there was a pit-closure programme? I already had one piece of insurance under my belt, with a pit deputy's ticket. But another string to my bow wouldn't come amiss. I decided I might as well try and get on the parliamentary panel of the Yorkshire miners.

Not that I'd any serious intention of becoming an MP. I had no ambitions in public life at that time, other than as an official with the NUM. Besides, there were no fewer than fifty-eight nominations from Yorkshire pits for the twelve places on the panel – the elected nominees who would be first in line when a local constituency needed a candidate. It would be a tough job to emerge at the top of that fiercely contested heap. Still, it was worth a go.

In the event – and to my surprise – I came fourth. Fourth! Presumably my activities on the Yorkshire Miners' Council had been noticed by the other delegates, who in turn had reported back to their pits. It was certainly a pleasant feeling to do so well. For the first time, it occurred to me that maybe Westminster was not out of reach.

Meanwhile I had an education to get. In 1951 I won a Trades Union Congress scholarship to study for a year at the London School of Economics. To reach that stage, I'd had to complete a questionnaire, write an essay and go through a lengthy interview with Mr Wray of the TUC Educational Trust. Once again, I suppose, my motive was to equip myself for an uncertain future; but I was also very conscious of the fact that I'd missed out on a whole world of knowledge. I was really a late developer.

The scholarship, of course, meant a total upheaval in my family. I'd have to go to London, leaving my wife and child behind. It would be even more of a wrench, because by now we were installed in our own small prefabricated bungalow at 292 Carlton Road. Modest it may have been, but to us it was a palace – and all the more welcome because it came as such a surprise. I'd been campaigning for my pitmates who were living in digs, pestering the local housing manager, Sam Thomas, for more new houses to accommodate them. No doubt I was a bit of a nuisance to him. Anyway, when a new estate was finally built at nearby Smithies, Madge and I visited the show house and wondered who'd be lucky enough to live there. We were open-mouthed when Sam called us into his office a few days later and presented us with the keys.

Despite the opportunity I was being offered, I wasn't enthusiastic at the thought of leaving my home behind. What's more, I'd have to get by somehow on an allowance of just £4 a week, to cover rent on my digs, food, hire purchase and to look after Madge and baby Susan as well. Of course we questioned whether we could possibly manage on such a tiny sum, but in the end decided to give it a try. As ever, Madge was solid in her support, but it didn't take long before it dawned on us that we'd bitten off more than we could chew, especially on hire purchase repayments. I had no choice but to appeal to Mr Wray. We just couldn't get by on £4. He kindly allowed us an extra 10s a week; and with that Madge and I decided we would somehow see it through. Madge also took a part-time job at Woolworths to help us get by.

So began the strangest year of my life so far. For weeks on end, I'd scrape by in London, sharing digs in Clapham with three other trade union students, beavering away at books on politics and trades unionism, writing essays, doing research and from time to time preparing and delivering lectures. I couldn't have taken it more seriously; when I first encountered Locke and Rousseau it began to dawn on me how very little I knew, and what a struggle it would be to grasp the half of it.

Our tutors were Professor Basset and Ben Roberts and they certainly didn't make it easy for us. Roberts, who was mainly in charge of our course, was an abrasive, bossy type. He knew trade union theory all right, but he hadn't a scrap of real working experience. His manner frequently upset our little group and he never really got the best out of us. We were not immature undergraduates, after all, but married men with official union duties and serious responsibilities in our workplaces. We were desperate to make the best of the educational opportunities offered to us, every one of us aching to absorb what learning we could. Yet he'd invariably talk down to us, with a condescension bordering on contempt. None of us even felt comfortable during tutorials. Perhaps it's just as well that there was no final exam; just a long, hard stint of concentrated political and trade union study. But it was a grounding, basic and necessary. And it was to stand me in good stead later on.

My only breaks in that long year were when I managed to get home to see Madge and my daughter. I couldn't afford to travel properly, of course, but I came to an arrangement with my brother-in-law Haydn Jones, a long-distance lorry driver. On the occasions when his trips allowed it, he'd pick me up on a Friday night at High Barnet tube station and take me home, then take me back to London overnight on the Sunday. The deal could only be worked every two or three weeks and invariably meant long, gruelling journeys up the A1, sometimes in fog or rain, ten or eleven hours on the road with just the odd stop for a rest in some transport café lorry park. But it was worth it to get home.

We were still struggling to live, even though Madge was running a tight ship. We'd been wildly over-optimistic in thinking that the extra 10s a week would keep the wolf from the door. So in my vacations from the LSE I'd go straight back down the pit. Those stints not only helped to supplement my meagre allowance but also maintained my qualification for free home coal. We were just about managing.

During one vacation, my two-year term as pit delegate expired. I stood again and was re-elected. It was a rare bright spot in my life at the time. At home our financial situation was still bleak. By Christmas 1951 we were really struggling. Madge had been absolutely wonderful about my course at the LSE and had made every sacrifice possible; but there was no money in the house for seasonal cheer. More importantly, we hadn't anything to buy a Christmas present for little Susan.

I was in such a state about it that I nerved myself to go and see Joe Hall, President of the Yorkshire miners. Joe was a good soul and a courageous man; he was always ready to go underground at times of disaster and help the rescue teams. Not surprisingly, he was an excellent leader of men and kept a firm grip on the Yorkhire Miners' Council. But he was a formidable character all the same. It wasn't easy to go to him, cap in hand.

Afer a bit of a wait at the Miners' Council Offices, I was eventually ushered into his presence. He was a well-made chap, round and balding, with a somewhat off-putting habit of rolling his tongue around his loose dentures. We knew each other, of course, though not well. After the usual exchange of greetings, I nervously explained my problem. Was there some kind of fund I could appeal to – for my child's sake really – to get us over Christmas?

Joe didn't hesitate. He pulled out his wallet and handed me a £5 note. 'Here thee are, lad. We'll find a political fund o' some sort to claim it from.' I could hardly believe it. I stammered my thanks and scurried back home in delight to tell Madge the good news. We bought Susan her present, our worries eased at a crucial time. I've always been grateful to Joe for that. But I never knew which fund supplied the fiver. I've thought more than once that it may well have come from his own pocket.

I completed my year at the LSE with some relief, but also with regret at having to say goodbye to my room mates Pat Fisher and Bill Monaghan, with whom I was good friends. Pat, now sadly deceased, went on to become quite a senior figure with the TUC at Congress House, and Bill became a lecturer at Glasgow University. Another notable figure on my course was Norman Stagg, later Deputy General Secretary of the Union of Post Office Workers.

But for me it was back home to 292 Carlton Road, the pit and the Yorkshire Miners' Council. It was a busy, contented life, especially as I was earning a reasonable wage again. I still wasn't sure what the future might hold.

In 1952 my mind was made up for me. The Labour Party at

Bridlington on the Yorkshire coast was looking for a new parliamentary candidate and called on me to attend a selection conference. I went, more out of curiosity than anything else, and somewhat to my surprise won the nomination.

At first I didn't think it would make any difference to me. The seat certainly wasn't easily winnable. The Tory MP, Richard Wood, was not only highly popular in the constituency but sat on a majority of 42,000. Still, the local Labour activists were a wonderful bunch of people. The more I saw of them, the more I enjoyed working with them. I'd go up for a weekend every month, attending meetings, speaking whenever I got the opportunity, generally making myself known. It was good fun explaining and defending Labour Party policy, especially in True Blue territory. I even began to think of chipping away at that apparently impregnable majority. I was now twenty-eight and it seemed to me that with energy and persistence I might actually manage to grab the seat by the time I was forty. I'd still be relatively young. I had finally caught the political bug.

But then, maybe it had always been there, below the surface. When I won the Bridlington nomination, I'd told the local party that I was on the Yorkshire miners' panel and that if a miners' seat became vacant I'd like the chance to attend the selection conference. So I suppose the possibility of a career at Westminster must have been in my thoughts even then. Generously, the Bridlington party agreed my condition. They wouldn't want to stand in my way if there was a chance of a winnable seat elsewhere.

Neither they nor I had the slightest idea how soon or how dramatically that chance would come.

4 The Road to Westminster

It started out as a routine meeting of Labour's Executive Committee in the Co-operative Rooms in Barnsley, in late 1952. All the local party stalwarts were there, including our newly-elected, miners-sponsored MP, Sydney Schofield. Everything seemed much as normal, until without the slighted warning Syd threw the room into uproar.

Quietly, he announced that he was applying for the Chiltern Hundreds and resigning his seat. We all gazed at him, dumbfounded. He had only been our MP for a year. There was no obvious reason for him to go. He'd been a miners' delegate from Glass Houghton colliery in West Yorkshire, a solid, dependable type, only forty years old. With a rock-solid majority of 18,000, he should have been set for life.

At last the party chairman, the bluff, genial Alderman Andrew Wright, broke the stunned silence. 'Pull thy socks up, lad,' he growled, not unkindly. 'We're all with thee.'

But Syd wouldn't be budged. 'My socks have never been down, Mr Chairman,' he insisted. He was determined to resign, and that was that.

Of course we were shocked. At the 1951 General Election, our veteran MP, Frank Collingridge, had collapsed and died while addressing a meeting at Woods glassworks in the constituency. Sydney Schofield had then fought and won the seat in the by-election which followed. Now the local party was faced with a third unexpected upheaval in little more than twelve months. I can't deny that there was dismay and some anger at what Sydney was doing, though later I learned that at Westminster he had always felt like a square peg in a round hole. His father had committed suicide. His wife loathed the political life with all its inevitable separations. So after brooding unhappily in the House, he had come to the view than enough was enough.

All credit to him, though. Once he made that decision, he stuck to it. After he resigned, he went back to his pit, became Branch Secretary of the NUM, moved on to be General Secretary of the Yorkshire Miners' Union and ended up as National Vice-President of the NUM. What a recovery! Man, know thyself. Syd certainly did, and helped make trade union history in doing so.

But that night in the Co-op Rooms I wasn't thinking so much of Syd's predicament as of the huge opportunity which had suddenly presented itself. I knew there was a chance, however slight, that I could replace Syd, and in my home territory too. Since I was still only twenty-eight I understood that many would consider me far too young, but it was worth having a go. I raced back home to tell Madge what I had in mind, half expecting her to tell me not to be so daft. But she reacted as she's always done: 'You know what's best. Do it. You'll get my backing.'

So the slog began.

First, I had to get the Miners' union nomination. I knew it wouldn't be easy, even though I was on the NUM parliamentary panel. There were eleven other miners in the field, most of them more experienced in politics and union affairs than I was. Somehow, I had to make an impact in the numerous pits around Barnsley, all of which would send delegates to a special selection conference. But it was midwinter in 1952–53. There was snow on the ground, long distances to be travelled. I had no vehicle to call upon, not even a bike to help me.

Perhaps in the end, that lack was an advantage. Had I approached the delegates too openly, it might have done me more harm than good, especially as they were all much older than me. Over-energetic canvassing can be a bit off-putting. So, denied the opportunity to put myself about as much as I would have liked, I turned instead to the local papers, inundating the newsdesks of the *Barnsley Chronicle*, the morning *Sheffield Telegraph* and the evening *Star* with details of my qualifications for becoming the next MP. I might be young, but I was the local man, lived in the constituency, was an elected union official with experience in the Labour Party and was a voluntary lecturer to boot. Sometimes, when listing my virtues, I nearly succeeded in impressing myself!

Meanwhile, an anti-miner campaign was developing in the constituency. With the abrupt resignation of Sydney Schofield, word was out that NUM candidates were liable to let the side down. Why was the local Labour Party being plunged yet again into the expense and trouble of a by-election? Fingers were being pointed in one direction only; and the most vehement finger-jabber of all was Alderman A.E. McVie, JP, leader of the Labour group on the council, Chairman of the Bench, a governor of the college and one of the kingpins of the entire area. He had no doubt at all who should be our next Member of Parliament: Alderman McVie. In fact it was said that he already held so many positions that if he gave them up to go to Westminster, the problem of local unemployment could be solved overnight.

But it wasn't just McVie who had doubts about the miners. Many local unions felt the same, perhaps inspired by a little understandable jealously at the influence of the all-powerful NUM. Besides, they could point to the fact that Syd Schofield hadn't done much for the area. He was rarely seen locally and didn't even live in the constituency (though in fairness, he was having a house built locally at Monk Bretton and therefore must have intended to do so). It all meant that whoever emerged as the official miners' candidate wouldn't necessarily succeed in winning the Labour Party nomination.

That wasn't my only worry. On the eve of the miners' selection conference, I was tipped off that Jack Wood, an official from a neighbouring colliery to my own, was plotting to scupper the whole proceedings. His plan was simple enough: after all the parliamentary hopefuls had made their speeches and taken questions, he intended to move a resolution saying that none of the nominees had enough experience to represent the Yorkshire miners at Westminster, and suggesting that no vote was taken that day and that the panel should be widened before a final decision was taken. Cunning old Jack. He wasn't on the panel, but was undoubtedly experienced. Clearly his resolution was an attempt to throw his hat into the ring at the last minute. But would it work?

I lost no time in going to see the Yorkshire miners' President, Alwyn Machen. When I told him what was happening, his response was quite firm: there would be no delays and no interference with the usual protocol. One way or another, the decision would be taken next day.

The following evening was all hubbub and excitement, a crowd of reporters, press photographers, miners and onlookers all jostling outside the Miners' Hall in Barnsley. In spite of the anti-NUM sentiment which had been stirred up in the constituency, everybody knew that this was a crucial meeting. Whoever won the nomination that night would have a flying start in becoming Labour's candidate in the by-election.

I was more nervous than I had ever been. No fewer than ten of the twelve members of the miners' parliamentary panel were to appear that night. I was somewhat overawed at the strength of the oppposition. There was Dick Kelley, a prominent union leader in South Yorkshire, Edwin Wainwright and David Griffiths, well known figures from pits just outside my town, Alan Beaney, a widely respected miner, delegate and former Methodist lay preacher. All made their names in the trade union movement and all eventually became NUM-sponsored MPs in due course. Then there was Harry Fish, a delegate and local politician who was also a feared fast bowler in the pit cricket league. Later he became

Mayor of Barnsley. Every one of them was in with a serious chance of winning. Nobody had the slightest idea how the contest would turn out.

The hopefuls were all invited to sit together in the executive room near the main hall. As always in such strained circumstances, we made polite small-talk, shuffled our feet, and assured each other that, no, we didn't really think we were in with much of a chance. In my own case at least, this was largely true. All the others were about fifty years old, since it was rare in those days to get on to the parliamentary panel until you had made a real mark in the union. And some of my competitors were already famous throughout the coalfield.

Because of the large number of candidates present, each of us was allowed only five minutes to speak, with another five minutes for questions afterwards. I got through my ordeal in a bit of a daze, giving the delegates the speech I'd rehearsed for days beforehand, answering questions as best I could and returning to rejoin my fellow candidates afterwards without the faintest idea of how well or badly I'd done. There was nothing for it then but to wait.

The waiting dragged on. There was no sign of a result. My colleagues began fidgeting, wondering what was happening. A tied vote perhaps? I had a pretty good idea what was going on behind those closed doors, but I said nothing.

As it turned out, I was right. When all the speeches were done, Jack Wood made his move, suggesting that the whole selection procedure should be postponed. But the Chairman, being forewarned, was ready for him. He had the rulebook beside him and had studied the relevant part of the constitution. There was no room for any delay and no reason either. He ruled Wood's motion out of order. If Jack had any allies in his plot, they were silenced. The votes were then counted and the result announced at last: Roy Mason 24; Edwin Wainwright 4; Harry Fish 2. (Later, Jack Wood became one of my most stalwart supporters).

What a night. I was overjoyed. I had aimed so high, never really expecting to hit my target first time. After talking to the reporters waiting outside and grinning for the photographers – a new experience, that – I dashed out of hall and into a waiting taxi. In spite of all my previous nervousness and doubts about my prospects, I'd taken the precaution of booking a cab in advance. Just in case. I hadn't been a scout for nothing; be prepared. I wanted to rush home to Madge and break the news. I can still see the delight on her face.

But now the real fight was on.

I knew I couldn't count on the support of the smaller unions. Alderman McVie and his friends had done their work too well. Besides, there was some genuine resentment over the way Syd Schofield had so suddenly decamped. On top of that, it soon became clear that I couldn't rely on the powerful Transport and General Workers' Union either. There had always been a gentleman's agreement between the NUM and the T&G not to tread on each other's toes and always to support the other union's nominees. Not this time. One of the key local T&G leaders was Councillor Harry Dancer and he clearly fancied his own chances for the seat. I knew I was up against it.

Then matters took a turn for the worse. Harry suddenly withdrew from the race and threw in his lot with Alderman McVie. The pact meant that local opposition to the NUM was uniting under a formidable leader. It was beginning to look as though the unthinkable might happen: the Barnsley seat could be seized by a non-miner.

I had a lot of canvassing to do. I stopped work at the pit, even though I couldn't afford it. After all, this was the opportunity of a lifetime for me. It might even be the disgrace of a lifetime, if I let the constituency slip away into anti-NUM hands. So somehow I had to survive on no income and hardly any savings. I didn't even have a bank account.

I was so strapped for cash that I might have been tempted to feign illness or an industrial injury to get basic – and temporary – social security payments, but of course that was impossible. Everbody from the local councillors to the colliery management knew exactly what I was doing. I hadn't the remotest chance of getting away with a bogus claim. Looking back, I'm relieved the option wasn't there.

Still, I wasn't fighting the battle on my own. Madge was with me all the way. And I was lucky enough to have two good friends on my side. Arthur Williams and Jim Burns were both well-respected, hard-working party men. Better still, Jim had an old van and offered to drive me round on the canvassing trail. It was a godsend. The constituency was blanketed in snow at the time and I would never have managed to reach the outlying villages without Jim's help. So my days fell into a pattern: in the mornings and afternoons, I'd tramp around the town making what contacts I could with party activists, union officials, anyone who had influence in picking the next Labour candidate. In the evenings, we would pile into Jim's van and chug off along icy roads to the furthest-flung corners of the constituency. It was an exhausting business.

Worrying, too. The more people I approached, the clearer it became that the NUM had lost friends. Again and again, I encountered bewilderment and dismay at Syd Schofield's action. A typical reaction came from the Moulder's Union, representing workers at quite a few light engineering firms in the town. The Moulders had six votes on the Labour Party selection committee, votes which had always swung automatically behind any candidate the miners nominated.

This time, it would be different. I was told that, yes, the Moulders understood that the town depended on coal. But they also felt let down by the NUM. So instead of committing their six votes to me, they intended to plump for the candidate who made the best showing on the night. Fair enough, of course. That's democracy for you. But as a young, untried parliamentary hopeful looking at an opportunity which seemed to be evaporating in front of my eyes, I wasn't in much of a mood to be philosophical.

On the big night – again, held in the main hall of the miners' offices – I still had no real idea of what the outcome would be. Sensing the mood of the constituency, the NUM had sent out circulars to all branches, urging them to ensure that their full delegation turned up. It only added to my feeling that the result would be desperately close. It was going to be a straight fight between my old foe, Alderman McVie, and me. Others had shown an interest, but one by one they had all fallen away. The hall was packed, with no fewer than 272 delegates present. I knew I could count on the ninety-nine miners' votes. The rest? I could only keep my fingers crossed.

I was called in to speak first: fifteen minutes to make my case, plus question-time afterwards. Andrew Wright was in the chair. He was an old buddy of McVie's and I knew I could expect no favours from him. Trying to conceal my nervousness as best I could, I talked of my credentials in the party and the union movement, my experiences at the LSE and my commitment to the people of Barnsley. I did my best to satisfy the anti-miner element, pledging to stay at Westminster for the long haul and making it clear I intended to go on living in the constituency.

So far, so good. My speech seemed to go down well enough and the questions afterwards posed no difficulty. Until the very end. Then Harry Dancer of the Transport Workers stood up and asked me to express my views on German rearmament.

I knew at once that this was the moment which would make me or break me. Harry was well aware that I had been beating this particular drum in countless lectures for the National Council of Labour Colleges. His question was designed to shoot me down in flames. Few of the delegates present knew the line I'd been taking; they would certainly disapprove once I answered. After all, it was only eight years since the war had ended. Auschwitz and Belsen still haunted the public mind.

Well, there was nothing for it. I had to say what I thought. And why. I explained the need to build a strong, democratic Europe in the face of the growing Soviet threat. I stressed that a major nation like Germany couldn't forever be kept down or treated like a pariah without fearful consequences in the future. After all those lectures, I knew the subject backwards, going through point after point without yielding an inch. My audience may not have agreed with a word, but at least it got a full reply, with no dodging. Still, as I made my way back to the executive room, I couldn't help feeling that my parliamentary career had ended before it had even begun. I sat gloomily alone until Alderman McVie returned from his presentation. Then it was a matter of hanging on for the result.

After a long, strained wait, during which McVie and I said little and avoided each other's eyes, we were called back into the main hall. I couldn't tell anything from the delegates' faces. I mounted the stage, heart thumping, hoping I wouldn't let my disappointment show if I lost. The Chairman read out the figures: Roy Mason, 148. Alderman McVie, 124. I'd made it. Just. With a majority of twenty-four. The rest of the meeting blurred into a flurry of congratulations, back-slapping, commiserations to my defeated opponent, photographs and interviews with the press. Once again, I couldn't wait to dash back to my little prefabricated bungalow to tell Madge the news.

Only next day did it dawn on me how close I had come to defeat. I was told that the Moulders' leader had asked Alderman McVie the same question on German rearmament which Harry Dancer had thrown at me. Mac had seemed flustered, simply replying that he would abide by the official Labour Party policy prevailing at the time, whatever it happened to be. It didn't go down well. He immediately lost the six votes of the Moulders – which had previously been leaning in his direction – and probably a handful of others as well. As it turned out, the delegates had preferred straight, sincerely held views – even if not particularly popular – to no views at all. That's the thing about electoral politics: you can never tell.

So I plunged head-first into the by-election proper. From an outsider's point of view, it couldn't have been an especially interesting contest. Barnsley was one of the safest Labour seats in the country, so the outcome wasn't remotely in doubt. Moreover, the Tories were solidly established in government; nothing that happened on my patch would make the slightest difference to them. Still, I fought the campaign as if the fate of the nation depended on it. I conducted factory meetings, both inside and outside the works gates, pithead meetings, meetings in school and village halls; I did walkabouts and canvassing; I talked endlessly to the press, shook thousands of hands and kept on going when my throat was raw, my feet aching and I could hardly tell one day from another.

Because of the nature of the constituency, nobody was really interested in my opponents. The voters wanted to know what I felt, how I saw things. I became the target of every active Tory in Barnsley – not that there were very many – with questions intended to trip me up or make me look foolish. I loved the challenge; but as the campaign wore on, I did begin to wonder why I was bothering to appear on election platforms with my political opponents. I don't think it was arrogance; I simply felt I was giving them the kind of public exposure they would never have managed on their own. In later life, I came to the conclusion that joint appearances were a waste of time. My motto towards Tories, Liberals and all other challengers was 'unknown they are and unknown they shall remain'. The only time I ever willingly appeared on a platform with an opponent subsequently was at the election count. I was always happy then to pat the arms of defeated candidates and offer the usual commiserations.

A somewhat rough attitude? Maybe it is. But then, politics is a rough old trade.

It's never rougher than when you're facing your first count in your first election. I know they say in Barnsley that you don't count the Labour votes: you weigh them. In such rock-solid Labour seats thay also claim that the electorate would vote for a donkey if it wore a red rosette. But when you're the candidate, it doesn't seem remotely so clear-cut. I paced up and down the Civic Hall, watching the votes being stacked, full of nerves even though it was obvious that I was going to win by a mile.

And so it proved:

Roy Mason (Lab): 29,283
Geoffrey Whittaker (Con): 10,905
Labour majority: 18,378

It was March, 1953. I was twenty-eight years old and a Member of Parliament. It was a moment of triumph, right enough; but in the midst of all the cheers, I couldn't help wondering how in the world I was going to afford my train fare down to Westminster.

5 A New World

In the end, the cost of travel, which had bothered me so much, turned out to be the least of my worries. Members of Parliament, I discovered, were entitled to travel vouchers. But there was no secretarial allowance, no help with postage or telephones or any of the other things necessary in the job. A Member was expected to do it all on his salary of £1,000 a year. Fortunately, parliamentary colleagues were well aware of my plight and rallied round with offers of assistance. All I had to do then was work out how to survive for a month, until my first parliamentary pay cheque arrived. After weeks of canvassing without a penny income, it couldn't come too soon.

Our financial situation was desperate. I'd spent almost every penny of my meagre savings. Madge and I were barely living and worrying about how to keep our daughter properly clothed and fed. So there was nothing for it: we'd have to appeal to Madge's father, Mr Ernest Sowden, for help. It hurt my pride to go to him, cap in hand; but he was very good about it. I received the good news in one of Madge's letters to me at Westminster: 'Anyway, I must retire now with my water bottle. . . . P.S. Dad has put the money down. It is £50.' That really was a lifesaver. Without that help, I don't know how we would have kept body and soul together in those first few weeks of my new career.

Finding somewhere to live in London proved less of a problem than I had expected. There was of course no question of Madge joining me during the parliamentary week; we couldn't have afforded to keep two homes going. But a number of my new colleagues, all former mineworkers, understood the difficulty. They introduced me to the West Central Hotel in Southampton Row. It sounded a bit grand, but in fact in was one of the cheapest places in town – run, I think, by the Salvation Army. It cost 16s 6d for bed and breakfast – and had become a kind of club for MPs from the coalfields. A whole group of them had made it their London base: Bernard Taylor, Albert Roberts, Harold Neil, Horace Holmes, all old miners. A least I wouldn't be lonely.

I was sworn in as Member of Parliament in my best suit. In fact it was my only suit, the suit I had worn at my wedding, eight years before. Madge was watching from the Speaker's Gallery upstairs, but Dad stayed at home on what was certainly one of the proudest days of his life and mine. He didn't have the money for the fare from Barnsley and I was in no position to help. Not that he would have accepted anyway; but to this day I wish he could have been there.

I was nervous, naturally enough. That morning I'd practised the procedure with Horace Holmes, the MP for Hemsworth and Willie Whiteley, the Chief Whip, learning how to stand with my two sponsors at the Bar of the House, how many paces to step forward, when to bow to the Speaker, 'Shakes' Morrison, all the rest of it. Nerve-racking stuff: I was convinced that the eyes and attention of the whole Palace of Westminster would be focused on me every inch of the way.

To begin with, it seemed I was right. There was a satisfying growl of approval from the oposition Labour benches when I was called forward, a show of indifference from the government side. That was all right with me; the Tories were the enemy, after all. I did my bowing and pacing without mishap and stood at last by the Despatch Box where I was to take the Oath. That was when my illusions began to crumble. I'd expected the whole place to listen in rapt attention as I read the words in suitably ringing tones; but it wasn't like that at all. No sooner had I arrived at the Clerk's table than everybody in the Chamber started chatting to each other, exchanging gossip, telling jokes, ignoring me completely – most disconcerting. It began to dawn me how much of an unimportant newcomer I really was. Before I had time to digest the disillusioning moment, I'd taken the Oath and found myself behind the Speaker's chair where I was given a brisk handshake and a quick word by the party leader, Clement Attlee. So that was that: my big moment over and done with. I couldn't help feeling deflated.

Next day I was in the tearoom, trying to look as though I belonged, when Arthur Moyle, Parliamentary Private Secretary to the party leader, came up to me. 'The boss wishes to see you,' he said. It was a knee-quaking moment, a bit like being summoned to see the headmaster when you know you've done something wrong. Not that I had any particular reason to be worried; but in those days Prime Ministers and leaders of the opposition seemed like giants. I was a bag of nerves as I followed Arthur to my unexpected appointment.

I was ushered into a large room, behind the Speaker's chair. Attlee sat in the far corner, mostly hidden behind a substantial oak desk. I could just see the top of his bald head peeping over the top. It reminded me of the old Chad cartoons, where a little humpty-dumpty of a man peers over a wall with a 'Wot?' slogan scrawled on the brickwork. In this case it could have read: 'Wot, no decent suit?' or maybe 'Wot, no money?' But there wasn't time to dwell on such irreverent thoughts. I had to cross a wide, wide expanse of carpet – a lesson, that, in one of the ways leaders maintain their authority – to stand nervously in front of the great man. He looked up at me. 'Morning, Mason,' he barked. 'You're a young chap with a big majority. You're going to be here a long time. I just want to give you two pieces of advice. First of all, I want you to specialize. Take Tom Williams as your example.'

That made sense. Tom was one of the most successful ministers of agriculture we'd ever had – and he'd come from the pits, like me. That was the point Clem was trying to get across. At that stage, in 1953, we had thirty-one ex-coalminers in the Parliamentary Labour Party. No wonder he urged me to specialize; I'd be lost in the scrum otherwise. But he wasn't finished yet.

'Secondly,' he went on, fixing me with a sharp eye, 'Stay out of the bars. That's all.' And with that I was out, feeling somewhat relieved that my ordeal was over. Still, it was good advice. I've followed it, more or less, ever since.

But now I had to get on with learning how to do my job properly. I'd spend hours in the House watching and listening as the grand figures of the day showed what they were made of: people like Winston Churchill and Anthony Eden on the government side, Attlee and Aneurin Bevan on ours. All had made their mark on history during the war or in the years following. All spoke with authority and knowledge. All were household names, setting a standard it would be hard to match.

And before I could even make the attempt, I had to see to it that my constituency was properly represented. What was most important, it seemed to me, was that I should be seen regularly in every corner of Barnsley, making myself available to anyone who had a problem. So I began turning up at village fêtes, galas, Sunday school shows, functions of every imaginable kind, including a monthly surgery in the Town Hall. Gradually, I developed a system. I divided the constituency into manageable segments and every weekend, when I went home, I'd ensure that I visited two or three of them, going to local churches, chapels, pubs, anywhere people could get hold of me if they needed a question answered or a complaint sorted out. During the parliamentary recess, I'd advertise in the local press, letting it be known that I was prepared to visit people at home if they were blind, disabled or found it difficult to get out and about. In those days I was very much the roving MP with a travelling surgery; but it kept me in touch.

Madge never complained at my frequent absences. She must have been fed up occasionally, as I rushed here and there, always with someone to see, something to do; but she never made a thing of it, not by so much as a word or a gesture. I hope I never took her for granted. Without a wife's support, life would have been pretty miserable, as poor Syd Schofield had discovered.

At Westminster I was gradually beginning to find my feet, helped along by the miners' group of MPs, which in those days contained such legendary figures as Nye Bevan, Jim Giffiths, Tom Williams, Wilfred Paling and Ness Edwards. Such men had been senior ministers in the last Labour Government and two in particular – Tom Williams and Wilfred Paling – were always ready with helpful advice.

My main worry then was when to make my maiden speech. I learned pretty quickly that I would have to choose between two competing theories. The first argued that a new Member should pipe down, keep his eyes and ears open, immerse himself in the procedural bible of Erskine May and never get on his hind legs until he'd mastered all the arts of parliamentary protocol. The second recommended, just as forcefully, that a new MP could only be part of the club once he had spoken and been heard. If he had something to say he should just get on with it, never mind the ins and outs of procedure.

It was a bit of a dilemma right enough, not helped by the fact that Tom and Wilfred insisted on giving me contradictory opinions. Tom was a cautious fellow, studious and reliable. No doubt that was why Clem Attlee had urged me to follow his example. His view was that I had plenty of time to play myself in. Wilfred on the other hand was a bit of a firebrand and encouraged me to get on with it without delay. In the end, eagerness overcame caution and I decided to give it a go. I wasted no time in telling my regional Whip, Horace Holmes, what I intended to do and he fixed it up with the Speaker. It was too late then to back down.

It's a strange fact that no matter how often you may have performed in public, a maiden speech in the House of Commons is still an ordeal. I'd made at least thirty substantial speeches during my by-election campaign and answered hundreds of questions, many from Tory opponents trying to trip me up; but as my big moment approached I felt unusually weak at the knees. Since the House was debating the Finance Bill – which would give legal effect to the measures proposed in the recent Budget – I knew the chamber would be pretty full. And that many present would be far more knowledgeable than me about the finer points of economics.

Still, I'd spent fourteen years underground. I understood the difficulties and needs of working people – better anyway than most of the Tories sitting on the government benches. I kept reminding myself that I'd been sent to Westminster for a purpose. By the time the Speaker stood and called: 'Mr Roy Mason!' I'd almost talked myself out of my apprehension.

Hoping that I wouldn't be given away by a quiver in the voice, I began in the usual way by promising, as parliamentary convention demanded, to be both brief and non-controversial. Well, I managed to be brief. The other half of the equation was a bit beyond me.

Fundamentally, I thought that a Tory budget was once again redistributing wealth from the poor to the rich. I argued that it pandered to the instincts of greed and fear in the nation.

It was probably a speech more appropriate to the Labour Club in Barnsley than the floor of the Commons, but I sat down, feeling that I'd not done too badly. At least I hadn't broken down and disgraced myself. One or two colleagues murmured words of encouragement. But what really made my day were the cards of congratulations I received later from Hugh Dalton, Hugh Gaitskell and Rab Butler – two former Labour Chancellors of the Exchequer and the then Tory Chancellor. I don't think I've ever felt so flattered, or so exhilarated. It didn't really occur to me then that such messages might be the normal exchange of parliamentary courtesies. It seemed to me that I was on my way. A few days later I spoke again, this time on the subject of the Entertainment Tax, with a comment on Barnsley Football Club's transfer of Tommy Taylor to Manchester United. I considered myself a full member of the parliamentary club at last. Mind you, I didn't get any congratulatory notes this time.

With the ice broken, I became every inch the busy politician; contributing to debates in the chamber, speaking at meetings of the Parliamentary Labour Party, questioning Ministers, immersing myself in constituency work. Before very long I felt confident enough to start campaigning on issues which directly affected the people I represented, such as the case for a new, modern hospital in Barnsley or the need to get rid of the muckstacks which had been such a feature of my childhood and which still disfigured all the coalmining areas of Britain.

I learned soon enough that there was a price to pay for making a nuisance of myself. Some of my colleagues thought it absolutely impossible to get rid of muckstacks and regarded me as mad for trying. I had to put up with a fair bit of teasing in the tearoom for suggesting that Barnsley could be made as pleasant as Devon. I didn't win many friends either for nagging ministers about the need for a new hospital; I dare say my colleagues thought I was just trying to push Barnsley to the head of the queue. Nor were they best pleased when I started getting press publicity for my efforts, especially through Graham Cawthorne of the *Sheffield Telegraph*. It's amazing how petty and jealous politicians can be; any one of my fellow MPs could have achieved the same amount of coverage, if they'd bothered to speak to journalists.

Sometimes the competitiveness reached ludicrous levels. I was stopped in the corridor one day by a somewhat worried-looking Tony Benn. He asked for my date of birth, as earnestly as if the fate of the Western world depended on the answer. When I told him, he beamed in relief and delight before scurrying off. He was still, by a few months, the youngest member of the Parliamentary Labour Party. Phew!

I don't think I ever played the game of schoolboy self-promotion to that extent. Not consciously, anyway. If some of my fellow MPs thought me a mite bumptious, it was all a bit of a front on my part. Just as when I'd been in the pits, I covered up any inward doubts and uncertainties with a show of confidence. Besides, if I had any tendencies towards conceit or pomposity, they would have been pretty well squashed in two encounters with Winston Churchill.

The first came when he knocked me down. Literally. Whenever I was in the chamber, I always sat on the third row of the opposition benches. During the course of one late debate, a division took place at midnight. Churchill, the Prime Minister, was still there, waiting for the vote. When the time came, he rose to his feet and ambled towards the Bar of the House, on his way to the Division Lobby. I got up too, and came down the steps, momentarily hidden behind the bulk of the Serjeant-at-Arms' chair. As I emerged from behind it, Churchill hit me with a surprisingly solid shoulder – accidentally, of course – and sent me sprawling to the floor. There I was in my suit – still my one and only – rolling around in the dust and grime of a carpet which must have been trodden by hundreds of MPs that day. Not very dignified. Churchill helped me to my feet and brushed me down without a word. I should add that we were both stone cold sober.

Our second encounter did even more to put me in my place. It came in a moment of intense political excitement, after it was discovered that the Government was secretly developing the hydrogen bomb. There was uproar in the Labour Party, partly because of its growing anti-nuclear sentiment, partly because it felt that such major issues should be debated openly. A motion of censure was put down. If the governmment lost – admittedly an unlikely eventuality – there would have to be a general election. Even if that didn't happen, Churchill and his ministers would be on the rack. So it wasn't any surprise that the chamber was absolutely packed for the debate, MPs jostling on the green leather benches, crowding each other at the Bar of the House, even sitting on the steps in the aisles.

Following Attlee's advice, I'd begun taking an interest in defence and nuclear issues and so – more in hope than expectation – I sent a note to the Speaker, telling him that I'd like to contribute to the debate. I scribbled down an outline of what I wanted to say, without for a moment thinking I would be given the opportunity.

Clem Attlee stood at the Despatch Box first, giving a powerful, clipped performance which lasted just seventeen minutes – he never was one to spin things out – and was greeted at the end with a thunderous roar of 'Hear! Hear!' from our benches. Then it was Churchill's turn, the grand old man himself, defending the government with all the passion and eloquence at his command.

I wasn't really listening. Amid all the tumult and shouting between the two sides, I had been passed a note by the Yorkshire Whip, Horace Holmes. The Speaker intended to call me as soon as the Prime Minister sat down. I found myself gulping, partly in sheer terror, partly in anticipation of what would be the most important speech of my career.

So much for anticipation. Churchill finished his oration, to mighty yells of approval from his own side. I only just heard my name being called. I was on my feet, straining at the leash, ready to give the House the benefit of my wisdom. Unfortunately for me, the House had other ideas. Once Attlee and Churchill had spoken, few wanted to hang around for the words of the Honourable Member for Barnsley. There was a great rush for the doors, a seething crowd of MPs surging out to their offices, to the bar, the smoking-room, the tearoom, the library – anywhere, it seemed, to avoid listening to what I had to say. I was left in a sadly depleted chamber, my moment of glory gone.

It was a chastening experience, one which reminded me yet again that at Westminster I didn't count for very much. But I'm glad of it all the same. I'd witnessed and followed Churchill's last major speech as Prime Minister. Before long he would retire at last, to be succeeded – disastrously – by Anthony Eden. For now, though, he sat hunched on the front bench, stony-faced, as I launched into my attack on the government and all its works.

In the end, as expected, the censure motion was lost. The debate was reported as another triumph for Winston Churchill, with only a few throwaway references to the part played by Roy Mason. Not that I was downhearted for long: I still had my campaigns to keep me busy.

The general election of 1955 was called not long afterwards. Once again I started pounding the pavements, determined not to lose a single potential vote. In the country at large, the Labour cause wasn't prospering; but in Barnsley at least, I meant to see to it that the Tories were beaten out of sight. In my election address, I made a point of the need for a new local hospital and promised that I wouldn't rest until the ugly old muckstacks were levelled and landscaped. I knew I'd end up looking pretty foolish if I failed to get those pledges honoured. But by now I had the bit between my teeth.

Back at Westminster – still in opposition, after the disappointment of Labour's nationwide defeat – I claimed my usual place below the gangway and set to work. I was beginning to feel like an old hand, no longer needing the advice of my elders and betters. Ready for anything.

I was now concentrating even harder on defence matters, spending hours in the library reading up on policy, military equipment, our commitments overseas, every detail I could absorb. In the end I became a very junior member of George Brown's shadow defence team, a minor promotion which thrilled me no end. Maybe I was making up for the disappointment of not being allowed to join the armed services during the war. Anyway, I found my new studies fascinating and sometimes disturbing. Never more so than when I discovered how callously the Army was being treated by Whitehall.

I could hardly credit it. When a soldier died on duty in Germany, the military authorities virtually washed their hands of him. If the bereaved family wanted a funeral in Britain, it had to meet all the costs of flying the coffin over. Our troops, in fact, were being treated with the shabbiness miners were once shown by the private coalowners.

It wasn't on. Why should parents or other grieving relatives have to pay for their loved one to have a decent burial on British soil? After all, it would be a simple matter to take out a couple of seats on a normal trooping flight to accommodate a stretcher or a coffin. So I started raising the issue in the House at every opportunity. During one major defence debate, I spent the whole of my speech damning ministers for their indifference to the plight of service families. I could see that they found it embarrassing; the Tories, after all, liked to proclaim their devotion to the cause of the armed forces. But it still took months before they gave way and conceded that soldiers' bodies would be brought home free of charge. I took some satisfaction from the part I'd played in shaming them into doing the decent thing.

I hadn't forgotten my other causes. On the hospital issue, I put down dozens upon dozens of parliamentary questions, talked endlessly to the press, nagged and complained to ministers whenever I got the chance, secured an adjournment debate to spell out the inadequacies of hospital provision in Barnsley. The government must have been thoroughly fed up with the whole business. One day the Health Minister, Enoch Powell, was queuing behind me in the tearoom and asked me to come and see him in his office afterwards. I found him sitting behind a desk full of paperwork. Somewhat wearily, he explained that I was adding immensely to his workload. Thirty questions in three weeks, he thought, was a bit much. Every one of them had to be sent to the Sheffield Regional Hospital Board for comment, then passed on to the Barnsley Hospital Committee for a more detailed reply. After all that, the whole bundle of papers came back to his office, where his officials added still more supplementary briefs. It was all adding up to a huge amount of work. He looked me in the eye and said: 'Please stop. Your hospital is being placed at the top of the priority list and I promise it won't be dislodged short of war.'

A great moment. At times like that, I suppose all politicians feel they've achieved something special. I certainly did. I felt it again when in answer to my questions the Minister of Housing and Local Government, Harold Macmillan, produced his circular, *Spoil Heaps*, which began the long process of land reclamation throughout the coalfields. It was a dream come true. From the day I'd put out my first election address I had been campaigning as hard as I knew how to get rid of the muckstacks, those vast mountains of dirt, waste and slurry which surrounded every coalmine, belching out filthy, sulphurous fumes whenever they caught fire. Every family in every coalfield hated them for their ugliness and smell. The names may have changed from region to region – muckstacks in Yorkshire, bings in Scotland, pitheaps in Wales – but the feeling against them was universal. They were a blot on people's lives. So of course I was delighted that at last the Government proposed to do something about them. Every local authority received a circular ordering them to check their muckstacks. Today, there's hardly one to be seen, the length and breadth of the land. It still gives me a buzz to walk through fields and woodland where once there was nothing but rock, clod and filth. To have played a part in such a transformation is what makes politics worthwhile.

It certainly wasn't worthwhile in terms of money – not to begin with, at any rate. For me, the mid Fifties were a time of almost unbearable financial strain. I never went near the MPs' dining room, where there were starched white tablecloths, a waitress service and meals which seemed impossibly expensive. Instead I'd make do with snacks in the cafeteria. Tom Williams was moved to take me aside with the advice: 'Never economize through the stomach, Roy.' Well, he was a wise old bird, but it wasn't as though I'd much choice in the matter. Madge and I were living on hire purchase and up to our ears in debt. On top of that, I was still repaying the £50 borrowed from my father-in-law. In my desperation to raise some extra cash, I even asked the National Coal Board if I could claim the pension I was owed after fourteen years underground. The answer was that I'd have to wait until I was sixty-five. Then, but only then, I'd be awarded 1s 6d a week! In a black humour, I decided to let the future take care of itself. I cashed my pension entitlement in for a lump sum of £26. Just £26 for fourteen years underground! At least it kept the wolf from our door a while longer.

In fact my poverty was such that in 1956 it drove me to threaten the office with an embarrassing diplomatic incident.

I didn't start out with the intention of causing trouble. On the contrary, I was delighted to be picked as a member of a Parliamentary delegation to the Gold Coast, a place generally known then as the white man's grave. I'd never been to tropical parts before; now I was to see one of the more exotic corners of the British Empire, a country preparing itself for full independence within the Commonwealth. A great opportunity; but once my initial excitement had subsided, it began to dawn on me that I would probably need special clothing to cope with the African sun. So it proved. Well-travelled colleagues told me that I'd need lightweight underwear, a white suit, sandals, a soft hat, the full kit. It didn't sound as though it would come cheap.

Somewhat concerned, I rang the office of Duncan Sandys, the Commonwealth and Colonial Secretary, to see if the government could help out. A polite official said that he would make enquiries. Later that day he sent me a message on a pink telephone slip. Yes, all was well. The official allowance was £40, enabling each member of the delegation to tog himself out in style. Great news. I wasted no time rushing off to tell Fred Willey and Lance Mallalieu, the Labour colleagues who would be coming to the Gold Coast with me. Forty pounds! It seemed a fortune to all of us. Off we hurried to buy our gear, feeling pretty pleased with life. Certainly I'd never before spent so much on clothes.

Three days before we were due to set off, the axe fell. Duncan Sandys' Parliamentary Secretary stopped me in the corridor and told me his office had made a mistake. The tropical kit allowance was for civil servants only. It didn't apply to MPs. I just stared at him. 'That's unbelievable! Parliamentarians get nothing?' He nodded apologetically. I could feel my temper rising. 'And civil servants get forty pounds?' He nodded again, looking even more sheepish. I just had to let rip. 'Right! I intend to ask questions in the House about this. And you'll have to disband the delegation. We won't go!' I was steaming. Not only had I been saddled with a bill I couldn't pay. I'd unwittingly dropped two of my colleagues into the mire as well.

I spent the rest of the day trying to get Duncan Sandys on the phone. Unsuccessfully, which in retrospect was probably just as well; I'm not sure that a display of rage would have helped my case. By this time, the whole of Westminster knew that a ferocious row was brewing. I didn't care. I felt I had been pushed too far. I was still in the grimmest of moods next morning when quite by chance I bumped into Sandys behind the

Speaker's chair. He didn't need any telling. As it turned out, his private office had already tipped him off that the Gold Coast delegation was in a state of open mutiny. Before I could launch into my tirade, he hurriedly told me he would rectify the problem. Within a matter of hours, his office confirmed that all of us would get our allowance. A tremendous relief all round; and I still think that the MPs who stepped off the plane at Accra later that week were the best-dressed delegation ever to represent the House of Commons overseas.

One of the consequences of this episode was that I gradually found myself taking on the role of unofficial shop steward for backbench MPs. In alliance with Ray Mawby, the Tory Member for Totnes – and a former trades unionist – I began campaigning for better salaries, proper pensions and allowances to cover the cost of telephones, postage and secretarial help. Nowadays such things are taken for granted: back then, many thought Ray and I were asking for the moon. When I produced my pamphlet *A Pauperized Parliament*, there were sniffs of disapproval from all sides, Labour as well as Tory. We were seen as pushy and undignified for banging on about money; but then, it's always easy to be lofty about such matters when you've plenty of your own. Ray and I wouldn't be put off though. We kept on campaigning and ignored the jibes. In the end, of course, we won our case in every particular. Ray deserves a lot of the credit. It must have been particularly difficult for him, a working-class lad in a party full of condescending toffs. But he was a good man, as genial as he was tough. I could never quite understand how he came to find himself sitting on the Tory benches.

The second outcome of the Gold Coast trip was more serious. Almost from the moment we stepped off the plane to observe the independence elections, it became clear to me that the country wasn't remotely ready. The people were very largely illiterate. There was no tradition of democracy, no developed adversarial system of politics and precious little understanding of what it was like to run a nation state. Perhaps I was just naïve. It was, after all, the first colony I had ever seen. But I didn't trust Kwame Nkrumah, the man who would almost certainly emerge as leader after the elections. It seemed to me that London was rushing its fences, too eager to get rid of a colony which needed more time. My suspicion was that Ghana – as it was to become – would slump more or less immediately into dictatorship.

It was a point of view which I guessed wouldn't go down well in the Labour Party, but I was determined to air my views. On my return, I met Hugh Dalton in the tearoom and told him of my concern. He advised me to go and see the Speaker, 'Shakes' Morrison. 'Stay in the Chamber,' said Morrison, 'And your voice will be heard.' He was as good as his word.

And so I spoke in the debate on the Bill of Independence and warned that all the high hopes for the new country were likely to be sadly disappointed. I didn't coin the term 'One man, one vote, once'; but that's what I meant. It's no satisfaction to me that I was proved right, not only about Ghana but virtually every other African country that shook off European rule. Still, being right isn't necessarily an advantage in politics. As soon as I sat down after that speech, I knew that I had mortally offended many of my colleagues. People like Fenner Brockway and the anti-colonial Left – the theoreticians and ideologues who'd read all the books and knew all the 'correct' reponses to each and every issue – took to cutting me dead at every opportunity. In the tearoom, they'd turn their backs as ostentatiously as they possibly could; in the corridors they would stalk past unspeaking, their noses in the air. Fortunately for me, I still had plenty of friends, people who for the most part had earned their living in factories or the pits and knew that life wasn't quite as straightforward as the textbooks made out. So I wasn't alone.

But the minor difficulties I had to endure were only part of a more widespread nastiness creeping into the party. At all levels. The heady optimism of 1945 had all but evaporated as the Fifties wore on. Now we seemed to spend more time fighting each other than opposing the Tories. With the growing influence of the Left, under the charismatic influence of Aneurin Bevan, the Labour benches in Parliament were sinking deeper by the day into a swamp of petty hatreds, self-indulgence and spite. Bevan himself was a giant of a character, eloquent, passionate and full of fire. He was capable of great personal generosity, even to his opponents, as I was later to discover. But many of those who followed him were cut from shoddier cloth. Under the influence of their bitterness and self-righteousness, the atmosphere in the parliamentary party was often ugly. There was no doubt that the Bevanite group was trying to take over the parliamentary party as a prelude to imposing its own version of pure, undiluted socialism on the whole country. Those of us who would not sign up to the left-wing agenda – unilateralism, uncritical support for the Soviet Union, knee-jerk anti-Americanism, opposition to the then Common Market – were damned as right-wingers or even class-traitors. Argument developed into disdain and disdain into personal hatred. Those of us on the so-called 'Right' grew used to being cut dead by our supposed comrades.

To be fair, the anatagonism wasn't all on one side. Backbenchers like the London MP Frank Tomney hated Bevan's minions with a far greater loathing than anything they felt for the Tories. He took the view that if the Left took over it would rupture the party and it might never recover. I shared his gloomy outlook; it was one of the reasons I voted against

Bevan and in favour of Hugh Gaitskell in the leadership contest of 1955. For all his ability and charisma, Nye was soundly beaten.

But by this time I had almost grown used to the viciouness of the fight. It couldn't be escaped. Yet again, I felt driven to take sides in a party which seemed determined to tear itself apart.

The issue, inevitably, was defence. There were many on the Left who saw the NATO alliance as a capitalist and militarist conspiracy, people who were wilfully blind to the aggressive nature of Soviet Communism and whose hatred of the Americans went beyond all reason. They seemed to me little better than the appeasers who had given Hitler a free run in the Thirties. And in their eagerness to defy party policy and undermine the leadership of Hugh Gaitskell, they were going a fair way towards making Labour unelectable.

The day came when they went too far. The occasion was a defence debate, one of those tense, crowded confrontations in the Commons when the Labour front bench was desperately trying to present a coherent, united front. The party had imposed a three-line whip for the vote at the end. Every MP had been warned that defiance simply wouldn't be tolerated. Not this time. If support for the official policy wasn't rock-solid, then our defence policy would be seen by the voters – quite understandably – as a shambles.

But the Left never did seem to have much sense of loyalty – or of self-preservation. At the end of the debate, George Draddock, Emrys Hughes, Sydney Silverman, S.O. Davies, Ernest Fernyhough, Victor Yates and John McCovern, ostentatiously refused to march into the voting lobby with the rest of us. In effect, they were daring Gaitskell and the leadership to do their worst.

I was never in any doubt about the outcome. It was inevitable. Even so, the seven rebels weren't going down without a fight. At the very least, they would have their day in court.

I think the entire membership of the Parliamentary Labour Party turned up for the 'trial'. The Grand Committee Room off Westminster Hall was a packed, seething mass, every chair taken, every corner crowded. I managed to get a perch on one of the windowsills with three colleages, all of us squashed uncomfortably together. Just in front of us sat Bevan, his face set. Though he had not defied the whip, he passionately supported the rebels' cause. The atmosphere was electric.

One by one, the rebels rose in their places to explain themselves. But the outcome was never really in doubt. Labour would never again be an effective political force if the rebels escaped punishment. The pity is that Bevan himself didn't seem to understand that.

In the end, the vote against him and the others was overwhelming, 131 to 93. He swung round to look at me as I put my hand up to have the whip withdrawn. He was clearly shocked at the outcome; shocked that I, as a fellow miner, had joined the ranks of his enemies. Moments later as we were thronging out – most of us in a subdued frame of mind – he rounded on me, brandishing a great ham of a fist in my face. 'I'll never forgive you for this,' he snarled. 'Never.' He was on the verge of tears.

But not long afterwards, when I was deep in trouble, he did forgive me. He forgave me with a display of generosity for which I've always been grateful. I disliked Nye's politics; I couldn't help admiring the personality of the man himself.

My spot of bother blew up with an article I wrote for the *Sunday People*, in which I complained about the enforced idleness of trades-union sponsored MPs, me included. It wasn't our fault: many of us wanted to be more active. The trouble was, our respective unions simply wouldn't let us. Again and again, whenever we wanted to make a point or kick up a fuss, the message would come down from the leadership of the NUM, the T&G, the Boilermakers or whoever: don't make a speech on this; don't ask a Parliamentary question on that. Their argument was simple. We were intruding. They could knock on any Minister's door at any time and demand to be heard. They didn't want to muddy the waters by letting MPs get involved.

I could see their point, of course. On the other hand, that attitude was stultifying the efforts of a whole group of parliamentarians. It reduced our influence. It didn't seem right to me; but I never dreamed I would provoke such outrage just for saying so.

There was uproar in the Trade Union Group of MPs when the *People* article appeared. The very next day, the Executive Committee met in Room J under the Chamber in what was to all intents and purposes a drumhead court-martial. I was working in the library at the time, blissfully unaware that I was on trial. Or that I'd been pronounced guilty in my absence. The first I knew of it was when the Bermondsey MP Bob Mellish appeared as a grim emissary. 'The Trade Union Executive wants to see you downstairs, Roy,' he announced. 'Now.' It wasn't an invitation I could refuse.

The atmosphere in Room J was grim. I entered to a collective glower. Bill Williams, the MP for Openshaw was in the Chair. George Brown, my boss on the defence team was there, as stern-faced as the others. Their message was uncompromising. I'd have to back down. I was ordered to write a letter to the *People* for publication the very next Sunday, explaining how I'd got it all wrong. It wasn't just humble pie they were forcing on me; it was a double helping.

I dug in my heels and told the executive there wasn't a chance of an apology. I stood by what I had written. I'd only said what needed saying; and if I backed down now, I'd only succeed in making myself look silly. By now the others were looking more than ever like a conclave of hanging judges. They were certainly angry as I was sent away. I had an uneasy feeling that I'd let myself in for real trouble.

And that's how it looked like turning out. When I had left, the executive decided that the issue had to be brought before the whole Trade Union Group. Not only that, but Nye Bevan would be invited to address the meeting on the relationship between sponsored MPs and their unions. The scene was set for a very public drubbing. Some of my comrades could hardly conceal their satisfaction that too-big-for-his-boots Roy Mason was about to be taught a lesson.

I went to the meeting expecting the worst, coming in late, sitting at the back of the room, huddling down in my chair to make myself as inconspicuous as possible. If ever there was a moment for Nye to take his revenge, this was it. But as he developed his theme, I started to sit up. Far from damning me up hill and down dale, he seemed to be taking my side. This wasn't revenge at all. It was almost a blessing. Most of what I had written in that *People* article, Bevan declared, was accurate. Of course there were problems between sponsored MPs and their trade unions. It was foolish to pretend otherwise. I felt the tension draining away. The mood in the room was changing. There would be no drubbing after all. As I was walking down the corridor afterwards, mightily relieved at my escape, Nye placed his arm round my shoulder. 'There you are, lad,' he said. 'I can't do better than that for you!'

Perhaps if we'd all managed to show each other that kind of generosity rather more often, the Fifties might not have been such a disaster for the party. I still cringe when I look back on the opportunities we squandered through lack of discipline, feuding and the endless parade of personal animosities.

Take the Suez crisis of 1956. That could and should have been our moment. Here was a Tory government conspiring with the French and the Israelis – though of course we didn't then know about the secret meetings – to invade Egypt and topple its leader, Gamal Abdul Nasser. Sure, Nasser had acted recklessly in taking over the canal; but the armed response from Britain and the others was a supreme folly, worsened by the fact that the government hadn't even managed to square the Americans first. The result was outright opposition from Washington, international embarrassment and the near collapse of the pound. The outcome was a humiliating withdrawal and political chaos at home. British public opinion was divided, confused and angry. And to make matters worse, the whole shaming episode served to divert attention from the brutal Soviet rape of Hungary.

I'd never before witnessed greater rage in the Commons. The House was in such a state of tension that it had to be suspended for a time. People sometimes complain about the rude and raucous behavior of MPs; but at times of crisis, in matters of war and peace, life and death, they have no choice but to show their feelings. Ministers deserved the storm of angry barracking which greeted them whenever they tried to speak. I think every MP in the chamber knew that the government was lying through its teeth about the origins of the débâcle. Everybody understood the damage that had been done to the country's reputation and honour. We'd been made to look fools in the eyes of the world. I remember Hugh Gaitskell in full flight, proving what a great debater he was, lacerating Anthony Eden for his catastrophic misjudgement and the political disaster he had brought on all our heads. Every word struck home. You could see it in the eyes of the Tory front bench. And in the expressions of Eden's parliamentary supporters. They knew their leader had disgraced himself, his party and the country. They must have felt in their bones that their position was beyond recovery.

Yet recover they did, with our help. Eden resigned soon afterwards, sick, worn out and still clinging to the pathetic belief that he'd been right. The Tories were discredited and despised in the country. The new Prime Minister, Harold Macmillan, hardly seemed the man to rally the troops. All the Labour Party had to do was close in for the kill.

Instead, we turned on each other, tearing ourselves to tatters over NATO, nuclear weapons and the Common Market. We squabbled while the Tories slowly knitted themselves together, argued while Macmillan turned himself unchallenged into the cartoon image of Supermac, traded insults among ourselves while our lead in the polls began to evaporate. I wasn't really suprised when we lost the election in 1959 on Macmillan's boast that 'You've never had it so good.' We had been handed our chance on a golden platter and just thrown it away.

Party conferences in those years were a misery for those of us who wanted to concentrate on fighting the Tories. Bevan would invariably pop up with a speech that entirely contradicted the official policy of the parliamentary party. He'd go to union conferences too and deliver grandstanding attacks against Hugh Gaitskell and the Shadow Cabinet. The Left, of course, loved him for it. People like Arthur Scargill and Mick McGahey, rising stars within the NUM, made him a hero. I dare say the Tories loved him for it too, since it made their cause all the easier.

Like others on the so-called Right, I believed that Bevan and his acolytes had to be stopped, however great the personal attractiveness of the man himself. The cause was all the more urgent because of the growing demonstrations against nuclear weapons and the vast marches to

Aldermaston every Easter, with left-wingers like Michael Foot prominent in the forefront. Through the work I'd done on defence policy, I had become convinced that unilateralism was not only misguided but positively dangerous, because it would inevitably undermine NATO and make a Soviet attack more rather than less likely. I had no illusions at all about the criminality and brutality of the Kremlin leadership, or about its aggressive intent. After the Berlin blockade of 1949 and the savage suppression of the Hungarian uprising in 1956, nobody but a blinkered fool could possibly doubt the militaristic nature of Soviet Communism; but some on the Left managed it somehow.

Bevan himself wasn't so gullible. As Shadow Foreign Secretary, he began to see – more clearly than his followers ever could – the complexities of the nuclear issue, the nature of the threat and the importance of preserving the Western Alliance. It was to lead to a dramatic conversion. At the Labour conference in 1957, he stood defiantly at the podium, begging the party to maintain nuclear weapons. 'Do not send me naked into the conference chamber,' he implored. It was an act of extraordinary bravery and honesty; but of course most of his erstwhile followers loathed him for it. From that day on, they turned on him, damning him as a traitor to principle, growing ever more extreme in their hatred. We contracted the disease of 'splittitis'. It was an ailment which led us to electoral defeat in 1959 and very nearly cost us the election of 1964.

I couldn't, of course, foresee all those ugly consequences; but I understood instinctively that the fight would have to be fought to a finish. The left-wingers were not only playing fast and loose with the safety of the country and betraying their own people. They were also undermining the Labour Party and damaging its leader Hugh Gaitskell, a man I liked and admired. In fact our relationship was so close that he was godfather to my second daughter, Jill, when we had her christened in the crypt at the House of Commons. So right up until he died I got stuck into Gaitskell's enemies – and mine – at every opportunity. By then, of course, the chasm between me and the Left was unbridgeably wide – particularly as I had published a couple of admittedly provocative pamphlets: *Why German Troops Should Be Allowed To Train in Britain* and later on *Polaris Yes, Yes, Yes*.

It not only made for more enemies in parliament; it inspired bitter animosities within my own union too. Particularly from a a former member of the Young Communist league and now a delegate from Woolley Colliery, called Arthur Scargill.

Scargill was by now a member of the Labour Party, but as far as I could see he hadn't changed his philosophy. He still seemed to believe in permanent revolution and appeared to think that the Soviet Union and

Cuba were workers' paradises. And of course he hated everything I stood for. Every utterance I made in favour of closer European co-operation or the need for a strong defence against the Soviet Union seemed to him evidence of class treachery. He was entitled to his views, of course; but I knew him for an enemy long before he made his move.

It came with a resolution which he managed to get through Woolley Colliery miners' branch, calling for consideration of Roy Mason's parliamentary future. Quite how many men voted still isn't clear to me; I'd guess about twenty or thirty members in a branch of around 1,500. But it didn't matter. The fact that an important Yorkshire pit wanted me sacked – because that's what it amounted to – had to be taken seriously. If my union turned against me, I didn't think the constituency Labour Party would be far behind.

So the day came when the Yorkshire Miners' Council sent for me, in what was to all intents and purposes a political trial. It was a bad moment, not because I thought I would lose, but because it seemed to me further evidence of the forces that were tearing the movement apart. However the confrontation turned out, it wouldn't do the union any good. Or the Labour Party.

Scargill spoke first, clutching a microphone in the body of the hall, watched by more than a hundred delegates and the platform party of senior officials. From the moment he opened his mouth, it was clear that he hadn't much of a case. I could see that the audience wasn't impressed. Half way through his speech, a chap named Fred Hansen called out: 'Throw in the towel, Scargill!' It might have upset him a bit, but he ploughed on gamely to the end, though without causing me any damage, as far as I could tell.

Then it was my turn. I knew I had to be on form. Scargill was a forceful character, used to getting his own way. He wouldn't have attempted a coup against me without sounding out some of the delegates first. But as I spoke, I became increasingly confident that the Yorkshire Council was on my side. At one stage, somebody – it might have been Fred Hansen again – shouted, 'Hear that? Throw in the towel, Scargill!' When the vote was taken, Scargill got eight and I got ninety-eight. I think he took it hard. He wasn't accustomed to losing, but on that day he lost and lost badly. I don't believe he ever forgave me for the rest of my political life. It was the beginning of an enduring enmity which would lead to many a confrontation in the future.

He wasn't my only opponent within the union. Some time later, in 1971 I went with Madge to the NUM conference in the granite city of Aberdeen, where the miners were preparing to come out in full-blooded opposition to Britain's membership of the Common Market. I couldn't have been more deeply dismayed. I was passionately in favour of our membership, because it seemed obvious to me that our long-term future lay in closer co-operation with our European allies. Mick McGahey, Scargill and all the other Communists and fellow-travellers in the union took the opposite view, on the grounds that a strong, united and prosperous Europe might prove inconvenient to their beloved Soviet Union. The sad thing was, they were in the ascendancy.

But I was determined they wouldn't railroad their views through without opposition. A 'No' decision by the miners, after all, would certainly have a major impact on Labour Party policy. So there and then I wrote a pamphlet on why the NUM should embrace the Common Market, had it printed, and stood outside the conference hall with Madge, handing it out to delegates as they arrived.

It turned out to be a wasted effort. During the debate, not one of the delegates supported my line. Overwhelmingly, the NUM rejected the Common Market as a bankers' ramp, an anti-workers' conspiracy and a threat to all the principles of socialism. It was a deeply depressing moment. I just wanted to get away.

I called a taxi to take Madge and me to the station. We got into it outside the conference hall and were just preparing to drive off when suddenly we were surrounded by a jeering crowd of Communists and left-wingers. McGahey was there, waving his arms. Others were thumping the roof. Some of them began pushing, rocking the vehicle from side to side. It was clear they meant to turn us over. Madge hunched down in her seat, managing to appear calm. I was seriously alarmed. Fortunately, our driver kept his head. He eased the taxi forward, very slowly. By this time, the mob was demented, pushing harder. There were no police in sight. The only help we'd get would have to come from our driver. He stepped harder on the gas. There was more thumping on the bodywork, more curses and yelling. Then somehow we were pulling away, leaving McGahey and his thugs behind. It was a thoroughly nasty assault by the Communists and their colleagues – and all because we'd dared to present an argument they didn't like.

As the fifties turned into the sixties, the Left redoubled its attack. The solid old certainties which had once been the bedrock of party policy began to crumble. Poor Nye Bevan died in 1960, worn out, I suspect, by all the fratricidal bitterness. More and more, the constituencies and the unions began parroting the agenda of the Left, until at the grisly party conference in 1961 they swept all before them. That was the year when Labour formally embraced the policy of unilateral nuclear disarmament, a decision which if implemented would begin to unravel the Western Alliance and present the Soviet Union with its greatest ever triumph in foreign policy. That was the year when, his back to the wall, Hugh Gaitskell roared defiance from the podium with his unforgettable promise to 'fight, fight and fight again to save the party I love'.

Tragically, he was never to get the opportunity. Shortly afterwards, he followed Bevan to the grave. For me, it was a devastating blow. I had not only lost a political mentor, but also a valued friend. Now we had a new party leader, in the young and energetic Harold Wilson.

Though his reputation was very much as a man of the Left, I had little hesitation in voting for him. It seemed to me that he was clever and confident, with more than enough guile to hold the extremists in check; and so it proved. In the beginning at least, the old Bevanite faction seemed ungrudgingly supportive. No doubt some of its members felt ashamed of what they had done to Bevan and Gaitskell; or perhaps they just sniffed the possibility of power. Harold Wilson was proving himself a truly formidable leader of the opposition; and under the weight of scandal and weariness, the Tory government was at last starting to fall apart.

By this time I was a full-blown front-bencher, Shadow Postmaster-General, no less. Like many others in the party I began wondering what it would be like to wield real power as a minister. This time, we surely wouldn't let the opportunity slip from our grasp. The Tories were increasingly bogged down in misfortune. They had sufferered an appalling scandal over John Vassall, a homosexual employee at the Ministry of Defence who'd been caught selling military secrets to the Russians. Hard on the heels of that calamity came the Profumo affair, when the War Minister was exposed for lying to the House over his relationship with that lady of leisure Christine Keeler, someone whose favours he shared with the military attaché at the Russian Embassy. To his great credit, Jack Profumo later became a pillar of goodness giving years of dedicated service in community work.

Back then though, nothing the Conservatives could do was right. Ministers were lampooned and lambasted by an increasingly exasperated press. There seemed to be a national feeling that it was time for a change. Satirical shows like *Beyond the Fringe* captured that mood. And the government's standing wasn't helped by the immense popularity of a revolutionary new Saturday-night programme on BBC television called *That Was The Week That Was*. Millions tuned in every week to see presenters like the young David Frost trample all over the old conventions of deference which had hitherto kept Conservative politicians safe. Suddenly, for the first time in an age, ministers discovered what is is like to be held up to ridicule.

Those were great days for the Labour Party. Harold Macmillan sensationally resigned in the middle of his party's annual conference, his reputation for languid unflappability torn to tatters. Better still for us, he was succeeded as Prime Minister by the 14th Earl of Home, an apparent throwback to the Victorian system of aristocratic government who seemed hopelessly out of tune with the times. Harold Wilson, meanwhile, was having a field day, dominating the Commons at the Despatch Box, reaching out to the voters, proclaiming a new Britain forged in the white heat of the technological revolution.

Labour was winning at last. We could all sense it. Alec Home tried to stave off the inevitable by hanging on to power until the last possible moment, but it was a forlorn endeavour. With the election of 1964, we knew we'd put an end to the Tories and their thirteen wasted years of power. Now it was our turn to govern; and I fully expected to play a central part as the nation's new Postmaster-General.

6 A Minister of the Crown

In all our excitement and anticipation of triumph, we'd managed to forget one of the most basic rules in politics: never count your chickens. Alec Home notwithstanding, Harold Wilson's brilliance notwithstanding, we came within a whisker of losing in 1964. As it turned out, Labour won fewer votes than in 1959, though the electorate was larger. We scraped into office on a minority vote, thanks largely to the 'first-past-the-post' principle of Britain's electoral system. Our overall parliamentary majority was five, nowhere near enough for comfort. In effect, the voters had put us on probation.

Not that my enthusiasm was dampened in the slightest. All that mattered to me was that after thirteen years with the frustration of opposition – eleven of which I'd shared as an MP – Labour was back in power. At last we could begin to get things done. I had no inkling then of the economic storms which would batter the new government, the sustained, speculative attacks on sterling, the erosion of the country's gold reserves or the need for harsh, deflationary budgets. I was eager and elated. Ready for anything.

I wasted no time getting myself down to Westminster. I knew very well that when Harold Wilson summoned a ministerial hopeful, his first point of contact would be at the House of Commons. I certainly didn't want to be hard to find. And sure enough, I eventually received a message to go across to Number Ten.

Not before time. I'd spent anxious hours watching as colleagues received their calls from on high, most of them returning with pleased expressions shortly thereafter, a few looking glum. I did my best to look nonchalant while friends, rivals and a few enemies trekked back and forth to their appointments with the Prime Minister, though I don't suppose my demeanour fooled a soul. I was so obviously on tenterhooks. When would my turn come? Would it come at all? It was quite a relief when the waiting was over at last.

I was full of optimism on the short walk across Whitehall and into

Downing Street. Clearly Harold was going to make me Postmaster-General, since I had shadowed that role in opposition and knew it backwards. I was confident I would make a job of it, though I'd made no preparations for legislation or anything of that nature. Still, it was a job, and a pretty senior one too, just outside the Cabinet. I'd have a whole department to run, a sizeable budget to command, real influence within the government and my own car with an official driver: more than enough to be going on with.

But I was still counting those chickens. When I was ushered in to see Harold in the Cabinet Room, he announced that he wanted me to become Minister of State at the Board of Trade. With special responsibility for shipping and shipbuilding. I couldn't conceal my disappointment. The Board of Trade? I barely knew where it was.

But Harold was an old charmer when he wanted to be. He made the job sound not only exciting but essential to the economic well-being of the country. Here was one of Britain's proudest industries, the key to our historic mastery of the seas, the basis of a trading endeavour which reached to every port and harbour in the world. Could I possibly turn down the opportunity to be part of such a mighty enterprise? Of course I couldn't. By the time I left Number Ten, all but a trace of my disappointment had evaporated. I returned to the Commons to sit and think about the task which had been thrust upon me.

I didn't have much time for pondering. Hardly had I settled down than I received a telephone call from one of the civil servants at the Board of Trade asking me across to my new domain. The building was in Victoria Street, a vast, artificially ventilated construction in concrete and glass, ugly as so many modern Ministries tend to be, but comfortable enough. And there was a touch of grandeur in the view; from my office on the sixth floor, I could see Westminster Abbey and Parliament.

But it was clear from the very beginning that I'd have no time to stand and stare. This was unknown territory, full of snares and the possibility of mishap.

My immediate boss was the President of the Board of Trade, the austere and somewhat forbidding Douglas Jay. He was an excellent economist and a first-class writer, regularly contributing financial articles to the national press. Very much respected in Parliament, he set a standard which I knew would be difficult to match. But he was always kind to me – and he had one fad which was very much to my advantage. He absolutely hated travelling, didn't like going abroad and was only too happy to delegate overseas trips to me. It meant that I had the opportunity to learn rather more quickly than most junior ministers.

And there was plenty to learn. I knew that the moment I was introduced to the Permanent Under Secretary at the Board, Sir Richard Powell, a well-built chap with the blaze of intelligence in his eyes and an immediately impressive personality. It struck me then how very powerful and formidable these Whitehall mandarins were. I had never met any of them before; but without a doubt they were the kingpins of government. I thought it would be a very long time before I had the confidence or experience to challenge their opinions.

Meanwhile, I had to grapple with the everyday realities of ministerial life, learning how to work with two private secretaries, a diary secretary and platoons of advisers who knew far more about the ins and outs of my new job than I did. Of these experts, none was more valuable to me than Amos Sutcliffe, a man who had worked in shipyards like Harland and Wolff and John Brown before being seconded to the civil service. With his hands-on experience always available, I gradually began to understand the complexities of the job I had taken on.

The tragic truth, I discovered, was that British shipbuilding faced ruin. Yes, we still had the great yards on Clydeside, Belfast and the Tyne. Yes, we had naval building at Rosyth, Devonport and elsewhere. Yes, there was plenty of construction capacity in smaller firms all around our coasts. But almost the whole of it was clapped out, obsolescent, overmanned and incapable of meeting the challenge from overseas.

The shipyards were in a bit of a mess, burdened by years of under-investment, by a multiplicity of competing trades unions, by restrictive practices, poor management and outdated working techniques. In this regard, they were worse than the pits. Electricians contested with engineers, who in turn did likewise. There were endless demarcation disputes over who did what. Whenever I visited a yard, I felt a growing sense of doom.

What I remember most clearly from those first few months is the sheer backwardness of our operations: old-fashioned welding, old-fashioned riveting, men in flat caps which they doffed whenever their bowler-hatted bosses walked past. I once went to a lunch where the owner of the yard stood at the end of the table with a great tureen of soup before him. We guests, along with everybody else, had to pass our plates along for him to fill. I doubt if you could find more old-fashioned, antiquated aloofness than that. I was tempted to do an Oliver Twist and ask for more.

It was just as old-fashioned on the union side. Often I'd hold mass meetings in local halls or cinemas. I'd preach the doctrine of productivity, the need to build ships more cheaply and on time, the importance of matching what our competitors – particularly the Japanese – were doing. I don't think it made a scrap of difference. The audiences would listen, of course. They'd applaud too. But change their restrictive practices? Not a chance.

I became even more worried for the future when I visited Japan. What I saw over there deepened my dismay. I was staggered by the progress they had made, how far they had left us behind. Every part of every yard was controlled and run by engineering graduates who certainly didn't need any lectures on productivity. They were all into critical path analysis techniques, making sure that in the pipewelding shop, in the bulkhead shop, in every part of the building of a ship, the materials were ready on time, delivered on time and produced at the agreed cost. Or less. I thought back to the yards in Britain, where each block of steel was cut and shaped individually; the young and clever Japanese were knocking out those same shapes six at a time. That wasn't the end of it. Unlike us, they could weld a bulkhead without having to lift it up and turn it over. In fact there didn't seem to be a single job in shipbuilding which they couldn't do faster, more efficiently and cheaper than us.

I was in a pretty bleak mood as I flew home. I had seen the future and frankly it terrified me; and the more I saw, the more pessimistic I became. It wasn't just the Japanese who were trouncing us. In Denmark they'd started building ships in spanking new dry docks, instead of on old-fashioned slipways. In Russia, they were making a name for themselves with fast, glamorous hydrofoils. And in Britain? The bosses still wore bowler hats. Their flat-capped underlings spent much of the day touching their forelocks. And when they weren't doing that they squabbled with each other over who did what.

If we couldn't wake our ideas up, we'd certainly be done for. What we needed – and urgently – was an utter transformation in our way of doing things, with a huge investment programme, the end of restrictive practices, better management, the amalgamation of smaller yards. The prescription was obvious enough; but in our system of democracy, no individual minister – let alone a mere Minister of State – can simply order such a drastic remedy. No, the only way forward was that good old British standby. I'd have to form a committee.

And so I did. I picked the veteran industrialist Lord Geddes to lead a team of independent experts, charging him with the task of seeing how we could rescue our ramshackle yards. Meanwhile, I made it my business to bang the drum at meetings of the Boilermakers, the Engineers, in fact any union which would have me. All of them listened to what I had to say. Some even agreed with me. But most seemed to think I was exaggerating the scale of the crisis. And time was slipping away.

It was more than a year before the Geddes Committee reported, with the recommendation that there should be a Shipbuilding Industry Board. I made sure that Joe Gormley of the NUM was a member, because the Board's work was bound to involve the pain of redundancy and the unions had to be on side. Government money would be available to encourage the privately owned yards to amalgamate and improve. The solution was sensible enough; but it seemed to me that it was too little, too late. The country had squandered a whole year before deciding the obvious. The shipbuilding magnates had never spent enough of their own money on bringing their operations up to date and were now relying on government handouts. The unions, though acquiescent in the need for change, were hardly enthusiastic. I thought even then that the writing was on the wall.

One of the lessons every new minister has to learn is that the rock certainties of opposition begin to look pretty threadbare when you're in Government. We had squeaked into power convinced we could do miles better than the Tories in what we'd derided as their 'thirteen wasted years', but almost from the first day we found ourselves mired in difficulty.

My own modest progress in tackling the problems of shipbuilding illustrates the point, though it was of course a sideshow. What really dominated our first seventeen months in power were the repeated assaults on the value of the pound, inspired partly by our tiny parliamentary majority and partly by the huge trade deficit we had inherited. That £800 million may seem pretty small beer by today's standards, but it was still the worst figure by a long way in the nation's peacetime history. And Harold Wilson's dogged determination to rule out the apparently easy option of devaluation meant that we wore in for a long haul before we could turn our trade around.

For me, the difference between the theory and practice of politics was summed up in a publicity stunt which very nearly went badly wrong.

One of my responsibilities at the Board of Trade was safety at sea, an issue which in my innocence I imagined could be handled by the shrewd stroke of a Ministerial pen. After all, could there be much more to it than ensuring that the regulations were sensible and enforceable?

It was in this rather complacent frame of mind that I decided to put on a bit of a show for the media. Since I had always got on well with journalists and broadcasters, it seemed a great idea to invite some of them to a night at sea on a trawler, where they could observe Roy Mason conscientiously going about his ministerial duties and demonstrating his concern for safety at sea. The event should make some splendid news pictures, at the very least.

We gathered on the quayside in the fishing port of Grimsby, a television camera-crew, three or four print jounalists from the national newspapers, George Deer, the MP for Newark and myself, all of us, I think, rather looking forward to the night ahead. True, the trawler on which we were to embark – the *Ross Tern* – seemed very small for a vessel which had to combat the rigours of the North Sea; but the five-man crew wore obviously old salts who knew their trade and the skipper cut a reassuring figure too. We slipped out of harbour at 11 p.m. on this pleasant night, in the best of spirits.

For the next few hours, all went remarkably well. In fact we landlubbers were all enjoying the experience of being far out at sea in such a small vessel. It didn't matter that there were no bunks for us, since we were all fascinated to see the way fishermen went about their trade. One or two of us, I suppose, may have felt a little queasy as we bobbed up and down, but that wasn't a problem for me. I've never felt sick on a ship, in a car or on a plane; and since I had no work to do other than appear wise and ministerial, the trip was rather relaxing.

I remember the skipper telling me that we were in good fishing grounds, some 40 miles off the coast. It was about 4.30 in the morning. He'd let down his onion-bag net over the side and was looking forward to a good haul. We observers were intent on keeping out of the way, while still making sure that we could see what was going on. That was when the tannoy squawked into life. Force 8 gale imminent, it said. Humber area.

Humber? That was surely us, wasn't it? Pressmen and politicians glanced uneasily at each other. The crew meanwhile were already pulling in the net, clearly anxious to get it on board and stowed away before the storm hit. They needed to be quick about it. Conditions were deteriorating with disturbing rapidity. The trawler was already bouncing up and down more vigorously than before. The wind was fiercer too, slamming across the deck. The crew were working with more urgency by the minute, almost in a frenzy to get the catch into the hold. Meanwhile the skipper was altering course for shore and safety.

Our boat was running into the teeth of the gale. I remember the vast green seas dwarfing us all, water thundering in furious tons across the deck, the vessel plunging down and sickeningly down into what appeared black holes in the ocean, the slow, painful struggle to climb out again. The rain roared, the wind howled. I was clinging for dear life to the radarscope, the skipper beside me with his arms locked around the wheel. We were the lucky ones. My companions were crouched down in corners, clinging to whatever was available and being horribly sick. Poor George Deer vomited and lost his dentures; for a few reckless minutes, the rest of us abandoned our handholds to scrabble around looking for them, while the deck reared up and down. It was like riding the big dipper at Blackpool.

In the radio room a crewman was bellowing 'Mayday! Mayday!

Mayday!' I remember wondering if anybody could possibly rescue us in such conditions. It seemed unlikely. Still, we were on course for home. The engines were still working. Our vessel was somehow managing to labour her way out of the deepest troughs. All we had to do was endure for a few worrying, unpleasant hours and we'd sail into the relative safety of the Humber estuary.

We limped into calmer waters at last, battered, bruised but grateful to be alive. One by one, members of the press party emerged from their corners and cubby-holes. Notebooks were produced. Cameras, too. The television crew started filming. There was an atmosphere of near hilarity, a natural reaction, I suppose, when people have come so close to the dangerous edge.

The merriment didn't last. One of the crew was down in the galley, cooking breakfast; before long, the smell of frying bacon and sausages was wafting up from below. I was suddenly starving and in my iron-stomached way looking forward to a bite; but almost to a man, the press contingent faltered. Cameras were put to one side, notebooks shoved in pockets. One by one, they staggered queasily to the rail to lean over the side, a picture of abject misery.

We sailed home to harbour at last, to be greeted by ambulances waiting on the quayside. Fortunately, we had no serious casualties, though some of our party needed to go to hospital for checks.

I returned to London a wiser man than I left it. I'd certainly learned more about safety at sea in those few, apprehension-filled hours than anything I could ever have gleaned behind a ministerial desk.

One of the consequences of that experience was that I started thinking about the quality of the lifejackets available to trawlermen and the Merchant Navy. The model then in use was a cork 'neckbreaker' which fitted under the chin and was capable of doing serious injury to any wearer who jumped into the water from a great height. It seemed to me a thoroughly unsatisfactory design, so I launched a nationwide competition to find a safer, more efficient alternative. When the various entries came in, I insisted on joining in the tests, which were conducted in a private swimming pool. There's nothing quite so invigorating as an hour or two spent leaping into the water from the top diving deck.

In the event – and without any arm-twisting from me – the clear winner was judged to be from McLintock's of Barnsley, a firm famous for producing eiderdowns, which had decided to have a go at lifejackets. It had done quite astonishingly well. Its new design not only avoided the risk of injury but offered a much higher chance of survival in the water, because it turned a man overboard on to his back within 30 seconds and then held his head above the surface. It was so impressive an advance, and with such export potential, that I decided to show it off in public in the Thames, appearing for the press and TV cameras in my bathers and lifejacket before plunging into the river. Our younger daughter Jill wasn't happy at the thought of Dad jumping in, but it was a great success as far as media coverage was concerned; yet it only occurred to me afterwards that while I might have been safe from drowning, it wasn't the healthiest of practices to swallow the murky waters of the Thames. Still, the new lifejacket was such an obvious improvement that nobody commented on the fact that it happened to be manufactured in my constituency. And it did become a great export-winner.

But there was little time to savour the moment. It was becoming clearer by the day that Harold Wilson was gearing up for another general election – and that at last he could look forward to the large parliamentary majority he craved. Why not? The opinion polls were firmly on our side. The Party was on its best behaviour, Left and Right working, for the moment at least, in a harmony they had never achieved under poor Hugh Gaitskell. The economy seemed to be looking up too. Harold was particularly proud of the National Plan, based on the promise of a growth rate of 4 per cent over the next five years. On top of that, we had set up the National Board for Prices and Incomes, which – naïvely as it turned out – we hoped would keep inflation under control. Even the sterling crisis had receded. In September 1965, the Americans had come galloping to the rescue with a massive support operation for the pound, a move which for the time being had sent the speculators packing.

And in spite of all the problems we'd encountered, we had an encouraging story to tell. Under our Rent Act, tenants at last had security of tenure. We'd abolished capital punishment – through a free vote in the Commons – brought in the Race Relations Act, pushed through considerable improvements in welfare and kept down unemployment. Sure, in our efforts to maintain financial discipline we'd been forced into some unpopular decisions, like imposing higher duties on whisky and cigarettes and cancelling that pride and joy of our aerospace industry, the highly advanced TSR2 warplane. Meanwhile cuts in the Navy budget and a dispute over aircraft carriers had provoked the resignations of the First Sea Lord and a junior minister called Christopher Mayhew. But I think we all sensed that public opinion was very much with us. Our optimism was confirmed at the Hull North by-election, when Labour romped home to a resounding victory.

It was the signal Harold had been waiting for. He opened his general election campaign on 1 March 1966. Four weeks later, he led the party to the second greatest triumph in its history, with a Commons majority over all others of ninety-seven. My own lead in Barnsley was very satisfying, over 14,000. At last we had truly established ourselves, to such an extent that some in the movement began talking of Labour as the natural party of government.

I quickly discovered what a difference a large majority can make: such a difference that within weeks of the election I found myself facing the most nerve-racking encounter of my career.

I'd plunged straight back into my ministerial duties at the Board of Trade after polling day. What I was looking forward to more than anything was an official trip to Moscow, which promised to be a pleasant visit of no overwhelming significance. In fact it was really a courtesy outing, returning the visit which the Russian Shipping Minister Viktor Bakaev had paid to London the previous year. Viktor was a rounded, jolly fellow and a good conversationalist. We'd got on very well; in fact he'd presented me with an intricate model of a whaler, carved from walrus tusks. I didn't think there would be the least problem when I saw him again.

I flew to Moscow in a relaxed frame of mind, accompanied by Amos Sutcliffe. With his expertise to back me up, I was confident that nothing could go seriously wrong. On the plane, he briefed me about the three dredgers we were building for the Russians and the problems we were having in getting some of the fittings which Moscow had promised as part of the deal. Routine stuff, really. When I walked into Bakaev's office soon after landing, I hadn't the faintest idea of what was to come.

We shook hands and chatted for a few minutes, but it was clear that something was up. Viktor wasn't quite his old, amiable self. I thought he must have something on his mind. So it proved. Suddenly he announced that I was to be given an audience with Aleksei Kosygin in the Kremlin. The following morning. At 9.30 sharp.

Like most politicians, I suppose I've developed some skill in concealing my feelings. But I'm sure my jaw dropped in astonishment and shock. Kosygin had replaced Nikita Khruschev as Chairman of the Council of Ministers and was now the head of the Soviet government. In effect, he was Tsar of all the Russias and certainly one of the world's most powerful men. Why on earth should he want to see me, a mere minister of State? I had the uneasiest feeling that I was being thrown into waters way out of my depth. I couldn't wait to get to our embassy for some much-needed advice.

I drove back in the company of the Commercial Attaché in Moscow, Alan Rothnie. Neither of us said a word. I'd already been warned in no uncertain terms to keep my mouth shut while travelling, since all vehicles were probably bugged by the KGB. Still, that silent journey gave me a chance to sort out my thoughts. I worked out that Kosygin must have issued his astonishing invitation because of Labour's thumping majority, which ensured we'd be in office for a few years. We had power. Presumably, he wanted to see at first hand what we were made of. I just happened to be the first British minister to visit the USSR since the election.

Of course I was bursting to unburden myself. Back at the embassy I was shown into a large room and – almost before the door closed behind us – began asking Alan what he thought. He held up a hand to silence me and pressed a button on the table. Immediately the room filled with chatter, the buzz and bustle of a cocktail party. That was another lesson for me. Even here, we had to assume that the KGB was listening. Somewhat chastened, I waited as officials were summoned for a murmured conference. They were clearly used to the probability of concealed micophones.

Eventually we all trooped down to the bowels of the building, where there was a secure room, swept every day for bugs. It was a spartan, unglamorous place containing little more than a green baize table, a scattering of chairs and a phone with a scrambler. But at last we could talk without fear of being overheard.

The first and most pressing task was to contact the Prime Minister and also my boss at the Board of Trade, Douglas Jay. It was beginning to dawn on me that the next day's encounter could be a significant event in Anglo–Soviet relations and I was growing more nervous by the minute. I found myself wishing I had more experience at this kind of thing. No doubt the diplomats who were urgently making arrangements all around me wished the same thing.

Still, the response from Douglas at the other end of a scrambled line was reassuringly matter of fact. I was to remind Kosygin of his own government's publicly declared policy, the need to rectify the imbalance of trade between Britain and the Soviet Union. This was familiar territory to me. I thought I could cope with that all right.

Harold's message was more of a challenge. On no account was I to leave the Kremlin without raising the question of Gerald Brooke, the young British teacher jailed for five years on a charge of smuggling religious and anti-Soviet literature into the USSR. Understandably enough, the savagery of the punishment had raised a furore at home. The government was under enormous public pressure to do something about it. Brooke's 'crime', after all, would not have been counted an offence in any Western democracy.

Once those instructions had been transmitted, it was the turn of the embassy professionals to sort me out. On no account was I to take notes into the meeting or make notes during it. Apparently there were cameras concealed in the Kremlin ceilings which would capture every scribble and doodle. I was advised that every word I uttered would be taped. Kosygin would certainly complain about British support for the Americans in Vietnam, the 'aggressive' stance of NATO and a whole host of other East–West issues; and here's how I was to respond. . . . It was about 3 a.m. before I finally managed to stagger off to bed, but it wasn't a restful night.

I was greeted at the Kremlin the following morning by a detachment of Red Guards, every man smartly turned out, with a sub-machine gun held at a precise angle across the chest. I was escorted along vast, carpeted corridors, past paintings and statues and the glitter of crystal chandeliers; but I was so focused on what I had to do that I hardly had an eye for the glories of an imperial past. We came at last to a pair of grand double doors and there waiting for us was Victor Bakaev and the top man himself. Aleksei Kosygin.

We sat opposite each other after a brief handshake and a few formal pleasanties. The leader of the Soviet Union turned out to be a grey, gaunt man, of little presence. He fiddled constantly with a paperclip, turning it round and round in his fingers. He not only seemed less impressive than Bakaev; he seemed to have less character than the interpreter sitting at the end of the table.

As the embassy staff had predicted, he began by berating me about British support for the Americans in Vietnam. I responded as I'd been advised. Then he had a go about NATO and again I replied with the official line on the Warsaw Pact. I felt sorry for the diplomats who spent their entire lives on this familiar rigmarole; but I remember being impressed by the accuracy with which my officials had forecast every move.

After these preliminaries, I raised the purpose of my mission – our wish to sell merchant ships to the Soviet Union. Kosygin had some muttered exchanged with Bakaev before returning to the attack. 'Britain is building three ships for us,' he declared, 'and they're all being delivered late.' He glared sourly across at me.

Thank Heaven for Amos Sutcliffe. I remembered the briefing he'd given me on the plane. 'Our problem is that we're buying £750,000 worth of parts from you to be installed on those ships. But I have to tell you that they are being delivered late.'

'Ah!' For the first time, Kosygin unbent with what might have been a smile. 'I expect my Minister to tell me when you're late – but not when we're late!' he said.

With that slight easing of tension, I took my chance. 'My Prime Minister has asked me to raise with you the case of Gerald Brooke and our deep concern. . . .' But the more I talked, the clearer it became that I was getting nowhere. Kosygin's face again took on a set expression. He said that the 'organ of power' – by which he meant the KGB – had determined that Brooke had been undermining the authority of the state. I tried to explain the Western concept of free expression, but it was hopeless. He simply didn't understand. Our definitions of democracy couldn't have been further apart. It gave me a depressing, first-hand insight into the nature of the Soviet regime. Poor Gerald Brooke served four years in captivity before the Russians let him go – in exchange for Peter and Helen Kroger, a pair of skilled and very senior spies who had been caught in Britain.

Still, if my encounter in the Kremlin didn't achieve any tangible result, at least I hadn't disgraced myself. And foreign trips can be full of pitfalls, as I discovered when I went on to visit Leningrad.

I was being entertained to lunch by the deputy mayor of the city and – a familiar ordeal in Russia – had been obliged to drink endless toasts in fiery vodka. Hardly a minute went by throughout the entire meal when somebody wasn't on his feet with a glass in his hand and a beam on his face to drink our health. Nastrovya! And of course it would have been impolite not to respond.

But I'd been warned. I kept nibbling bread rolls and bits of toast as blotting-paper. And when I could get away with it, I avoided draining my glass. As the drinking went on, I managed to stay more or less sober.

Sadly, my Private Secretary, Ken Jordan, was a little more rash. Trying to keep up with our hosts, he matched them glass for glass. Suddenly, he slumped sideways in his chair, quite out of it. Unconscious.

But one thing the Russians know about is how to handle such situations. At a discreet signal from the deputy mayor, two burly fellows appeared from nowhere, lifted Ken in his seat and carried the whole burden outside. Of course he had to put up with a fair bit of teasing as we flew home.

It wasn't long before I had another memorable encounter. Soon after my return, I found myself standing up to a very senior member of the Royal Family and doing it with a bluntness which I think suprised us both. But then, I've never been able to stand petty rudeness; and Prince Philip was undeniably rude to me. I think he deserved everything he got in exchange.

It happened like this. I'd been given added responsibilities for civil aviation matters at the Board of Trade and in that capacity was invited to address the biennial meeting of the Pilots' and Navigators' Guild, a very grand affair at the Guildhall in London, where the men were expected to wear white tie and tails, with the women turning out in formal gowns. Now I've always reacted against that kind of flummery, so I arrived in what I thought was a perfectly adequate dinner jacket. Perhaps that helped mark me as an outsider, though I couln't really have been anything else in a gathering which included such legendary figures as the night-fighter ace 'Cat's-Eyes' Cunningham and the flying pioneer Sheila Scott. Anyway, outsider or not, Prince Philip wasted no time in trying to make me feel like one.

As Grand Master of the Guild, it was his job to introduce me before I made my speech. All he was required to do was utter a few routine words of welcome; but from the moment he got to his feet, it was obvious that he was out to take the mickey.

'You'll have noticed,' he began, 'that our chief guest tonight is an elected member of the House. Mason, they call him.' I immediately sat up. His tone wasn't in the least welcoming. 'I hope he's a builder and not a destroyer,' the Prince went on. I could see that the audience was beginning to enjoy it. People were craning forward, the better to witness the sport. 'You'll remember that we had a Ministry of Civil Aviation once. And no doubt you'll remember the TSR2.' There were growls of agreement from the assembly. The decision to cancel that remarkable plane had hit hard. Still, it hadn't been me who'd taken the decision. Nor was I best pleased to be put in the pillory when I'd come along with a message of goodwill and amiable intent; and certainly not when the man hurling the rotten fruit was a royal personage who presumably thought I couldn't answer back. As the Prince continued with his barbed comments – wittily expressed, I'll grant him that – I began steaming.

It was my turn at last. I stood to polite applause and a haze of cigar smoke. The pilots and navigators had already enjoyed more entertainment than they could have expected. I began with the necessary preamble – Grand Master, Deputy Grand Master, bretheren, lords, ladies and gentlemen – and turned to look the Prince in the eye.

'Your Royal Highness', I continued, 'With a 27,000 majority in Barnsley and a 97 majority in the House of Commons, criticisms from you matter not!' I was doing my best to look genial as I said it, but he seemed stunned. He blinked and turned away. In the hall, you could have heard a pin drop. I doubt if anybody present had ever before heard a member of the Royal Family challenged.

Philip clearly understood that he'd gone too far. Afterwards, when I was having a drink with some Guild officials, he came across and expressed regret for mentioning 'those matters'. Then he launched into a story about my constituency. 'I was flying as co-pilot in a helicopter in your part of the world,' he said. 'The cloud base was a bit low, so we came down to work out exactly where we were and I saw the top of your football stand, with the message BARNSLEY BREWERY ALES all over it.'

'Yes,' I retorted. 'You've told me that tale before.' I turned on my heel and walked away. I was disgusted with him. We've met many times since and always got on well together; but on that occasion he'd crossed the line.

7 Climbing the Greasy Pole

A change of job was the last thing on my mind, that evening at Brown's Hotel, in January 1967. Still wearing my civil aviation hat, I was having a quiet and very private dinner with executives from the state airline, BOAC, discussing a possible takeover of a smaller company. Naturally enough, our discussions were commercially sensitive, involving millions of pounds; but I found it hard to concentrate after being summoned to the phone. It was Number Ten on the other end. Could I see the Prime Minister in the morning, at 10 o'clock? And by the way, would I mind coming in by the side entrance? I suspect the BOAC team found me rather distracted after that.

Next day I made my way through the unfamiliar corridors of the Cabinet Office building to arrive in the annexe outside the Cabinet Room itself. There was a uniformed messenger there, with two red Prime Ministerial boxes, but no sign of Harold himself. 'Hasn't done his boxes,' the messenger confided. 'I don't think he's well.'

Sure enough, Harold – in those days always a picture of robust health – was feeling under the weather. After kicking my heels downstairs for a few minutes, I was asked to go upstairs to his bedroom. There he was, still in bed in his pyjamas, an empty pint mug beside him. He didn't look particularly bad, though I discovered afterwards that he'd been ill for a couple of days, with only a handful of people knowing about it.

Well, he'd had a rough time of it in the past few months. No sooner was he back in Downing Street after the election than he'd had to cope with the first national seamen's strike in half a century, an event which he blamed bitterly on 'a tightly-knit group of politically motivated men' – by which, of course, he meant the Communists and their allies. The end of the dispute brought no relief. It was followed in short order by another economic crisis, with balance of payments difficulties, wages rising much faster than productivity and more pressure on sterling. Through it all, Harold had doggedly refused to consider the option of devaluation, a decision which caused considerable strains in Cabinet. There was even some talk – never very serious – of a plot to 'dump Wilson'. In a desperate attempt to hold the line, he'd been forced in July, 1966 to introduce a savage deflationary package, with swingeing cuts in government spending, new controls on hirepurchase, tight travel allowances and a legally-binding freeze on wage increases.

It never really worked. Unemployment kept going inexorably up. Sterling was still weak. Party left-wingers, who had been growing increasingly restive since the seamen's strike, were seething with resentment. I wonder if, in his heart of hearts, Harold suspected that the game was up and that sooner or later he would have to devalue.

Still, he seemed chirpy enough that winter morning, pyjamas and a sickbed notwithstanding. 'Roy,' he announced, 'I'm going to move you. Denis Healey is making changes at the Ministry of Defence and I want you to go across as the first Minister for Defence Equipment. You'll have a big budget: Army, Navy, Air Force, all their kit. What's more you'll have a salary increase of £2,000, because you'll be a senior minister of state.'

I didn't hesitate. I'd had no idea that there were two minister of state grades. Or that I'd been on the lower rung. Besides, I was being offered a big, brand new job. And the extra £2,000 a year wasn't to be sneezed at.

I got to know Denis Healey well in my fifteen months at the MoD. I found him a formidably intelligent boss, a man who ran his department with the efficiency (though not necessarily the quietness) of a Rolls-Royce engine. He'd stand no nonsense from his junior ministers or his officials – and certainly none from the generals, admirals or air vice-marshals. I think that they were sometimes intimidated by him. But he was highly respected, not just for his brainpower but for his sheer knowledge of defence matters. He understood what life was like on the front-line, too. He'd been a beach-master at Anzio – not a job for the faint-hearted – and had been decorated. Fortunately, we got along all right; it might have been a pretty uncomfortable stint otherwise.

Mind, he could be a crude beggar. I remember sitting on the front bench with him once, trying to listen to the exchanges in the House. But he was having a very audible conversation with Roy Hattersley. Unwisely, I turned to him and said 'Ssh.' He just glared. 'Eff off!' he snarled, though – being Denis – he was rather more specific about it. I remember thinking that I hadn't used language like that since I came out of the pit. But then, he was the intellectual, not me.

Still, I had other things to occupy my mind. One of the things I came to appreciate at the department was the enormous significance of the British arms industry. This wasn't a struggling, failing enterprise like shipbuilding, but a thriving, high-tech sector of the economy which not only sustained our armed forces but contributed hugely to our export trade.

One example. On a visit to Tehran, where I had a private audience with the Shah, I signed a deal to sell the Iranians no fewer than 1,200 tanks. Admittedly, that was a particularly big order; but it does illustrate the scale of a sales effort which supplied military hardware – frigates and jet fighters, helicopters and field artillery, small arms and communications equipment – to allies all over the world.

I never seriously questioned the morality of it. In a very dangerous world, Britain has a strategic requirement for an armaments industry. It needs to equip its forces with the very best kit – and do it as inexpensively as possible. It needs to sustain overseas allies. How else can that be done while keeping costs down, except through a vigorous export policy?

I have to admit though that the safeguards intended to prevent rogue regimes getting their hands on lethal weapons aren't always foolproof. Today's ally can sometimes – quite unexpectedly – become tomorrow's enemy. It's a sobering thought that some of the tanks sold to the Shah must eventually have ended up under the control of the Ayatollah Khomeini. Not a happy thought; but I certainly never acted as cynically or recklessly as the Tory Ministers who were later embroiled in the arms-for-Iraq scandal.

Still, my concerns back then were mainly focused on the difficulties faced by the government. In spite of his long, dour rearguard action, Harold had finally been forced to capitulate, devaluing the pound on Saturday 18 November 1967. The news came as a shock. I was still too junior to play any part in such a decision, but however inevitable it may have been I knew it wouldn't do our reputation any good with the voters. Not after the painful struggle to avoid it. Not when it was accompanied by deflationary measures which among other things imposed heavy new charges on NHS prescriptions, abolished free milk in secondary schools and postponed the raising of the school leaving age. It wasn't the most pleasant of duties to defend all that to the disappointed members of Barnsley Labour Party.

But before too long, I had more cheering things on my mind. In 1968 I was invited to join the Privy Council, an entirely unexpected honour which meant that in future I'd be formally known as the Right Honourable Roy Mason. Right Honourable! I know that in these disdainful days it's fashionable to turn up one's nose at such archaic symbols; but I'll bet there's not a single Privy Counsellor, including the professional egalitarians like Tony Benn, who doesn't secretly thrill to the title. It has, after all, a very special ring to it.

Rehearsed in everything I had to do, my head full of instructions and advice, I arrived at Buckingham Palace for my introduction, joining my fellow Right Honourables in an ante-room. When we were all assembled, the President of the Council, Dick Crossman, left us to see the Queen privately. This, it turned out, was the way it had always been done.

After a few minutes, those of us remaining were all shepherded into a line, according to our seniority. As low man on the totem pole, I was at the end. Somebody pressed a Bible into my hand, for the purposes of taking the oath. At a given signal, the doors to the Queen's room were thrown open and we marched in, still keeping to our allotted positions in the line. The Queen was sitting behind her desk on our left as we formed up before her like sentinels. Or perhaps like schoolboys summoned to see the headmaster. We bowed.

There were two low, cushioned stools, placed on the floor between politicians and monarch. I'd learned all about them during rehearsals. I was keeping an eye on the Clerk to the Privy Council, the gentleman who'd led me painstakingly through the ritual. He was the one who would give me the signal when it was time to do my stuff. Naturally I was anxious not to miss my cue.

He gave me a discreet nod at last and I moved forward from the line to kneel on the first cushion. The Bible was in my right hand. The Clerk read out the oath and I swore it. Then it was time to stand, transfer the Bible to my left hand and kneel on the second stool. The Queen approached and extended her hand, palm down. My part then was to take her hand and bend over it, barely brushing the back with my lips. Thus the ceremony of the kissing of hands. It's the hard bit which comes next.

The new Privy Counsellor must then rise and make his way back to his place in the line, but without turning his back on the monarch. It's quite a feat, walking backwards, avoiding the stools and getting into position once again. You need a good sense of direction. There are horror stories of new members who never quite made it, members who stumbled over the obstacles or misjudged the location of the line to barge into their ministerial colleagues or tread on unseen toes. Fortunately, I managed without mishap to stand with the others with some relief as the Queen signed a batch of Bills into Royal Assent (including the one introducing a decimal currency). After that, we all bowed once more and trooped out. My first session of the Privy Council was over. Throughout the rest of my ministerial career, I'd attend a meeting every few months.

In time, those occasions became a little less stilted. Dick Crossman, who had a bit of a penchant for reform, was keen to introduce a note of informality and after discussions with the Palace came up with a solution.

He was particularly anxious that I should be there for what was being billed as a special occasion, so – after some juggling with my parliamentary diary – I did as he asked.

My class at Carlton Spring Lane School. I'm sitting in the third row from the front, sporting the ribbon on my chest which denotes me as a class monitor

Scouting was my schoolboy passion, taken so seriously that I went on to win more than 20 proficiency badges, the bushman's thong and gold cords before going on to become a King's Scout

Miners' cottages in Long Row, Carlton, with my pit and the hated muckstacks in the background. In the foreground is Carlton's Working Men's Club, of which my dad was a committee member

In uniform as Flight-Sergeant in the Royston Flight of the Air Training Corps, 1943. To my bitter disappointment, I was never allowed to go on and join the RAF

With Marjorie and Susan admiring baby Jill after her christening in the crypt at the House of Commons. Hugh Gaitskell and Harriet Slater MP were her godparents

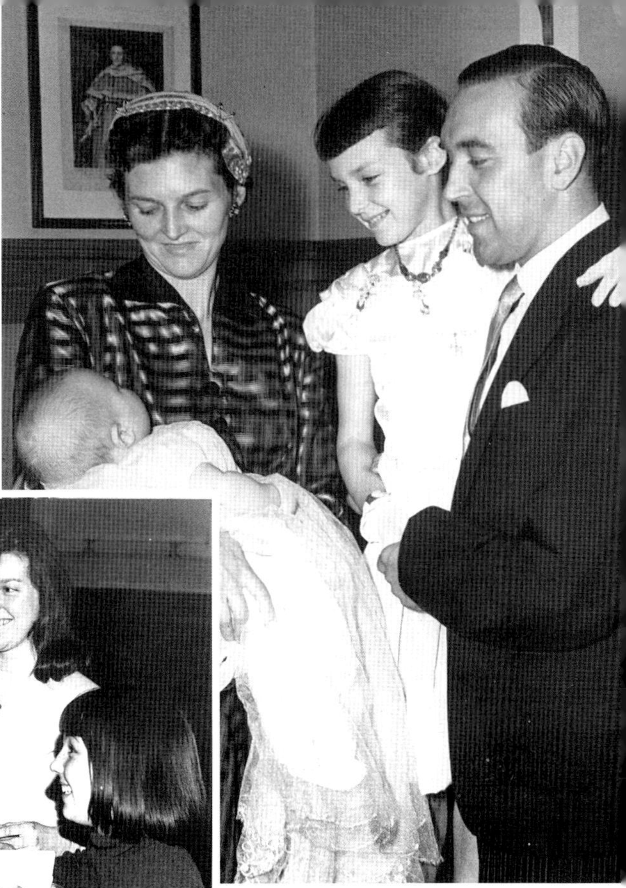

Electioneering was always a collective effort in my household. Here my family helps out with the preparation of my election manifestos for posting, 1964

The family gathering after celebrating our 50th wedding anniversary, in 1995. From left to right: Allen Duke, Susan Duke, Caroline Duke, Steven Duke, Marjorie, me, Kevin Martin, Jill Martin and their son Andrew

Arthur Scargill unveiling a plaque in remembrance of the miners who died in the 1936 Wharncliffe Woodmoor (Old Carlton) pit disaster, with my wife, me and the Mayor of Barnsley, Harry Dancer, looking on

On the canvassing trail with Marjorie in the 1979 General Election, when Margaret Thatcher swept to power. In the background is Inspector Pat Thomas

Canvassing in Old Town, Barnsley, with Councillor Arthur Butler. The smiles aren't in response to any political message: I'd just offered to get the coal in!

On the coal-face as Minister of Power, 1968. I'm in my old workplace, Wharncliffe Woodmoor 4 and 5 pits, New Carlton

With my Parliamentary Private Secretary, Pat Duffy, after our Harrier flight to Brough in Yorkshire, where the maritime version of the plane was to be developed

Leaping into the River Thames in 1965, to try out – and publicise – a successful new lifejacket design. This version, produced by a Barnsley firm, became a great export-winner

Waiting to hear the summons for the Queen's Speech on the Government front bench with other members of Jim Callaghan's Cabinet. The former Prime Minister, Harold Wilson, sits beyond the aisle, blowing his nose

On walkabout in Belfast, 1977. The alert soldier in the foreground illustrates how dangerous the streets of the Province could be then; but I thought that to be seen in public was part of the job

The one that didn't get away ....
With my record-breaking durado, caught off the island of Mauritius

The Privy Council proceeded as it always did, with ministers lined up, the bows, the signing of Bills and all the rest of it. But instead of taking our leave at the end, we were all ushered into another room, where we had drink with the Queen. This was Dick's new broom in action and a great success it was. We'd never had refreshments before; in fact I was under the impression that in all the centuries of Privy Council meetings to date, none of its members had been offered so much as a cup of tea. Well, we always liked to think of ourselves as the party of radical reform.

Shortly thereafter I was on the move again. When I'd been at the Ministry of Defence for about fifteen months, Harold sent for me and told me he wanted me to become Postmaster-General, the very job I'd expected to be given in 1964. I jumped at the chance. Though the post was not quite of Cabinet status, I'd be running my own department in St Martin's Le Grand, master of all I surveyed. Every day when I arrived at the office I'd be saluted by a uniformed commissionaire. I'd have my own car and driver too, instead of making do with vehicles from the pool, like other junior ministers. On top of all that, I'd have my own car telephone, a great rarity in those days. I felt that I had arrived at last.

It could be great fun too. When Glasgow Celtic became the first British football club to win the European Cup, I made sure that we issued a special stamp to commemorate their achievement. There's an undeniable pleasure in being able to agree such small gestures without having to ask permission.

But even in such an apparently placid department there could be pitfalls, as I discovered when I decided that the vans used by Post Office engineers should be painted yellow. I had learned that the old green livery could be a bit of a traffic hazard, since the vans couldn't easily be seen when they were travelling along leafy country lanes. They were having too many accidents, so a change of colour seemed the obvious solution. But there was absolute hell to pay in Parliament. My critics thought I was about to paint everything yellow: phone boxes, pillar-boxes, postal delivery vehicles, the works. I did my best to explain that I had no such ambition in mind, but I doubt if all the suspicions were laid to rest. On matters affecting the Post Office, backbenchers could be quite astonishingly prickly.

They weren't the only ones. I still remember with some irritation how Roy Jenkins, the Chancellor of the Exchequer, complained at the way I was handling one issue in my department.

Obviously I've always been involved in trade union affairs. I'm a born-and-bred trades unionist. So of course I took an interest when I found that Post Office workers were in a dispute over their pay. They weren't rewarded wonderfully well for what they did and I couldn't help showing some sympathy for their case. Especially as they weren't asking for an outrageous increase. What I didn't know then was that my few murmured words of understanding would find their way to the Treasury. Or that they would cause uproar.

I went home to Barnsley for the weekend blissfully unaware that someone had gone tittle-tattling to the Chancellor. My first inkling that something was amiss came just as I arrived home on that Friday afternoon. Would I please get myself back to London on Sunday morning for an urgent meeting with Roy Jenkins at 11 Downing Street? I suppose it's a measure of my naïvete at that time that I still had no idea why he wanted to see me.

To say that he dealt with me sternly would be an understatement. He sat behind his desk and denounced me up hill and down dale. Apparently I'd strayed into territory that was none of my business. I had challenged the government's financial strategy, interfered with the public sector borrowing requirement, spoken without thinking and behaved in every respect in a manner unworthy of a minister. I just gaped at him, flabbergasted. It genuinely hadn't occurred to me that a few sympathetic words to underpaid workers would provoke such a reaction. I didn't think the matter was that serious. In fact I was so taken aback that I didn't even get angry. I just listened to Jenkins' pompous and bossy lecture and then left, chastened. Of course he knew far more about the financial ramifications of the episode than I did; but it was unnecessary, I thought, to treat me in such an overbearing and unpleasant way.

Not that I had much time to brood over the encounter. I'd been PMG for barely three months when everything changed.

I was at home in bed and fast asleep when the telephone began ringing in the hall downstairs. Dragged awake and not in the brightest of moods, I looked at the clock. Two o'clock on a Sunday morning. Madge was stirring too, but I told her not to bother answering. 'It'll be some drunk wanting to pester me,' I told her. 'He'll get fed up and ring off in a minute.' But the ringing went on and on. And on. At last Madge could stand it no longer. She got up and went downstairs grumbling, ready to give the caller a piece of her mind. I was dropping off again when she called up: 'It's Downing Street!'

Oh. That woke me up all right. I rushed down to the hall as fast as my feet would carry me. On the other end of the line was Harold's private secretary. The Prime Minister wanted to see me privately for lunch at Chequers later that day. At one o'clock, without fail. And no, he couldn't tell me what it was all about.

Well, this was a bit of a poser. I'd never before been summoned so abruptly – and certainly not in the middle of the night. Could something have gone catastrophically wrong in my department? I didn't think so; but I needed to be sure. So I rang my Private Secretary and got him out of bed. It was now 2.30 a.m. but apart from a little initial bleariness he was all attention. I asked him to run through the events of the past three months, to check for potential ticking bombs. The yellow vans? A minor administrative detail. The spat with Roy Jenkins? Over and done with. Any other issues? Nothing that would engage a Prime Minister's interest. I mumbled apologies for waking him and hung up, baffled. What could Harold be up to? And how could I get to Chequers? I couldn't summon my Ministerial car, since nobody was supposed to know about the meeting.

So I spent the next few minutes – and it was now about 3 a.m. – trying to persuade my local cab firm that I was indeed the Member of Parliament and a government minister. And that I needed to get down to Chequers by lunchtime. The firm took a bit of persuading. Evidently I wasn't the only person in Barnsley to get calls from drunks in the small hours. Still, at last my bona fides were accepted and I was promised that a taxi would be outside my front door at nine o'clock.

I spent the drive down chatting idly with the cabbie, trying not to worry too much about what lay ahead. We arrived half an hour early, so the driver stopped at the front gates of Chequers and we got out to sit on the bonnet and have a smoke. Bang on time – it always pays to be punctual with a Prime Minister – I was knocking on the front door.

As it turned out, Harold wasn't ready for me. The WAAF sergeant who answered told me that he was taking an important phone call, but would I like a drink while I was waiting? She brought me a gin and tonic and I hung around in the hallway trying to appear nonchalant. Harold appeared a few minutes later, looking rather tired, I thought. 'A spot of trouble, Roy,' he began. 'Ray Gunter resigned last night.'

'Oh.' My first reaction was relief that the trouble had nothing to do with me. But I wasn't surprised that Ray had thrown in the towel as Minister of Power. Many of us had seen it coming.

'I've had a word with Roy Jenkins and Michael Stewart [the Foreign Secretary] and we all agree that you should be approached to replace him. And of course you'll be entering the Cabinet.'

I just stared. This was easily the biggest chance I had ever been offered: not only a place in Cabinet, but responsibility for running the industry where I'd once worked as a pit boy for 19s 6d a week. I should have grabbed the opportunity with both hands. Instead I smelled a rat. 'There's something wrong, isn't there?' I found myself saying. 'Are there any skeletons in the cupboard?'

'Let's walk outside,' said Harold. He led the way into the rose garden while I frantically tried to work out why I was feeling so suspicious. I knew that Ray had been having a terrible time at Power. According to tales I'd heard from the corps of ministerial drivers – probably the best intelligence system in the whole of Whitehall – the man wasn't up to the job. He'd been neglecting his red boxes, hadn't been reading many of his briefs and didn't really have a grip on his department. He'd been getting by on the strength of the old boy network; Ray was well in with trade union leaders like Frank Cousins and understood how to deal with the TUC General Council. But those advantages couldn't keep him going for ever, in a job which demanded a grasp of high-tech issues like North Sea gas exploration and nuclear power. In the end, he'd taken to the bottle, which of course made his performance even worse. I assumed that when he'd stormed out of his Cabinet post – at around midnight, as it turned out – he'd been under the influence. And probably mighty glad to get rid of a job that was on top of him. Still, none of that really explained why I had such an uneasy feeling about the job I had just been offered.

But in that long walk round the Rose Garden, Harold was adamant. Ray had gone because he was no longer enjoying the work. There were no skeletons. So on that basis I pushed the doubts to the back of my mind and said I would be delighted to take on the new role.

After that, it was as jolly as could be. Before we went in to lunch, I telephoned Madge with the news. Harold, meanwhile, had arranged for my successor as Postmaster-General, John Stonehouse, to join us afterwards for coffee. It was a relaxed and enjoyable end to an episode that had begun in some trepidation.

Next day I discovered that my suspicious instincts had been absolutely right. I went into the Ministry of Power building in Millbank that Monday morning full of the highest expectations. By mid afternoon, I was thinking of resigning.

Almost the first document I saw on my desk was all about an announcement that would shortly be made. A new nuclear power station was to be built at Seaton Carew, on the Durham coalbed. It was a terrible shock. What was being proposed might not have amounted to a skeleton in the cupboard as far as Harold Wilson was concerned; but to me it felt like a betrayal. I was a former miner. I remained a member of the NUM. I knew the anger and despair that would be felt in the pits when it was learned that coal was to be spurned in favour of a nuclear station. And what would certainly add insult to injury was the fact that the thing was to be built on top of a mountain of coal.

Emotion is the worst possible guide to policy-making. But when I remembered the hardships of my childhood friends and neighbours, my dad's ruined body, the dead men dragged from disasters underground and all the hopes which mining communities placed in a Labour Government – their government – it was impossible not to respond emotionally.

I made an immediate appointment to see Harold in his room at the Commons that night. To be fair to him, I don't think he expected the intensity of my reaction. I told him I'd find it difficult to make the announcement about Seaton Carew. 'It will be the death-knell of coal,' I told him. 'That's how people will see it.' I pleaded with him to let me take the whole issue back to Cabinet, where I'd give a presentation on why a coal-fired station would be so much better.

Harold was courteous but firm. 'I'm sorry,' he said. 'You can't do that. We've had four or five Departments examining every aspect of this. We've had a cost benefit analysis, we've looked at the impact on coal and we've decided that nuclear power is the fuel of the future. The decision in Cabinet was unanimous.'

Unanimous! That was a blow, since a prominent member of the Cabinet was that tribune of the people and self-proclaimed friend of the miners, Tony Benn. It was clear to me that the battle of Seaton Carew was already lost, beyond hope of recovery. And to add insult to injury, I was advised that I ought to seek the views of T. Dan Smith before making the announcement. Smith wasn't an MP – far less a minister – but he was a real power in the Labour Party through his dominance of local government in the North-East. Evidently the Prime Minister didn't want to make a move without informing this guru in advance. As it turned out, Smith was on holiday in Yugoslavia and I had to send a courier to him with the Seaton Carew brief. His reply was that he welcomed the development and the many jobs which would accompany a new nuclear power station. So much for the miners. The episode didn't make me any happier about having to announce the project. Smith, incidentally, was later embroiled in a major fraud scandal and sent to jail.

So my career as Minister of Power had got off to a miserable start. But at least I had a weapon left to ensure that such a thing couldn't easily happen again.

'I've had lengthy discussions with my officials about all this,' I told Harold. 'Do you know, there's not a single power station can be built in this country – coal, oil or nuclear, it doesn't matter – unless I give it a licence?'

He looked a little taken aback at that, so I repeated the words. 'Unless I give it a licence. And I'm telling you now. It might not be good government, but I've got to be true to myself. I'm not going to give a power station licence in this country until there's another coal-fired station back on stream.'

Well, Harold may have been somewhat startled by this mutiny from the newest member of his Cabinet, but he accepted it with good grace. Perhaps he felt a little guilty for not appreciating that Seaton Carew was for me a real bone-rattler of a skeleton in the cupboard. Or perhaps he just thought it best not to meet trouble until he had to. After Seaton Carew, there was no immediate urgency about the next power stations to be built.

And so began months and months of obduracy in my department. We were coming under increased pressure from all kind of groups – the electricity industry, engineers, people like the boilermakers – urging the need for more power generation. But they preferred stations to be fired by oil or nuclear reactors. So I wouldn't budge. I dare say I was cursed by everybody in the industry. Apart, of course, from the miners.

Meanwhile, I was gradually becoming accustomed to my new status as a member of the Cabinet; and a pretty lowly status it was, to begin with. I had no briefing before attending my first meeting, no idea of what to expect. In fact I had never even sat in the Cabinet Room before. I was so innocent that when I was assigned a place on the Prime Minister's side of the table – three places along – I was rather pleased. It took a while before it dawned on me that it was just about the worst spot to be, because it was impossible to catch Harold's eye. Still, I knew enough that first time to keep my mouth shut and my opinions to myself.

Some of my new colleagues I warmed to at once as I observed how they operated. Jim Callaghan in particular became my mentor. In fact I think any minister could have learned a lot from watching him in action. He had no stock of nastiness in him, never indulged in backbiting or petty behaviour. In fact he was one of the rocks on which the Wilson administration was founded. It was a tragedy that he'd eventually be driven to oppose Harold over the woefully misguided scheme hatched by Barbara Castle to 'solve' the problem of unofficial strikes through legal sanctions.

A few of my other colleagues impressed me too. I very much liked Cledwyn Hughes, Secretary of State for Agriculture. Bob Mellish, the Chief Whip, struck me as a good man, solid and dependable. And I liked George Thomas, the Welsh Secretary. They may have been Harold's men, but they were never acrimonious. The Environment Secretary Tony Crosland was a decent chap too. He smoked a lot, but always looked and sounded a comfortable, sensible man.

I wasn't too sure about some of the others. The trouble with Tony Benn, I always thought, was that he tried too earnestly and too hard to be working class. Of course he hadn't the faintest idea of how to do it and would insist on pint pots of tea in the tearoom, copying what he obviously imagined to be a proletarian habit. Besides, I'd never quite forgiven him for selling the pass over Seaton Carew. Then there was Dick

Crossman, a brilliant theorist no doubt, but not on my plane at all. As for the Employment Secretary Barbara Castle, I found her quite a sly character, always using wiles and wheedles and seeking private meetings to get her own way. I'd decided never to trust her long before the *In Place of Strife* débâcle.

As one moves up in the Cabinet pecking order, one shifts to a different seat around the table. Later on, as Defence Secretary and then Northern Ireland Secretary, I found myself sitting next to Barbara Castle and Tony Benn and discovered that both were taking copious notes of our private views on the great issues of the day. As eventually became clear, they were assembling material for their diaries – even though they and everybody else had been warned by Harold Wilson that such behaviour was unacceptable. On that occasion, the Prime Minister said that in future members of the Cabinet should leave their notes behind at the end of meetings. Barbara Castle started making a great show of doing this, but I was told by one colleague who sat near her that the papers she left behind tended to be blank. Obviously she and Benn weren't taking the slightest notice of Harold. Perhaps they thought that when it came to it he wouldn't push the issue to the point of an open row – and I suppose they were proved right. But as far as I was concerned, they were cheating on their colleagues. If that kind of thing had happened in a committee meeting of a miners' lodge, the culprits would have been sent to Coventry and kicked out for splitting on their mates and making money out of it.

But I didn't have the time to worry too much over personalities. I was too busy running my own department. And discovering some of the frustrations of high office.

Here's a small example. Shortly after I arrived at the Ministry of Power, I had the opportunity to influence the appointment of a new Director of Industrial Relations for the National Coal Board. It seemed to me an excellent idea to move somebody from the NUM into the post. It would at least ensure that the board and the union understood each other's thinking and might well lead to an improvement in relations throughout the industry. So I wrote to the NUM – my own union – and asked if they would like to nominate a member of their Executive for the job.

My letter was ignored, so after a couple of weeks I wrote once more. Again I was ignored. Evidently some people in the higher reaches of the union were too prejudiced to seize the opportunity being offered. Well, I didn't propose to hang around forever. I just sent for Cliff Shepherd, the white-collar representative of the NUM Executive and offered him the job. He was delighted and served both the Coal Board and the entire industry well for a number of years.

In retrospect, I should have taken some warning from the strange attitude of my old union comrades. It was the first sign of the nastiness which was to come from that quarter. But I suppose I was too busy and preoccupied. Particularly over the future of the power stations, a dispute which seemed to be dragging on forever.

Well, I wasn't going to give in. One of the things which concerned me most as Minister of Power was the rate of pit closures. The decisions, of course, had nothing directly to do with me. They came under the remit of the National Coal Board. But I couldn't help being dismayed, especially as the head of the coal division at the ministry, a chap called Williams, seemed happy to treat the miners as mere units of production, points on a graph. His attitude hurt and angered me. I lived in a coalfield and knew very well what impact the closures were having on pitmen and their families. They deserved better than cold analysis from a distant official in London. In the end, I shuffled Mr Williams sideways, putting him far away from any responsibilities for coal.

But that didn't solve the underlying problem. The pits were still being closed down. In my time at the ministry, no fewer than thirty were shut, bringing the pain of redundancy to thousands of my former colleagues. I hated what was happening, fretting in my office as death sentences were passed on this pit and that. I was beginning to learn all about the limits on ministerial power.

I had a chance to stem the tide when I called a major conference at Sunningdale, where leaders of all the industries for which I was responsible – coal, gas, nuclear generation, electricity, steel – would look at their power requirements. The occasion wasn't specifically designed to help coal, but I hoped that the discussions would lead to a slowdown in the rate of pit closures. From that point of view, It proved a reasonably successful exercise. I didn't get everything I wanted, but at least those present were left in no doubt about my attitude. In subsequent months, fewer pits came under the axe, though still too many for my liking.

Sometimes there were irritating distractions from the job in hand. One of the features of government at that time was the atmosphere of intrigue which hung over Whitehall, with rumours of plots to dump Harold and replace him with somebody more acceptable to the City and industry. It was mostly a lot of nonsense, foolishly given credence by some of Labour's most notable conspiracy theorists, like Dick Crossman and the absurd George Wigg. Nevertheless, there was unease in the air, with stories of a shadowy group called Great Britain Limited, which apparently had ambitions to bring about a national government. Among those involved in this daft enterprise were people like Cecil King, the then Chairman of Mirror Group Newspapers and – of all people – Lord Mountbatten.

I had better things to do than give any mind to such over-excitable rubbish – until the day Alf Robens, Chairman of the Coal Board, gave a TV interview in the North-East coalfield which seemed to support the King–Mountbatten agenda.

I was quite incredulous. On the face of it, Robens was in clear breach of his contractual undertaking as boss of the NCB not to engage in political controversy. His offence was all the worse, since as a former Labour MP he couldn't take refuge in a claim of naïvete. From my home in Barnsley that Friday night I sent a signal to my private secretary telling him to make sure that a full transcript was on my desk by Monday morning. And to arrange for Alf Robens to be in my office at 3 p.m.

When I read the script I became even angrier. There was no doubt at all that Alf had stepped way out of line. I marked passage after passage in which he'd trampled all over his obligations to remain politically neutral. Presumably he thought he was enough of a heavyweight to get away with it. Or perhaps he imagined that I wouldn't dare take him on.

He came in at three o'clock without the faintest idea of what awaited him. In fact he probably thought I was going to help one of his friends to become Deputy Chairman of the Coal Board. I soon disabused him of that. I told him that what he had said was quite unacceptable and showed him the offending passages. 'I've no compunction in saying this, Alf,' I told him. 'Harold Wilson is aware of what's going on. If you do anything like this once more I'll sack you.' He was sitting on the armchair to my left, fidgeting, throwing one leg over the arm, trying to appear confident and in control. In fact he seemed to be treating me as if I were his junior. But I had the power to get rid of him and he knew it. He was pretty deflated when he left. That day he'd suffered what was probably the sternest warning of his public life. He never strayed over the line again.

But that wasn't much of a consolation when the pits were still closing and my hopes of building a new coal-fired power station seemed as forlorn as ever. Though I was still stubbornly refusing to grant new licences, the Electricity Board seemed equally stubborn in its determination not to give way. It was an old-fashioned stand-off, with neither side willing to yield an inch.

To my relief it all ended suddenly and quite unexpectedly, in a simple deal and a brisk handshake. I was visiting a power station in the South of England, in the company of the Deputy Director of the Central Electricity Generating Board. After our morning tour of the plant, we were assembling for pre-lunch drinks when he asked for a private word and took me to one side.

'Look,' he said. 'I'd like four licences for new stations. I want two oil-fired and one nuclear. And I'll give you a coal-fired station to go with them.'

At this point, one of the local officials approached to say that lunch was being served. My host got quite agitated. 'Go away!' he barked.

'Coal-fired?' I asked, once we were alone again.

'I'll give you Drax Two,' he promised.

'Right. You're on. That's a deal.' We shook hands on it and I went back to my ministry in the best of moods. Drax Two would be built alongside the existing Drax One and in fact became the biggest coal-fired generator in Western Europe. It was the best possible news the coal industry could have. I was very much looking forward to making the announcement on the floor of the Commons.

I never got the chance. Two weeks after the deal was made, I was made President of the Board of Trade. The Ministry of Power was absorbed into a giant new Ministry of Industry and Technology, run by Tony Benn. It fell to his deputy, Harold Lever, to run the coal division and he it was who eventually made the statement about Drax Two. I can still remember him blinking with pleasure as the cries 'Hear! Hear!' erupted from the Labour benches at the news. I doubt if he'd ever before been greeted with such noises of approval.

Good luck to him. I was left to reflect on the way I'd been lumbered with the miserable announcement about Seaton Carew. I'd love to have redressed the balance with a farewell flourish of good news about Drax Two. Still, that's the way it goes. In the life of politics, you can usually expect more kicks than pennies.

This time, my appointment to another department hadn't come as a surprise. Earlier that year, I'd been chief guest at the Durham Miners' Gala and at the end of the official dinner, Harold came to sit beside me. 'You're ready for more responsibilities, Roy,' he murmured. 'You'll be first in to see me when I do my Autumn reshuffle. I'll be offering you one of two jobs.' Naturally I was pleased. There can't be many politicians who don't enjoy basking in the Prime Minister's favour.

In the event, I had no difficulty deciding which job I wanted. As part of his reshuffle, Harold was creating a vast new Ministry of Industry and Technology under Tony Benn. My old job at Power would be absorbed into this, but there was nothing to stop me moving across – still with a seat in Cabinet – to continue looking after coal. What did I think?

Well, I wasn't too thrilled. I'd no longer be in sole charge of my own department. And I certainly didn't fancy being subordinate to Benn. 'What's the alternative?' I asked.

The alternative, as it turned out, was much more appealing: President of the Board of Trade. I didn't hestitate. Harold was especially anxious to improve the country's export performance and with an election on the horizon so was I. Healthy balance of trade figures would not only improve job prospects in the country but impress the voters too. It's ironic that in the end the electorate wasn't impressed at all, largely because I insisted on a policy of honesty. In fact after our defeat in 1970, some in the party tried to pin the blame on me.

But that little upset was way in the future. From Day One in my new job, I made a point – almost obsessively – of seeking out customers around the world. Unlike my old boss at Trade, Douglas Jay, I enjoyed travelling abroad. And so I beat the drum for British textiles in Australia, British electronics in Asia, British engines in Europe, British chemicals in North America. I opened trade fairs in Hong Kong, Korea and South-East Asia. On average, I undertook an overseas mission every fortnight. It always seemed to me that such relentless activity must be doing some good.

Not that my efforts always endeared me to the country's industrialists. In between those trips abroad, I and my number two at the board, Lord Wilfred Brown of Macrahanish, were embroiled in a ferocious battle over the proposed new National Exhibition Centre. This was a crucial project, a scheme which would provide a showcase for the best products this country had to offer, an up-market bazaar for all the world. The trouble was, British industry didn't want it.

Actually, that isn't quite true. Our industrialists, entrepreneurs and financiers did want it. Passionately. But they wanted it in London, close to their homes and their company headquarters. They were genuinely horrified to discover that I was quite serious in my determination to promote this development in the regions. It was as part of this approach that I decided that the new NEC should be built in Birmingham.

As far as I was concerned, it wasn't an especially difficult choice. We had examined the road, rail and air links, the hotel accommodation, the availability of land and all the rest of it, in exhaustive detail. Birmingham fitted the bill admirably. Just as importantly, the council was desperately keen – so much so that it had actually put up a little money for the project. It seemed to me high time that our second city got a fair crack of the whip.

Not all my Cabinet colleagues agreed. The Chancellor, Roy Jenkins, took a lot of persuading. So did the Environment Secretary, Tony Crosland. But after seemingly endless exchanges of letters, memoranda and technical submissions, I managed to wear them down. Birmingham was to get the prize.

I might just as well have confessed to high treason. There was uproar when the decision became known. The large and powerful London lobby was furious in its opposition. No fewer than seventy-one of the largest companies in the land signed a petition begging the government to site the NEC in the capital. For months on end, I was snowed under with submissions assuring me that there was simply no trade outside London, that foreign buyers simply wouldn't risk the hazardous journey to the Midlands.

Perhaps I exaggerate the anti-Birmingham prejudice – but not by much. The episode offered a fascinating insight into the way these quite distinguished metropolitan people really viewed the rest of the country.

I even encountered opposition from my own party. When I made the announcement in the Commons, the majority of London's Labour MPs sat in grumpy silence. But a claque of backbenchers from Manchester barracked me throughout. That response was far more wounding than anything said from the Tory benches, from which Sir Keith Joseph denounced me in fine style.

Still, I had one crumb of comfort. The day before I was due to make the announcement, the leader of Birmingham City Council sent me a telegram. It read: 'Please, Minister, don't die before 3.30 tomorrow afternoon!'

In the event, the protests soon faded. Within weeks of my statement, all seventy-one firms which had damned Birmingham from the rooftops changed their minds and let it be known that they would after all back the new National Exhibition Centre. Today the NEC is a great success and it's hard to imagine that it could have been built anywhere else.

Sometimes there were welcome diversions from serious ministerial activity. I'd been fascinated by the possibility of space travel, ever since I had given talks on the subject in the early Fifties. As a backbench MP, my interest deepened when I had the chance to meet the first man in space, Yuri Gagarin and the first woman, Valentina Tereshkova. Now I was to be given an even more thrilling opportunity. After the American moon landing, Harold Wilson arranged a reception for the astronauts at Downing Street and knowing of my enthusiasm asked Madge and me to act as hosts for the evening and receive all the guests. I think it counts as one of the most exciting moments of my life, to shake the hands of Neil Armstrong, Buzz Aldrin and Michael Collins, men who'd done and seen things which were once the stuff of science-fiction fantasy.

In other respects, my concerns were much more down to earth. The political landscape in 1969 was dominated by ferocious battles over two great issues of principle: Dick Crossman's ambitious plans for the House of Lords and Barbara Castle's ill-fated proposals to reform the trades unions. In the end, the government had to abandon both; but not before sustaining wounds from which it never recovered. No doubt we should have forseen the consequences; but then, General Hindsight never lost a battle.

Like the majority of Labour MPs, I firmly agreed with the Crossman scheme to reform our upper chamber. It seemed to me absurd that Lord Tomnoddy and his many friends should play a part in the national legislature, just because they happened to be their fathers' eldest sons. Under Dick's proposals, the right of hereditary peers to sit in the chamber would be phased out and we'd have a two-tier House of Lords, with voting and non-voting members. Very up to date. Shouldn't such a measure whistle through, with little fuss?

But like almost everybody else, I'd reckoned without the intervention of the two most brilliant parliamentarians of the day, Michael Foot on the Left and Enoch Powell on the Right. Between them, they tore the Bill to pieces – Enoch because it offended his romantic view of the Lords and Michael because he thought it would lead to a vast increase in the power of Prime Ministerial patronage.

The destruction of the Crossman reform at the hands of this extraordinary pair was certainly the most devastating display of backbench power I've ever seen. Unfortunately, it did nothing whatever for the reputation of the government, which was left looking baffled, confused and outmanoeuvred.

And then there was the Barbara Castle mess. She called her White Paper on trade union reform *In Place of Strife*. She should have called it *In Place of Common Sense*. It was a disaster from the beginning and did more to undermine morale within the government and the party than any other event in Harold Wilson's first six years.

Some of us – notably Jim Callaghan, but also including Fred Lee, Dick Marsh, Tony Crosland and myself – thought it would all end in tears. It wasn't that we were under any illusions; I knew perfectly well that the unions could be overbearing, undemocratic, out of touch with their members and sometimes remote from economic reality. But wouldn't it be better to encourage them to reform themselves, rather than try and bully them into submission?

To be fair to Barbara, there was hardly much enthusiasm for self-regulation. The Royal Commission on the Unions, set up under Lord Donovan in 1965, had found that collective bargaining in Britain was hopelessly crude and outdated, needing a fundamental shake-up. That was bad enough; but the problem was made far worse by the rash of unofficial strikes in the country, strikes which nobody had much idea how to control. In the absence of any great initiative from the union side – and with the public firmly of the view that something had to be done – Barbara no doubt thought it right to steam ahead with proposals for legal sanctions against unofficial strikers and fines on recalcitrant unions. Bold proposals. But then, she had Harold Wilson on her side.

So began the months and wearisome months of rows, rumours, negotiations, disagreements in Cabinet and mutterings against the Prime Minister. I believe that Jim Callaghan, who led the opposition to *In Place of Strife* seriously considered resignation at one stage. Morale in the parliamentary party slumped. I myself was depressed, since it seemed to me that legal sanctions wouldn't stop unofficial strikes, only create martyrs. And I hated the way relations between the party and the unions were being placed under such strain.

Of course it couldn't go on. We were knocking the stuffing out of ourselves. Slowly – painfully slowly – the view grew in Cabinet that the penalty clauses in Barbara's legislation had to go. Meanwhile, the TUC moved at last, with what I thought were quite significant changes in its attitude towards unofficial strikes and inter-union disputes. It was enough to secure an agreement.

There was such a feeling of relief in the party. I think we all saw a new beginning. The tragedy is that the opportunity achieved after so much pain was thrown away. The unions failed to read the writing on the wall; and in later years that failure to reform themselves landed us with the Winter of Discontent and the years of Thatcherite triumph. It's just as well that none of us can look into the future.

But back then we weren't remotely concerned about Margaret Thatcher. She was merely a somewhat obscure shadow education minister. Our interest lay in Ted Heath, leader of the opposition and the man who might – if the opinion polls were to be believed – topple Wilson from power.

Yet even after *In Place of Strife*, I don't think any of us took his challenge too seriously. He had none of Harold's brilliance or ease. Socially awkward, prickly, utterly lacking the common touch, Heath seemed an unlikely winner in the rough-and-tumble of an election campaign. True, the polls showed Labour lagging behind. But they'd been doing that since the beginning of 1967. We had grown used to bad news from that quarter. Perhaps that's why we allowed ourselves to be so woefully led astray.

In the Spring of 1970, our luck changed. For the first time in three years, Labour took a lead in the polls. It seemed the opportunity Harold had been waiting for, the chance to snatch a third term. Fortune appeared to be smiling on him at last – except for the situation at the Board of Trade.

Just as Harold was clearing the decks and preparing himself to ask the Queen for a dissolution of Parliament, it became uncomfortably clear that the next set of trade statistics would hand a propaganda weapon to the

Tories. The Prime Minister, the Chancellor and I all knew that they would make the most of it. Our problem was that the monthly balance of payments figures would show a deficit of £30 million – peanuts by today's standards, but enough in an election campaign for the opposition to damn us as a bunch of incompetents.

One or two of the government's advisers thought there might be a way out of our dilemma. The major part of the deficit was caused by the cost of two Boeing airliners which we had ordered from the Americans at £9 million each. So why not just cancel the order, thereby avoiding embarrassment on the hustings?

I wish I could say that I turned the idea down purely out of honesty and a sense of propriety, but it wasn't quite like that. True, I thought the idea was a bit of a stunt and not worthy of a serious government. But more to the point, too many people knew about the order, in the Board of Trade, in the Treasury and in the airline industry. When the details leaked out, as they surely would, we'd be accused of cooking the books. Better an embarrassment which might be contained than a full-blown scandal which certainly couldn't. Harold Wilson and Roy Jenkins agreed with me that we would just have to bite the bullet.

I've no doubt that the poor trade figures did adversely affect us in the run-up to polling day. In fact after our defeat, some of the wiseacres in the party lost no time in attributing the defeat to Roy Mason, the man who couldn't or wouldn't manipulate the figures.

Me? I don't believe the decision made that much of difference. The truth is, Labour had been performing badly in the polls for years. We made the mistake of seizing on a sudden – and inexplicable – improvement in the Spring of 1970 as evidence of a fundamental shift in public opinion. On top of that, we underestimated the skilful way Ted Heath – the awkward and supposedly unelectable Ted – would use television. Throughout the campaign we believed what the pollsters were telling us – and at one stage our lead was 13 per cent – without paying enough attention to what we were hearing on the doorstep. Even in rock-solid Barnsley, the clues were there. In the last few days of campaigning, I began to see that the tide was turning against us; but by then it was far too late. I held on to my seat easily enough, with my majority slightly down. Elsewhere, the political map of Britain was turning blue. The Tories were home with a parliamentary majority of thirty-two.

8 Treading Water

Madge and I sat watching television all night on Thursday, 18 June, disheartened and upset as the results flooded in to confirm our private fears. In the bleary light of Friday, we saw Ted Heath triumphant on the steps of Downing Street and the parade of new ministers emerging to beam at the crowds. My successor at the Board of Trade turned out to be a Scottish farmer, Michael Noble. He seemed a pleasant chap and of course I wished him well, but it was hard to resist a gloomy grunt when the news came through. Few politicians take kindly to the loss of their jobs.

Still, moping isn't my style; and besides, I had unfinished business in London. At 5.30 on the Sunday morning, my wife and I began the long drive South, hoping to get to the Board of Trade before anybody else turned up. I was anxious to clear out my office in privacy. The last thing I wanted was to run into any of my old officials – or to make small talk with my ministerial replacement.

I found the caretaker at 1 Victoria Street and got him to open a back door for us. Madge and I took the lift to the sixth floor, clutching a couple of cardboard boxes. We packed all my personal belongings as quickly as we could and got out of the place without meeting another soul. Not the most dignified of exits, but then no minister should expect a ceremonious departure. In ancient Rome, when emperors drove in triumph through the cheering crowds, a slave would stand behind him in the chariot to murmur: 'Remember you are only a man.' Our way of reminding politicians not to get too big for their boots is just as effective. Ministerial careers can end in cardboard boxes and a furtive creeping out of the back door; well, you shouldn't join if you can't take the joke.

And there are compensations. There really is something liberating about losing office, once the initial disappointment has worn off. No more red boxes demanding your attention in the small hours, no diary secretaries to fill every moment of every working day, no more issues demanding an urgent decision, no more the exhausting, unending round of meetings or the burden of relentless paperwork. When my daughter

Susan graduated in Theology, Hebrew and Greek from Bangor University, I'd had to beg Harold Wilson for a day off Cabinet so that I could be there. Now I was free of all that. Though still with front-bench responsibilities. At last I had the space for family and friends and leisure which no senior minister can enjoy if he's doing his job properly. My wife and daughters no longer had to put up with family weekends disrupted by red boxes.

Of course I loved being at the heart of government; no point in denying it. When I hear ministers complain about the personal sacrifices they've had to make, I can't help wondering why they don't mention the enjoyment, the interest, the sheer exhilaration of high office. Few politicians really want to spend all their lives on the backbenches. They dream of the authority and power which office brings. And it's not entirely a question of brute ambition. Most MPs undoubtedly hope to get on, but equally they want to contribute something. Isn't it the case that most of us hope to leave this world a better place than we found it?

Still, the ministerial workload is formidable. I'd found it necessary to get into the office early, usually around 8.30 a.m. My private staff used to operate a shift system to keep up and open the safes, since they usually had much further to travel than I did. Then it would be non-stop until the small hours of the following morning. I rarely finished my boxes much before 1 a.m., because I had to deal not only with my own department's affairs but keep abreast of what was going on in other ministries. In fact I'd say my work almost doubled, once I moved up into the Cabinet. It's a hard learning curve, with little room for relaxation. I might have enjoyed the odd drink – but never at lunchtime. Under no circumstances. After all, I could have been called upon at any time to make a statement in Parliament if some emergency blew up. There's nothing so damaging in politics as the sight of a minister slurring his words.

But it's not the politicians who pay the price. It's their families. Both my daughters said to me: 'We never saw you, Dad.' How could they, when I was away from Monday morning until Madge picked me up at Doncaster station on Friday night? Even then, the pressure wasn't off. I had Labour party meetings on Friday nights, constituency surgeries on Saturday mornings, business with Cabinet colleagues when they came visiting the coalfields; and always, always, I had those red boxes to do. At least two of the things would arrive by special messenger on the Saturday morning. He'd be back again by 4 p.m. on the Sunday to pick them up. There weren't many family outings at weekends.

The one time I insisted on setting aside was Sunday lunch. For a couple of hours or so, the four of us would sit round the table, talking about the small incidents in our lives, listening to music, catching up with each other, just being a family.

Madge was the rock on which our lives were built. She kept busy while I was away at Westminster, involving herself with the Girl Guides, the Brownies, the disabled and all manner of things besides, including being a governor of three schools. She was the one who brought up our daughters, kissing away their troubles, going to the concerts and speech days and school plays I could hardly ever attend, just being there. Keeping the family together. And that wasn't the end of it. She took her City and Guilds exam in cookery, stood in for me at dozens upon dozens of public functions, dealt with constituency problems, attended meetings on my behalf and kept me in the closest touch with whatever was going on in Barnsley. That's been the pattern throughout our marriage. Even when I was Secretary of State for Northern Ireland, she flew back and forth to the Province to carry out 101 public engagements. She even presented a Royal Charter to one borough, when I couldn't be there because of a three-line whip in the House.

So I'm not exaggerating when I say there are compensations in losing office. I might have been treading water as far as my political career was concerned, but in terms of family life, the years after Labour's defeat in 1970 were a pleasure. I even discovered a new interest which was to develop into a lifelong passion: fly fishing. I now had the chance to spend the occasional day at the lake or by the riverside, where I'd go after rainbow trout and brownies, all cares forgotten. There's nothing on earth like returning home after a successful day to enjoy a newly caught supper.

Constituency work too was always absorbing and worthwhile. One of the real satisfactions in an MP's life is the ability to lend a helping hand when it's needed. I've never tired of it. It was at this time, for example, that I started arranging free film shows every month for pensioners and the disabled in Barnsley, with firms and individuals sponsoring the entertainment. I'm pleased to say that after nearly thirty years I continue to be involved and those shows still go on.

Making a difference is what it's all about; and you don't necessarily need government office to do that. In the late Sixties, Madge and I had come across a local couple who had four sons, three of them tragically afflicted by muscular sclerosis. We used to visit the boys at their family allotment, as they sat in their wheelchairs feeding the hens and racing pigeons. Their lives were sadly restricted, but it so happened that at that time, Lord Snowdon had designed a powered chairmobile which would give the disabled far more freedom of movement. I thought it would be a great idea to obtain one for a trial with these lads. I set about raising the funds through Green Shield Stamps, which were then given away with groceries and petrol as an incentive to customers. With the help of local schools, working men's clubs, Scouts, Guides and other bodies we collected enough to buy one of the new chairmobiles and in the foyer of the Ritz Cinema put on a special demonstration of how well it worked. It was a great success, but of course one chair wasn't enough between three disabled boys. And what about other local people who might benefit? Barnsley's Medical Officer of Health was there, so I asked him for an assessment of how many disabled people in the area could handle a chairmobile. He came up with a figure of thirteen. So I managed to get thirteen firms in the town to sponsor one each. It was a tremendous act of generosity on their part, ending with a mass presentation of chairmobiles to people who would in future have at least a measure of independence. A great day for them and for me; one of the happiest, I think of my political life.

There were other pleasures in those years. When Harold appointed me Shadow President of the Board of Trade, he gave me the latitude to appoint promising newcomers to my front-bench team. It meant that I became a bit of a talent-spotter and since my job had such a wide remit – shipping, shipbuilding, tourism, films, general trade matters – I had plenty of opportunity to try people out. And so I brought the young John Prescott on to the front bench to deal with a particular shipping matter on a Friday morning. It gave me quite a kick to see how thrilled he was. In fact he invited his father down to sit in the Strangers' Gallery and watch him perform at the Despatch Box. He did very well, too. I also brought Albert Booth in to handle shipbuilding affairs and Stanley Clinton Davis to cope with legal matters. They all went on to distinguish themselves, with John becoming Deputy Prime Minister, Albert entering the Cabinet and Stanley going to Brussels as one of our Commissioners in Europe.

But it wasn't all sweetness and light. Even in opposition there are pitfalls, as I discovered when I led an official delegation to China which ended in recrimination, embarrassment and a pointed diplomatic snub.

It was, without question an important all-party visit, the first from Britain since the turmoil of Mao's Cultural Revolution. The Labour nomineees for the trip were Michael Meacher, Joel Barnett and myself – all front benchers – plus the senior backbencher, Bob Sheldon, and the Labour peer Lord Chalfont.

In fact Chalfont posed a bit of a problem. Right at the beginning, the Foreign Office tried to ensure that he was appointed delegation leader, presumably on the grounds that he was a peer of the realm and knew how to handle a pair of chopsticks. I disagreed. Chalfont wasn't in my view a proper politician at all. He'd been defence correspondent for *The Times* when Harold Wilson brought him quite unexpectedly into government as Minister for Disarmament. It was a bit of a gimmick. Besides, Chalfont had never been in Cabinet and I had. It wasn't a question of pulling rank, but I understood that the Chinese wouldn't take kindly to a delegation led by somebody so obviously a political junior. It still amazes me that the Foreign Office seemed incapable of grasping the point. Anyway, it soon backed down when I made my position clear.

In retrospect, I'd probably have been better off saying nowt and letting Chalfont have the honour. As things turned out, it was his blurting out of an embarrassing truth which set the seal on a disastrous trip.

At first, everything went swimmingly. One morning, I remember, Michael Meacher came rushing into the breakfast room quite excitedly and declared; 'I've discovered a new fruit!' With that he proudly put three pomegranates on the table. Gently, I explained that for years one of the treats enjoyed by working-class children was picking out the seeds of a pomegranate with a pin. He seemed quite disappointed. But such distractions apart, it was a hard-working few days. We visited factories and farm collectives, got on very well with our hosts and were looking forward to a meeting with Chou-en-lai, certainly the most powerful figure in China after Mao himself and hugely influential in the country's relations with the outside world. That encounter, without doubt, would be the highlight of our trip.

It was on an excursion to see the Great Wall that things went badly wrong. The Chinese had arranged the excursion as a treat for us, a rare break from our working tour. Of course they were immensely proud of the Wall and keen for visitors to see and admire it.

We arrived in our long, sleek limousines and stepped out to study this great wonder of the world. Like almost everybody else who comes to the Wall, all of us naturally intended to walk along a stretch of it. All of us, that is, except Joel Barnett and Robert Sheldon.

They emerged from the cars, took one look and just turned their noses up. They made their opinion very evident by saying: 'We haven't come all the way to China to look at a pile of stones.' With that, they got back into their car and ordered the driver to take them back to Peking.

I felt like running after them and dragging them back, but it was impossible to provoke a scene in front of the bewildered Chinese. I just had to watch, cringing at the discourtesy of it all, as this pair – both of whom eventually became senior Treasury ministers – made their escape.

We didn't have to wait long for the consequences. The Chinese were clearly appalled at what they saw as a deliberate insult. Almost before we knew it, the meeting with Chou-en-lai was cancelled. Instead of improving relations between Britain and China, our delegation – or two members of it – had succeeded only in making them worse.

We flew home in a bleak, bitter mood. In an effort to limit the damage,

I'd got everybody to agree that there would be no public comment on the fiasco. It really was a question of least said, soonest mended. But inevitably, the media had got wind of something wrong. They were waiting for us when we landed at RAF Brize Norton: TV cameramen, reporters, print journalists, the lot. I was greeted at the foot of the aircraft steps by the station commander, who said that he had arranged a mammoth press conference and would I care to step this way? I glared at him. 'Well, you can just cancel it,' I growled. 'There'll be no press conference, no television pictures, nothing at all.'

So that was that. I thought I had succeeded in keeping the lid on. But as I was driving home to Barnsley, I switched on the radio for the news. To my astonishment I heard the voice of Lord Chalfont on air. Worse that that, he was spilling the beans without the slightest restraint, though like every other member of the delegation he'd promised not to do so. Perhaps he couldn't help himself. He was an old journalistic hand, after all. And it was a compelling story. But I'd think twice in future before going on so much as a trip to Blackpool in the company of Joel Barnett, Robert Sheldon or Lord Chalfont.

Still, all that was a bit of a sideshow. On the domestic front, things were going from bad to worse under Ted Heath and the Tories. To be fair, the Prime Minister had achieved a remarkable political success in negotiating the terms for Britain's entry into what was then known as the Common Market. Though Labour was becoming increasingly hostile to membership, I privately welcomed his statement on 17 June 1971 that a White Paper on our proposed membership was on its way. After all, I had fought and argued in favour of the European cause for years. In fact when the decisive parliamentary vote was eventually taken, in October 1971, I joined sixty-eight other Labour pro-Market rebels in supporting Britain's membership. It's the only time I've ever defied a three-line whip and I didn't much enjoy it. Apart from anything else, it gave more ammunition to Arthur Scargill, whose hatred for the European project was almost as intense as his dislike for me.

It was a moment of glory for Ted Heath. I hope he enjoyed it, because there wouldn't be any others. Elsewhere, things were beginning to go very badly wrong for him.

There's no doubt that the government had a mandate to reform the unions; the failure of Barbara Castle's *In Place of Strife* was still fresh in the voters' memory and they expected action. The problem was that the government's Industrial Relations Bill, published in 1971, was perceived as so savagely punitive that it stood no chance whatever of winning even grudging consent from the TUC or the Labour Party. It seemed that ministers knew no other way to proceed other than through clumsiness, arrogance and abrasiveness. So at the beginning of 1972, relations between government and opposition were at a dismally low ebb. They worsened further still with the publication of the January unemployment figures: 1,023,583. By today's standards, the number may be unremarkable; back then it was utterly devastating. Parliamentarians on both sides still had bitter memories of the hungry Thirties. The mood in the House was genuinely angry. At Prime Minister's Question Time, the Bolsover MP Dennis Skinner stood directly in front of Heath, snarling and brandishing a fist in his face. The uproar was deafening. The former miner Tom Swain hurled an evening paper with its damning headline on the Despatch Box. The Speaker had to suspend the sitting for a quarter of an hour.

It was against that background that for the first time since 1926, the National Union of Mineworkers voted for an all-out national strike. It was the last thing the government expected. Coal, after all, was an industry in decline; and for years, the NUM had more or less acquiesced, though with plenty of grumbles along the way. There was a general assumption that yet again the union would be bought off for a couple of pounds. But this time it was different. The union had a new leader in the tough and wily Joe Gormley. The Coal Board had a new Chairman in Derek Ezra, who was generally felt to be sympathetic to the miners' cause. Above all, the simmering resentment and frustration in the pits had to erupt sometime. The miners were ready for a fight.

At first nobody in Whitehall or the media took them seriously. There were confident predictions that the power stations had ample stocks of coal in reserve. Besides, it was asserted with equal confidence, the miners wouldn't hold out for long. Had anybody suggested that the dispute would drag on for six weeks, he would have been laughed to scorn.

For the Tories, that was yet another catastrophic misjudgement. They reckoned without the tactic of the flying picket, where hundreds and sometimes thousands of men would descend on power stations and other key points to prevent the transport of coal. The huge coke and coal depot at Saltley Gate became the symbol of NUM defiance, when Arthur Scargill finally achieved national recognition by asembling a crowd of some 15,000 banner-waving pickets, forcing the police to close the gates. But in fact ministers were already on the run. In spite of all those foolish boasts at the beginning of the strike, the reserves at the power stations were really down.

By now the government was close to panic. It had responsibility for wage settlements in the public sector, but in this case the job was clearly beyond them. I could see the desperation in ministers' eyes when I faced them across the floor of the Commons. Some were beginning to mutter about a political agenda behind the strikes, but in truth the miners – with the exception of a few firebrands like Scargill – weren't interested in bringing the Tories down. They just wanted decent treatment. Their pay had been badly eroded over the years. Their industry was facing increasing competition from gas, oil and nuclear power. When I had been in charge of coal, I'd done my level best to keep production up, but I had still seen at least thirty pits close. Under the Tories, that miserable process was accelerating. They'd not only started to import foreign coal but more than doubled the tonnage produced by opencast mines. And on top of that, they began converting coal-fired power stations and hiving off the profitable ancillary undertakings of the National Coal Board. They'd reversed every one of the policies I had pursued and as a direct result of their actions some 25,000 NUM jobs were being placed in jeopardy. No wonder the miners were in a mood to fight to the last ditch.

So was I. This was an industry in which ninety-two miners had been killed the previous year. Nearly 600 men were seriously injured. There were more than 82,000 accidents, all in the space of a mere twelve months. And that takes no account of the hundreds of men dying every year from the black lung disease pneumoconiosis, or the thousands of others wheezing and coughing out their lives because of conditions underground. You bet I was emotional. In one lengthy Commons speech I railed at ministers for their 'short-sighted, stupid, doctrinaire and provocative' policies. If parliamentary convention had allowed it, I'd have used more robust language.

In the event, the government paid dearly. It was forced to declare a state of emergency. The country was hit by a succession of power cuts. Businesses were suffering. Public support for the miners was growing by the day. The Coal Board was suffering huge financial losses. The miners showed no sign of yielding.

Ted Heath's initial determination to stand firm began to crumble. On 11 February, the Government announced an independent inquiry into the level of miners' pay, chaired by Lord Wilberforce. Within a matter of days, the distinguished judge came back with a recommendation of a pay award of more than 20 per cent. It was utter humiliation for the government. The whole Tory case had been blown apart. It was a quite stunning victory for Joe Gormley and the NUM – and without doubt the beginning of Ted Heath's downfall.

But he seemed determined to dig himself into a deeper hole. In November that year – almost in a state of despair at the torrent of pay claims which followed the miners' triumph – the Government completely overturned the manifesto on which it had been elected and introduced a statutory prices and incomes policy. No doubt Ministers imagined they were being tough and decisive; in fact they were courting disaster for themselves. From then on, they found themselves dragged willy-nilly on to the battlefield, becoming participants in too many industrial disputes for their own good or anyone else's.

Their misfortune deepened on 6 October, with the outbreak of the 1973 Middle East War. Inevitably, that set the cost of oil soaring and inspired fears over the security of our supplies. It was the worst possible moment to risk another confrontation with the NUM, but by this time the government was trapped in the consequences of its own folly. Two days after the war broke out, Phase Three of the prices and incomes policy was announced. It allowed a 7 per cent norm for pay increases – below the then rate of inflation. But already the miners were preparing a new claim of thirty-five per cent. The final act of the government's ill-starred decision to take on the NUM was about to begin.

To this day, the Heath years are remembered for the three-day week, imposed from 1 January 1974. Most of industry was forced into short-time working, heating in shops and offices was reduced, street lighting was dimmed, advertising hoardings blacked out. Television closed down for the evening at 10.30 p.m. and all this so that Heath could take on and beat the miners, who weren't even on strike at the time. They were merely operating an overtime ban. But Heath was clearly determined that in this confrontation there would be none of the erosion of coal stocks which had brought the government to grief in the previous dispute. It was another horrible miscalculation. It raised the stakes. It confirmed the impression of government intransigence. It threw down an open challenge to the pitmen. And incidentally it played into the hands of people like Mick McGahey and Arthur Scargill, who were already seizing on the dispute as a platform for their revolutionary rhetoric.

In fact it was the unholiest of messes, made even worse by the perception that a government which seemed so reluctant to pay the pitmen a decent wage didn't hesitate to hurl millions of pounds at the Arab states when the price of oil quadrupled.

I doubt if ministers ever dreamed they would preside over such a fiasco. I was Chairman of the Miners' Group of Labour MPs during the dispute and in company with the Group Secretary, Elfed Davies, was called in for a secret meeting with Willie Whitelaw, Secretary of State for Employment. It was clear to me that he personally wanted a solution – any solution – that would get the government off the hook. But Willie's a loyal old soul; perhaps more loyal than Heath deserved. He wouldn't budge on the question of making the miners a special case. Nor did he have anything of significance to say about the things which made pitmen so very different from other workers – the time they had to spend before their shifts waiting for the lifts to take them underground or the time they were obliged to spend afterwards in getting themselves clean.

So there was scope for a deal if the government really wanted one. Indeed the TUC had already made the unprecedented offer that if a deal was done with the miners, other unions wouldn't use it as an argument when negotiating their own settlements. But ministerial inflexibility was the order of the day. My meeting with Whitelaw followed the pattern of so many other informal exchanges during the strike: the prices and incomes policy was sacrosanct. And so the Tories conspired in their own destruction.

Throughout all this, I was as active as ever I'd been as a minister: making speeches, asking parliamentary questions, putting down Commons motions, harrying the government in any way I could. It struck me as odd that not a word of these activities ever found their way into the miners' journals. In issue after issue of the *Yorkshire Miner*, for example, I'd see reams of stuff about the activities of left-wing colleagues like Alan Beaney or Dick Kelley; but readers could be forgiven for assuming that Roy Mason spent his days idling. In effect, I had become a non-person. Naturally – and not just because of wounded vanity – I was irritated by such treatment. It struck me as petty and dishonest, a typical product of the vindictive Left. Indeed I'd sent tapes of my speeches on the strike both to the NUM and the Yorkshire NUM, but they were never acknowledged. Of course I couldn't know then that the attempt to airbrush me out of the record was only the beginning of a campaign which in years to come would plumb much murkier depths of nastiness.

But I had little enough time to brood. On 4 February, the result of the NUM ballot for an all-out strike was announced. An overwhelming majority – 81 per cent – backed the call. Three days later, Heath announced a general election dominated by the theme '*Who Governs Britain?*'

9 Defence of the Realm

It proved to be a damn silly question. The government is supposed to govern Britain; and if it runs whingeing to the voters as though in doubt of that answer, it can expect a pretty dusty response. Ted Heath went down to deserved and unlamented defeat and we were back in. Just. Without a Parliamentary majority to call our own. Labour: 301 seats; Tories 296; Liberals 14.

As before, I didn't want to hang around in Barnsley. If and when the call came from Downing Street, I intended to be immediately available. This time though, the drive to London had to be postponed. Heath was refusing to go gracefully and spent the entire weekend trying to cobble together some kind of deal with the Liberals and the Ulster Unionists to keep himself in power. He didn't actually resign until the evening of Monday, 4 March.

Impatience had overtaken me by then. I'd travelled to Westminster earlier that day to mooch around the corridors in the hope of picking up some titbits of gossip. As it turned out, it was well worth the effort. On one of my forays I bumped into Ted Short, who was to become deputy Prime Minister. He sidled up to me in a conspiratorial fashion and muttered from the corner of his mouth: 'I think Harold's going to offer you Defence.' Then he scurried away.

Vastly encouraged, I mooched around some more. Still no word. An hour went past. Then two. My phone remained silent. At last I went back to my digs in Clapham Common, deflated. Obviously Ted had got it wrong.

It wasn't until 10.15 that night, while I was having a cup of coffee with my landlady Emily Hall that Downing Street finally reached me. I raced round to Number Ten by cab, wondering at the lateness of the hour, anxious about the delay. After all, while Heath had been flailing around for support, Harold had enjoyed the luxury of a whole weekend to make his Cabinet plans. Could he have given somebody else my job?

I needn't have worried. Defence it was to be. For me, it would be like coming home. I'd cut my political teeth on defence issues, been a Minister in the department, knew the subject and the personalities well. I told Harold I'd thoroughly enjoy the challenge.

He looked at me a little oddly, obviously surprised at my enthusiasm. 'It'll be tough,' he warned.

He never spoke a truer word. In Labour circles, Defence was by far the least popular department in Whitehall. Many party members, not to mention an influential minority of our MPs, thought it a waste of money to maintain our military strength at such a high level of preparedness. Some wanted us to abandon our nuclear deterrent unilaterally, an attitude reinforced by a pervasive, knee-jerk anti-Americanism. A few colleagues had even managed to persuade themselves that the Soviet Union was a friend to mankind and posed no threat at all.

The quality of Labour thinking on the issue – if it can be called thinking – had been summed up for me in a resolution passed overwhelmingly at the party conference, the previous October. It called for cuts in Britain's military spending, 'initially by at least £1,000 million a year'. As far as I was concerned, that slash and burn approach was as reckless as it was ignorant. It would at a stroke cut our defence effort by more than a quarter. It would devastate our front-line forces, plunge NATO into crisis, wreak havoc with thousands of jobs in the defence industry and present the bullying militarists in the Kremlin with political opportunities they would find hard to resist.

But the pressure was such that the party leadership couldn't altogether resist it. Labour had gone into the election with a manifesto commitment to reduce defence spending to the level of our main European allies. It would mean achieving annual savings amounting to hundreds of millions of pounds over a period of time. This I thought would be manageable; and at least we weren't surrendering to the extremism of the party conference. After all, there was a sound case for examining our defence commitments. The country simply couldn't afford to go on spending such sums – 5.7 per cent of GNP in 1973 – when the economy was in such poor shape. In Cabinet on 14 March, Denis Healey warned, 'the country is confronted by an economic situation which might well be the worst which has ever been faced in peacetime.' Against that depressing background, even the Tories had been forced into defence cuts of £178 million shortly before the election.

That said, I hadn't the slightest intention of just hacking at the defence budget – warmly though such butchery would have been welcomed by left-wingers. Unlike them, I was very well aware of the threat posed by Soviet aggression. The invasion of Czechoslovakia and the crushing of the Prague Spring were still fresh in my memory; and there wasn't the slightest sign that Moscow was about to mend its ways. In the potential battleground of Europe, the Warsaw Pact powers confronted NATO with a marked superiority in men and conventional weapons – up to 40 per cent more soldiers in fighting units, a lead of 2.5 to 1 in tanks, more than 2 to 1 in aircraft and field artillery, not to mention formidable advantages in geography and the ability to reinforce the front line over short, secure routes. The West was outnumbered and outgunned. In my view it would be insane to drop our guard when faced with those kinds of odds.

I came away from Downing Street that night with plenty to think about. Somehow I had to honour our manifesto commitment while still maintaining our armed forces in fighting trim; and while I was about it I needed to satisfy Chancellor Healey's demands for spending cuts, keep the Left reasonably quiet and at the same time ensure that morale in the services didn't suffer. Fortunately for me, I'd been given a first-class team to help with the job – the tough and very able Bill Rodgers as my deputy, the Portsmouth MP Frank Judd as Navy Minister, Bob Brown running the Army and Brynmor John in charge of the RAF. All good men. In the Lords, an important member of my team was Desmond Brayley, a former regular soldier. I didn't know much about him, but Harold was very keen to have him and he had hands-on military experience as a former captain in the Royal Artillery. That was good enough for me. On top of that, the three key offices in Government were occupied by people I thought would be generally supportive: Denis Healey (in spite of his need for cuts) at the Treasury, Jim Callaghan at the Foreign office and Roy Jenkins at the Home Office. With a bit of luck, I thought, I might be able to square the circle after all; some ideas were already beginning to stir.

The very first day in my new office overlooking the Thames taught me something about military sensitivity. Like most new ministers, I was keen to make my surroundings as homely as possible, so I arranged for all my old, familiar mementoes to be delivered – family photographs, my collection of miners' lamps, other bits and pieces. Among these was the model of a whaler carved in walrus tusks, presented to me years before by the Soviet Shipping Minister, Viktor Bakaev.

Everything arrived as planned. Everything, that is, except my model whaler. Unbeknown to me at the time, all hell had broken loose when it was discovered that the thing was a present from Moscow. Security officials spent hours prodding it and poking it, examining it from every angle. Could the cunning Russians have planted a bug, on the off-chance that one day I might be in possession of state secrets? Unlikely though the proposition seemed, it was decided that no chances could be taken. My model was eventually removed to the bowels of the building, where a team of experts took it apart. At long length, my little ship was pronounced clear. All that remained then was to put the pieces back together again. I have to say that the lads did a brilliant job; you still can't see the joins.

I soon had more pressing matters to worry me. I'd only been in office a matter of weeks when I delivered a speech to mineworkers in Newcastle-under-Lyme, basically dealing with my plans for the department. In the course of my remarks I foolishly departed from the written text to comment on the situation in Northern Ireland. 'There is an undercurrent of feeling on the mainland from people who would like to see our troops withdrawn.' I observed. 'But until we can solve the problem in Northern Ireland, they will remain.'

I imagined that I was only restating government policy. I had no idea of the hole I had opened for myself. It wasn't until I arrived at the local railway station for my train home that the truth dawned. There was an urgent telephone message for me in the stationmaster's office; could I get in touch with Merlyn Rees, the Northern Ireland Secretary, right away?

Somewhat mystified, I contacted Merlyn, to find him furious. He left me in no doubt that by merely mentioning the possibility of troop withdrawals I had blundered badly, trodden with hobnail boots all over his turf and made an idiot of myself.

Very chastened, I could only express my regrets. But there was worse to come. My speech had provoked uproar, especially in Northern Ireland. The West Belfast MP Gerry Fitt announced that he was flying to London to protest personally to the Prime Minister. By now I was covered with embarrassment. At Cabinet the following Tuesday, Harold ticked me off personally, saying that he would be grateful if in future Ministers would stick to their own departmental remits. Well, I deserved it. On Northern Ireland matters, as I was later to discover at first hand, careless talk can be dangerous.

It was a hard lesson, underlined later by an open letter sent to me by Sinn Fein:

A Chara,

On behalf of the IRA we wish to place on record our deep gratitude for your help in our stuggle against the murdering thugs of the British Army (they have their mothers, but do they know their fathers?).

With your encouragement, we were convinced that a few more bombs in England plus those funeral caskets returning will signal the defeat of the British Army, when we resume hostilities inside the next few weeks.

We find it a savage irony that by coming to our aid, the blimps and the fur-coat brigade have proved themselves the best friends the IRA have ever had.

Is sinne,
Mairin de Burca, Tony Heffernan
Ard Runaithe

I promised myself I'd never again open my mouth on anything to do with Northern Ireland without thinking twice.

Meanwhile, I was beginning to grapple with the need for swingeing cuts in my budget, while still keeping Britain in the front rank of military powers. It was clear to me that it simply couldn't be done without a major defence review.

Harold was all in favour, though – perhaps typically – his key advisers wanted the review conducted on a confidential basis. 'An announcement that we were conducting a defence review would have an unfortunate effect,' the Permanent Secretary to the Cabinet Office, Sir John Hunt, wrote to Wilson. 'Especially on our NATO allies, who might draw extreme and incorrect conclusions about our intentions and some of whom might use this as an excuse for reducing their own defence effort.'

Sir John even had advice to the Prime Minister of what he should do if he was asked questions in the House about the review: 'You might think it sufficient to say that the government are reviewing closely all aspects of public expenditure, including, of course, defence, in the context of their overall programme, in order to see where savings may reasonably be required over the next few years.'

There speaks the voice of the true civil servant, obsessed with secrecy but with little understanding of the political realities. To begin with, an exercise like a major defence review would be bound to leak. And if a Labour government was caught conducting some hole-in-corner study into how to save money on defence, there would be hell to pay. The opposition – and more importantly the armed forces – would fear the worst. The government's arguments would be undermined before they were even put. I thought it best to be frank from the outset and said so. And that was understood.

Now I had to get on with the sheer slog of what was to become the most far-reaching review of our defences ever conducted in peacetime. Britain then was still in the afterglow of empire. We not only had a heavy presence in Germany to meet the Soviet threat but thousands of troops in Northern Ireland and a whole scatter of forces across the world. Contrary to what everybody imagined, we hadn't really withdrawn from East of Suez; we still had commitments in Oman, the Gulf, to CENTO and to SEATO, not to mention forces in Hong Kong, Singapore,

Malaysia, Brunei, the British Indian Ocean Territories and Mauritius. Other defence facilities included the use of South Africa's Simonstown naval base, together with assets in Malta, Gan, Diego Garcia and Mombasa. We were, in fact, still acting as a world policeman. And any attempt to shuffle off that burden would certainly provoke cries of pain among our allies unless we consulted every step of the way. Certainly there would have to be a lot of negotiations, probably a lot of withdrawals, some heartaches and a lot of unscrambling to do.

However, all these overseas commitments meant that I could make deep cuts without seriously affecting our military strength in Europe, where it really mattered. But tempting though the equation seemed, I wasn't going to prejudge anything. We would have to examine every option carefully. So I wasn't best pleased when the Chancellor, Denis Healey, stuck his oar in. I'd been planning to announce details of my review in Parliament, when Denis proposed that my statement should include the following: 'We accept as a starting point the decision taken by Her Majesty's Government in 1968 that our forces should be withdrawn from South East Asia. Discussions are proceeeding with our allies and other governments as regards the timing of this withdrawal.'

I knew very well what Denis was up to. When he was Defence Secretary back in 1968 he'd made some announcements about pulling back from East of Suez – but many of his proposals hadn't actually been carried out. Now, with his Chancellor's hat on, he was trying for another bite of the cherry in the hope of saving some easy money.

I disagreed. I wrote to Harold:

In previous correspondence I have set out my serious reservations about anticipating – at a time when the review is barely under way – the outcome for a specific area of our commitments. As I have already said, I think it would be quite wrong to tackle the review piecemeal and my intention is that we should look at commitments, capabilities and resources together. . . . There is also the important question of our allies. Consultation must be a necessary preliminary of a withdrawal from Singapore and will be much more easily carried out against a background of a comprehensive picture of our intentions regarding defence policy as a whole. There would also be a prime requirement to consult the Americans who need to consider carefully the impact of any decision that we may take. In view of the Chancellor's reservation, however, I think that it may be necessary to discuss this among colleagues. I suggest that the most appropriate forum will be the Defence and Overseas Policy Committee [of the Cabinet].

That was enough to see Denis off for the time being. With the support of Jim Callaghan at the Foreign Office, I got my way. My announcement of the review didn't include a word of what the Chancellor wanted me to say. I was pleased with my victory; but as I was bitterly to discover before too long, you can never safely ignore a Chancellor who is on the lookout for savings.

Nor could I ignore the machinations of the Left. In May 1974, the National Executive Committee of the Labour Party set up a working party 'on defence expenditure and the export of arms'. It would become the spearhead of a sustained attack on the government by people I came to regard with increasing distaste.

But other problems were crowding on me. In August 1974 I was taking a brief break with Madge in Madeira, when I received an urgent phone call from the department. I was told to pack my bags and get myself to the airport by first light, where a plane would be waiting to pick me up. And no, I couldn't be given any details of what was up. Security and all that. Intrigued – in fact rather worried – I had little sleep that night. We were at the airport well before the dawn, to be picked up by a somewhat old-looking RAF twin-prop plane. The sergeant loadmaster was somewhat abashed when we boarded, since the aircraft had only bucket seats, newspapers instead of proper tablecloths and no refreshments other than a sandwich or two. But, he was delighted to be able to write in his logbook that he had looked after the Secretary of State for Defence. 'I never expected that,' he said. 'Not in this aircraft.'

I learned then that the crisis in Cyprus had gone from bad to worse. A coup had been launched by the Greek National Guard. The troops, loyal to the military regime in Athens, had attacked the presidential palace and there were claims – later proved false – that Archbishop Makarios was dead. It looked very much as though the thuggish Colonels were determined to enforce the unity of Cyprus with Greece. Outright war between Greece and Turkey had suddenly become a real threat, with the landing of Turkish forces on the island.

I had a lot to think about on that flight home. We touched down in Oporto on the way, but I couldn't disembark. Security again. There was a car waiting for me when we arrived at Northolt and I was whisked immediately to the Cabinet Office Briefing Room (COBRA) to meet Harold, Jim Callaghan and the Chiefs of Staff. Jim was working overtime to prevent a full-blown war, but our immediate problem then was the fate of the thousands of British holidaymakers and other nationals on the island. Fighting was fierce. The airport had been seized and closed, so there was no possibility of our people making their own way home.

What we set in train was the biggest rescue operation undertaken by

British forces since Dunkirk. We arranged for the despatch of HMS *Devonshire* and HMS *Andromeda*, together with the Royal Fleet Auxiliary *Olna* as the spearhead of a gigantic armada of ships and planes with orders to evacuate not only our own people but other foreign nationals too – a total of around 27,000 civilians in all. Fortunately, we had the use of our sovereign bases at Akrotiri and Dhekalia, which enabled us to supplement the evacuation from the beaches with a huge airlift, using Hercules aircraft, VC10s, Britannias and Belfasts. In one day, the RAF brought out 2,000 refugees from forty-two nations.

It was a spectacularly successful operation in a dangerously volatile environment, with no lives lost. I thought the service people involved should have been awarded a peace medal in recognition of their achievement, but my proposal roused no enthusiasm among my colleagues. I still think that was a mistake.

But undeniably the crisis reflected well on the government as a whole. Not only had we proved decisive and efficient in getting the civilians out, but Jim Callaghan's efforts were crucial in bringing about a cease-fire on 22 July. The next day the wretched military junta in Athens resigned in disgrace, a very welcome development.

Not that we could afford to rest on our laurels. With our ultra-fragile parliamentary position, Harold had no choice but to go to the country as soon as the polls gave us a fair wind. It wasn't much of a surprise when he chose 10 October as the date for the second general election of 1974. What threw me into the deepest gloom was the content of our manifesto.

The words were unambiguous: 'Starting from the basis of the multilateral disarmament negotiations, we shall seek the removal of American Polaris bases from Britain.'

I was appalled. This was Labour at its reckless worst, swayed – in spite of the mention of multilateral negotiations – by the unilateralists, the Bevanite rump, the anti-Americans and the apologists for Soviet Communism. Needless to say, my views and those of my ministerial team had been ignored. Perhaps the fact that I had allowed underground nuclear tests in Nevada – necessary in my view to maintain the credibility of our weapons – put me beyond the pale as far as some colleagues wore concerned. After I announced the success of the test I came under ferocious attack from Labour Action for Peace – Arthur Latham, Frank Allaun, Bob Cryer, Hugh Jenkins and all the usual suspects – and from the Tribune Group.

Clearly I'd underestimated both the influence of the Left and overestimated Harold's willingness to stand firm. The consequence was that the party was now saddled with a manifesto commitment which I thought crazy. I couldn't offhand think of any other policy which would do more to undermine NATO or place our relations with Washington under greater strain. I couldn't help remembering the pamphlet I had published years earlier under the title: *Polaris, Yes, Yes, Yes*.

Resignation wasn't remotely an option. I wasn't about to hand a propaganda gift to the Tories at the start of an election campaign. Besides, if I stayed on at Defence I fully intended to shove the whole issue of nuclear weapons onto the back burner. If the Left erupted at signs that I was dragging my feet, that was fine by me. I'd fight the issue out in Cabinet if necessary. I was pretty confident of what the outcome would be. Barring any really sensational breakthrough in the arms negotiations between Washington and Moscow – in which case we'd obviously give up the Polaris bases, if that was what it took – my colleagues would stick firmly by the Alliance.

Most of them, after all, were perfectly well aware of the reluctance of the Soviet Union to live up to its professions of *détente*. Only the previous year, Leonid Brezhnev had told Communist Party leaders that while he saw ten to fifteen years of peaceful co-existence with the West, it had to be accompanied by an increase of economic and military power in Eastern Europe. He foresaw a time, probably by 1985, when the Warsaw Pact would be so strong that it could dictate the terms of its relationship with the West, leading to a worldwide increase in Communist influence. That open threat of political pressure backed by military force was one no British government could dare overlook.

So in my own personal election address in Barnsley I simply ignored the Polaris issue, contenting myself with a promise to 'reduce defence spending and divert resources to social welfare and productive industry'.

Oddly enough, our supposedly vigilant media didn't cotton on. Perhaps they had more pressing business on their minds. To be fair, so did I. A scandal erupted in my department barely a couple of weeks before the election and according to many of the news reports, it might just be enough to tip the outcome against Labour.

I was off the Northern tip of Scotland aboard the aircraft-carrier *Ark Royal* at the time, as part of my programme of getting out and about to see the forces in action. These things don't stop just because there's an election campaign. For a few hours I could forget the business of canvassing in Barnsley to enjoy the thrill of watching the Royal Navy show what it could do. Very impressive it was, too: a night exercise which involved our pilots finding the ship in pitch darkness and thumping their warplanes safely down on deck. I was watching from the bridge, full of admiration for the aviators and telling myself (a little guiltily) that however much the Government was paying them for their terrifying skills, it wasn't enough.

Though it was about 2 a.m. I would never have torn myself away from the spectacle but for a flash signal from the ministry. That brought me down to earth with a bigger thump than anything I had seen on deck. My Parliamentary Under-Secretary in the Lords, Des Brayley, was in deep trouble. Questions were being asked about the company he had built up before he entered government, the Canning Town Glass Works. The press had got hold of information that the firm was to be investigated by the Trade Department. There were suggestions of expenses fiddles, inappropriate commission payments, fingers in the till. I just stood there, suddenly remote from the naval drama going on all around me. This was serious. A hostile press could make mincemeat of the government over this in the run-up to polling day. After all, Harold had just made a speech warning party workers against Fleet Street plots to discredit the good name of Labour. The opinion polls were looking reasonably encouraging, but I knew the mood could switch in an instant. It wasn't impossible that we could lose on 10 October. And without doubt, my department would be saddled with much if not all of the blame.

At about 2.30 a.m., I got through to Des Brayley at home, telling him I would see him first thing in the morning. In the meantime, he was to stand fast. I had no idea then of whether the accusations against him had anything to them, but I didn't want him to do anything silly. As it turned out, I was preaching to the converted. I discovered later that to avoid the press contingent clustering around his front door, he had crept into the back garden, thrown his mac over the barbed wire on top of the rear wall and made his escape. He spent the next few days in anonymous bed and breakfast accommodation until the furore died down.

Meanwhile, knowing nothing of this, I was busily trying to limit the damage. I didn't want Des to go. He may not have been the most accomplished performer at the Despatch Box, but I had always found him a reliable member of the Defence team, with a fund of practical common sense. I hoped he would be able to come up with a convincing answer to the charges against him. At first light I helicoptered off *Ark Royal* to take a plane for London. I was in my office early to hear the story from Desmond's own lips. But he was a shattered man, broken by all the publicity. The more he spoke, the more my heart sank. There was no doubt about it: he would have to resign. That afternoon he went across to see Harold in Downing Street. By the evening it was all over, in a resignation described by the *Daily Express* as 'a savage punch at Labour's election chances'.

In the event, we scraped back. Just. Labour won only an additional eighteen seats from the Tories and had an overall majority of just four. For the Government, it was scant improvement on the position before the election and no cause for celebration. But for the Tory leader, Ted Heath, the outcome was disastrous. Less than five months later he was dumped by his party in favour of an untried and untested challenger called Margaret Thatcher. I don't think anybody in the Labour Party – least of all me – thought there was much to fear from her.

After our October disappointment I plunged back into the urgent business of completing the defence review – only to find myself almost immediately embroiled in an unexpected and most unwelcome row with Jim Callaghan, the Foreign Seecretary.

It erupted with a headline in the London *Evening Standard*: ' "Who Runs The Navy?" Jim demands.'

What had happened was that ships of the Royal Navy had been conducting exercises with South Africa's maritime forces. It was a prefectly legitimate operation under the Simonstown Agreement with the Republic, but obviously the kind of thing which in those apartheid days could be guaranteed to provoke the Labour Party. Worse still, our ships, under Vice Admiral Henry Leach, had apparently sailed into Cape Town harbour and fired a 21-gun salute to the South African flag.

Jim was reported to be angry and embarrassed by the incident and obviously blamed my department. So did the entire Labour Party. The NEC wasted no time in censuring the government.

But Jim was mistaken in pinning the blame on me. The arrangements for the joint exercise had been made by the Foreign Office and our Chargé d'Affaires in South Africa. Somehow, the arrangements hadn't been transmitted to the Foreign Secretary himself until it was too late. I made it my business to call in all my ministers and press officers to spread the word in the Commons tearoom and round Whitehall and get the department off the hook. But it was an uncomfortable experience to find myself at loggerheads with Jim Callaghan, who was not only a Cabinet ally but a friend. Fortunately, our relationship suffered no lasting damage; Jim's a big enough man to rise above such inter-departmental rows.

By now the long, hard slog of the defence review was all but complete. We'd had preliminary consultations with the Americans, our other NATO allies and with partners across the world, from Malta to Singapore. What we had achieved, I thought, was the best possible outcome: substantial savings which nevertheless preserved our core defensive interests in Europe and fully maintained the integrity of NATO. I was delighted with it, though I knew that some in my own party would complain that I hadn't gone far enough.

One area in which I did suffer a defeat was over the Royal Yacht *Britannia*. Though I am and always have been a convinced monarchist and believe in flying the flag, I had to defend my budget too. And for all the propaganda which always surfaces whenever *Britannia* is mentioned – that she could serve as a hospital ship in case of hostilities and all the rest of it – the blunt truth was that she served no defence purpose whatsoever. Her annual running expenses worked out at about the cost of keeping a frigate at sea. She was, in short, a luxury we couldn't afford. Not when active units in all services were being trimmed. I thought that retaining her would certainly provoke criticism of the kind which would embarrass not only the government but the Queen too.

Unfortunately for me, Harold not only refused to countenance my solution but didn't seem to think there was a problem in the first place. Unlike Tony Blair, who eventually did get rid of *Britannia*, he was a bit of a sentimentalist on all royal matters. It's pretty clear that he got on better with the Queen than any Prime Minister before or since and on this question allowed his heart to rule his head. So the answer from Downing Street was that *Britannia* must stay and continue to be provided for within the Defence budget.

However, you don't get anywhere in government if you're not prepared to fight your corner; and I had a powerful ally in the Chief of Naval Staff, Admiral Sir Edward Ashmore. He sent me a memo which opened up a second line of attack.

> Much of the case for retaining the yacht rests on its representational advantages and it is clear . . . that her running time is almost exclusively devoted to Foreign Office and royal business. The only two ministries to benefit from *Britannia* are therefore the Foreign Office and the Department of Trade and there is clearly a strong case for a subvention from these ministries. I therefore recommend that we should press strongly for the running costs to be borne pincipally on Foreign Office and/or Department of Trade votes. . . .

I wasted no time firing off a minute to Harold suggesting that these departments should stump up £1 million annually to keep *Britannia* afloat. Maybe the sum involved wasn't so very much; but I was fed up with the way my Cabinet colleagues seemed to think that Defence was a milch cow. At least now one or two of them might think twice before assuming that they could save their own budgets by demanding cuts in mine.

As it turned out, my attempt to turn the tables didn't get very far. Ironically, it was undermined from within my own ministry, by the Chief of the Defence Staff, General Sir Michael Carver. In a strong memo, he challenged the view put forward by both Admiral Ashmore and me:

> I am reluctant to take the line you recommend, on two grounds mainly. The first is that of our role in support of the Sovereign, one of the traditional duties of the armed forces and one which we cherish. The army contributes to this in many ways, some very much in public such as the heavy load of ceremonial duties in London and some lesser known ones behind the scenes. The Royal Air Force provides the Queen's Flight, special aircraft on other occasions and the Royal Air Force Regiment Colour Guard Squadrons. I feel that the Royal Yacht falls into the same catgory as far as the Royal Navy is concerned.
>
> The second is more material . . . raising the general issues of trying to charge other departments for activities of the services. It could be that it would be appropriate to do so in a wider context, for example of fishery and oil rig protection, hydrography etc, but . . . we could lose a great deal more than we would gain.

So that was that. With the Chief of Defence Staff in opposition, I hadn't a chance of getting my scheme through. And in retrospect, I think the General was probably right. If we weren't going to get rid of *Britannia* altogether, we would be better off shutting up and taking the financial consequences. Of course that still left the problem of Cabinet colleagues who wanted my budget trimmed even more.

The details of my review, announced in the Commons on 3 December 1974, showed that we'd be cutting defence spending as a proportion of GNP from 5.5 per cent to 4.5 per cent over a period of ten years. Drastic medicine; but most of those savings would be achieved by reducing or withdrawing our forces from far-flung territories. In this way, we would save vast sums in trooping flights, family accommodation, hospitals, schools and all the expensive ancillary services which help to keep our forces in fighting trim.

Sadly, my axe couldn't stop there. The spending constraints on me were so tight that other savings had to be found. I had to reduce the Navy's frigates, destroyers and mine counter-measures vessels by about one seventh. This was where the retention of *Britannia* seemed so unfair. The Army's re-equipment plans would be modified too, with the cancellation of the Vixen wheeled reconnaissance vehicle and a reduction in planned helicopter purchases. The RAF got off more lightly: in fact I managed to allow for some improvements in our air combat capability and to continue with the Tornado project in which we were collaborating with other European countries. Most important of all, in view of what happened eight years later when Argentina invaded the Falklands, I made sure that development and design work continued on the maritime

Harrier fighter. Of all the decisions I took at Defence, that was probably the most significant.

Given the huge pressure for much wider and deeper cuts, I believed I had done as good a job as possible. Britain remained a core, committed member of NATO. Our nuclear deterrent was still in place. Our forces were now much more focused on the real job in hand – keeping the Russians at arm's length. The Tories, of course, were officially critical of what I proposed, but I don't think their hearts were in it. Shortly after my announcement, I received a charming letter from Alan Clark, then the Tory MP for Plymouth Sutton (and later a noted diarist). He wrote:

May I say personally that given the stringent fiscal requirements that were imposed upon you, which of course I deplore, I consider that your review was a pretty creditable piece of work and I have already said as much on the *Westminster* TV programme which did very little for my personal popularity with the opposition whips [Aha, one crumb of comfort for me!].

But then, the real trouble over defence matters never really came from the Tory party. It came in all its reckless wrong-headedness from my own side; from the people who habitually used the word 'comrade' but hadn't a clue what real comradeship meant: the Labour Left. In the vote on the review, no fewer than fifty-eight MPs, led by the Tribune Group, marched into the lobbies against the government. It was clear to me then that far worse was to come.

10 Taking on the Left

As a bit of a relief from all the in-fighting, I'd begun doodling some possible designs for a new Ministry of Defence tie. Neckwear in all its permutations and possibilities had become a hobby ever since I was a junior Minister at the Board of Trade. In all my trips abroad, I had discovered that my overseas counterparts always wanted to talk about the British weather; whenever there was a social occasion in one of our embassies, I'd inevitably be buttonholed by somebody keen to make a point about the rain in Manchester or the fog in London. I suppose the idea was to make me feel welcome, since it seems to be the universal opinion that the British are interested in nothing else. But I was getting bored and fed up with it. So as a kind of diversion, I designed my first ever tie, with a motif which was meant to draw the question: what's that? At least it should make for a bit of variety in conversation.

My original effort was a tie for Labour MPs. After all, politicians don't have badges or ribbons to indentify them as such (perhaps just as well), so there seemed to be a niche in the market. Having come up with what I thought was an attractive motif, I submitted the design to the Labour Party Liaison Committee for approval. Once they had given the go-ahead, I had dozens of ties run up by the Barnsley firm of Midwood. They sold like hot cakes, with colleagues queuing up to buy. At cost price.

Once I'd got the bug I couldn't stop. I designed a tie for Chequers, taking the motif from one of the windows in the old house, and presented a whole batch – some blue, some burgundy – to Wilson. The first thing he did was send one to every former Prime Minister still living – Harold Macmillan, Alec Home and Anthony Eden – signifying membership of the premier's club. I designed a tie for the Speaker too, which he'd give away by the dozen whenever he made an official trip abroad.

I had been too busy in my first few months at Defence to produce something similar for the department, but I felt I should. It already had an official tie, designed by Lord Mountbatten, but I thought it an undistinguished, somewhat pock-marked affair. I was sure I could do better. In time, I came up with a motif which could be worn by the men of all three services and the central secretariat staff too. I was quite proud of what I had done, and brought the designs – again one in blue, the other in burgundy – into the office one Monday morning. The idea, I told my staff, was to get someone in the ministry to sell the ties and donate any profits to one of the service charities.

I waited a week and nothing happened. My officials obviously hadn't taken me seriously. 'Right,' I told them, 'I'm going to go down to the staff canteen and put my designs on the wall with the notice "This is the new unofficial tie for the ministry. Please apply to the Secretary of State." ' Well, they took me seriously then all right. Within an hour I had a visit from somebody in the army division asking if he could arrange the sale of ties on behalf of one of the benevolent funds. I gave him the go-ahead, of course. What's more, he ended up selling hundreds of them at NATO meetings, army get-togethers and defence exhibitions.

Unfortunately my more serious problems couldn't be solved so easily.

From the moment of the left-wing rebellion over the review, I knew that the battle was still to be won. My very success in preserving the teeth of our front-line forces was like a red rag to a bull. Some of my critics didn't think Britain should be a serious military power at all. Others were half in love with the Soviet Union and thought it should be trusted. All of them wanted the government to slash defence spending by £1,000 million, as demanded by the Labour Party conference in 1973. What made such views particularly dangerous was that the Left and its allies were in a dominant position on Labour's National Executive Committee; and before Tony Blair succeeded in knocking some sense into the party, the NEC had real power.

The attack on me and my department wasn't long in coming. A week after my review, the NEC Study Group (on defence spending, the arms trade and alternative employment) agreed to 'reconsider' its programme of work in the light of what I had said. What it meant, of course, was that it wanted to come at me again for not following the party conference line to the letter. It wanted much more drastic cuts in defence and never mind the consequences.

The mood of the Study Group was summed up in a letter sent by its chairman, Ian Mikardo, to party General Secretary Ron Hayward in January.

The main purpose for which the Group was sat up was to study and report on the political, defence and employment implications of the substantial cut in defence expenditure which would result from our getting down to the 'average per cent GNP' target as quickly as possible and at the same time pursuing the policy we laid down on nuclear weapons and bases.

Since then, of course, we have had the announcement of a government policy on defence cuts substantially different from the one we were envisaging.

If the National Excutive Committee is prepared to accept the government's policy . . . there would be no point whatever in our Group going on with its studies.

The only thing which would justify our going on would be a decision by the Executive that it would, notwithstanding the government's decision, continue to advocate the 'average per cent GNP' target reached within a period substantially shorter than ten years, together with the party's nuclear policy, and therefore instructing us to study the implications. . . .

So there it was. An open invitation to the NEC to launch a sustained campaign against its own government's defence policy. That letter sums up why the Party has been electorally so unsuccessful for most of this century. And why Tony Blair had no choice but to neuter both the NEC and the power of the party conference. We would regularly spend more time and energy savaging each other than ever we did in confronting our real enemies.

Needless to say, the NEC agreed that Mikardo's wrecking tactics had to be supported. He was, in effect, given a mandate to go gunning for the Defence department; and there wasn't the slightest possibility that he or his colleagues would listen to the facts of the case. Most of their views were set in concrete and had been for years.

He was all the more dangerous an opponent because he was a slick, clever operator, with a fair degree of personal popularity in the party. Besides, he had the ability to get away with behaviour which would certainly have covered most other politicians in embarrassment. I was with him, for example, on a parliamentary delegation to Poland in the Fifties, the first such visit from Britain since the Communists took over there. It was a fascinating trip, but one which Ian Mikardo didn't really experience. He slipped away from the rest of us soon after we landed in Warsaw and was hardly seen again until shortly before it was time to leave. We suspected that he had seized the opportunity to visit other Eastern Bloc countries, setting up trade deals on behalf of his own companies – and doing it at the taxpayers' expense. Though we had no positive proof that this is what he'd been up to, we knew there were no flies on Ian.

Apart from Mikardo himself, the Study Group's members included Tony Benn, who had just been converted to the unilateralist cause, Frank Allaun, for whom no defence cuts were ever deep enough and Michael Foot, the veteran Aldermaston marcher. They were joined by a whole clutch of academics, some of whom had a rigorous and informed approach to defence matters; but there were others whose judgement and understanding I trusted not one whit, together with a platoon of trades unionists who in general would follow the line of left-wing fashion.

To be fair, there were also a number of people on the Study Group – including Alan Lee Williams, Jim Wellbeloved, Geoffrey de Freitas and Rod MacFarquhar – who didn't swallow the Left's agenda. So long as they stuck it out, I hoped that the discussions might be conducted with a leavening of common sense. If the worst came to the worst, they might even produce a minority report at the end, which would take some of the sting out of Mikardo's objectives. But they tended to feel increasingly uncomfortable with the way things were going.

So, frankly, was I. Perhaps optimistically, I'd hoped that my review would mark the beginning of a period of stability for the forces, but I had reckoned without the Chancellor's problems with the public finances. In April 1975, Denis Healey announced that he had no choice but to demand savings right across the board. In the case of Defence, that meant a further cut of £200 million. To me, that was a really bitter blow and made something of a mockery of all the careful planning I'd done over the past year. I warned that such a swingeing cut coming so soon after the defence review would destroy confidence throughout NATO. The Americans had told me that the reductions already announced represented the limit that was tolerable. Other allies would be equally dismayed.

Summing up at the end of the argument, Harold proposed that 'instead of a cut of £200 million on Defence, there should be a cut of £110 million'. I knew that was the best I could get. Still, mine wasn't the only ministry feeling the pinch. I'd manage somehow. But I wasn't happy about it; and I knew in my bones that sooner or later Denis would be back for more.

In the parliamentary party things weren't much better. When the defence estimates were debated in March 1975, a group of Left-wingers, led by Stan Newens, Frank Allaun and a bearded Scottish unilateralist called Robin Cook put down a hostile amendment to my proposals. The following month, fifty-six Labour MPs voted against the Government in the Defence debate.

When today's New Labour is so studiously moderate in all things, it's sometimes hard to appreciate the sheer lunacy which informed so much of the party's thinking in the recent past. In June 1975, for example, the

International Committee of the NEC solemnly resolved that Mikardo's group 'should not discuss the political and strategic implications of cutbacks in defence expenditure'. That resolution was subsequently confirmed by the whole NEC.

Another paper put out by the Study Group attempted to explain why defence considerations shouldn't influence the defence budget:

> Unless the Labour Party has very clear ideas about how to carry out defence cuts, proposals for reducing the level of military spending are likely to be whittled away by impressive-sounding expertise in the Ministry of Defence, by domestic pressure from industry and the armed services and by external pressures from other members of the Alliance.

Oh, aye. The Labour Party couldn't be doing with expertise, from any quarter. Its prejudices might be upset.

In the same paper, we were assured that 'It is a mistake to believe that money buys security. On the contrary, a more rational defence posture might well be achieved with fewer commitments, less sophisticated equipment and hence less money.' And so the options which Mikardo and his friends wanted to examine included the cancellation or reduction of a whole range of major equipment programmes, such as the multi-role combat aircraft, the through-deck cruiser, the Polaris missile system and the Future Main Battle Tank. This last seemed a particularly likely candidate for the axe in the Left's terms, since 'British tanks have, in the past, proved a popular instrument for destroying Arab armies or terrorizing Iranian peasants'. I wasn't in favour of terrifying peasants either, be they Iranian or any other kind. But it would have been a waste of breath to try and persuade my critics otherwise.

It mattered though. I doubt if any British Defence Secretary has had to contend with such sustained drivel from within his own party – or had to take it so seriously. I had already seen what the ignorant Left was capable of, with the manifesto commitment to kick out the American nuclear bases. Now it was pressing for the end of effective British defences, the certain unravelling of NATO and an inevitable increase in Soviet power. If Mikardo and his friends got their way, a whole programme of surrender would be foisted on the party and perhaps – if ever we managed to win an election again – on the country too.

With all that going on, the referendum that June on whether Britain should remain a member of the Common Market seemed a welcome distraction. But as it turned out, that debate too involved me in yet another fierce battle with the Left.

I had never wavered in my belief that the country's future lay in Europe. I'd been banging that particular drum since long before I became an MP; so I wasn't going to sit on the fence now. I produced a leaflet for my constituency which asserted that membership of the Community was 'better for peace, better for progress, better for jobs, better for prices, better for Barnsley and better for you'. It wasn't a particularly popular line to take in South Yorkshire – in Labour circles at least – but I had a few allies who were prepared to campaign publicly with me: friends like Pat Duffy from Attercliffe, Alec Woodhall, the member for Hemsworth, Eddie Wainwright from Dearne Valley and Albert Roberts of Normanton. Together, I think, we presented a pretty powerful case.

It didn't go down well with the local NUM, by now increasingly under the thumb of Arthur Scargill. The result of the referendum – 17 million votes in favour of staying in against 8 million – was a bitter disappointment to him and the other anti-Europeans. Three weeks later they tried to take their revenge. On 25 June, the Yorkshire Miners' Council passed a resolution censuring me and rest of the 'pro' campaigners and instructing us not to speak against the union on major issues. Scargill himself claimed that by virtue of sponsoring MPs, the miners' union was entitled to tell them which way to vote.

It was a typical piece of folly, as he soon discovered. His words provoked uproar. Next day the Speaker, Selwyn Lloyd, ruled that they should be examined as a possible breach of privilege. Scargill was clearly in deep trouble and there he would have remained but for Joe Gormley, the national President of the NUM. Joe always was a much wilier bird than Scargill could ever hope to be and moved quickly to undo the damage. He issued a statement on behalf of the National Executive insisting that the NUM would never interfere with the freedom of action of any of its sponsored MPs. It was a rebuff – and a deserved one – for the Yorkshire Miners' Council and Arthur Scargill. But it was enough to get the man off the hook. The steam went out of the controversy and Scargill never was found guilty of a breach of privilege.

I suspected, however, that the affair might make things more difficult for me back in Barnsley. I had become very aware that the traditional hard Left in the constituency, together with the Trotskyite Militant Tendency and the miners' caucus were becoming ever more critical of the government in general and me in particular. They loathed the idea that Britain should have a strong defence against the Soviet Union. They hated the Common Market. They were forever demanding more nationalization. I believed that all these groups were in a minority, but they were certainly capable of uniting to make the most noise at party meetings. Sometimes things became very heated when I gave my monthly

Parliamentary report. As far as these Trots, fellow-travellers and Scargillites were concerned, anyone speaking in support of the government was guilty of class treason. But my local allies showed what they thought of them. At the party's annual general meeting they voted against them overwhelmingly. Every single party office – Chairman, Treaurer, Secretary and the rest – went to my friends and colleagues in the Centre or on the Right. It was another rebuff for Scargill and a relief to me. But I had an uneasy feeling that defeat would probably make Scargill more determined than ever to retaliate.

Certainly there was no let-up in the sniping from the Left at Westminster. Hardly a week went by without a hostile parliamentary question, a critical motion or more pressure from Ian Mikardo and his friends. What I was determined not to do was give them a shred of credibility or respectability. Right from the beginning, Mikardo's Study Group had been pestering two of my junior ministers – Bob Brown for the Army and Frank Judd for the Navy – to take part in its discussions. For some reason, it wasn't interested in hearing from Brynmor John, who ran the RAF side. Perhaps Mikardo imagined – erroniously – that he would prove less malleable than the others. In fact all my ministerial team shared the view that the Mikardo Group was the enemy of any sensible defence policy, intent mainly on finding whatever anmunition it could to fire against the government.

Harold Wilson knew it too, but – as usual – was wary of upsetting the NEC. His suggestion was that Bob Brown and Frank Judd could attend Study Group meetings if they wished, but purely to discuss the employment implications in the event of further cuts in defence spending. They were not to take part in any debate on particular cuts, or any examination of what types of defence equipment were being sold overseas and to whom. It was a typical Wilsonian compromise, satisfying nobody but upsetting nobody. I don't blame him. He had to keep the show on the road somehow. And why should he stick his head above the parapet, when that was the job I was paid to do?

In the end, Frank and Bob did the sensible thing, made their excuses to Mikardo and declined to attend his meetings.

That didn't stop the pressure, of course. For months thereafter, they received nagging letters from people like Jenny Little, the Labour Party's International Secretary and Keith Hill, also of the International Department, urging them to change their minds and join. To their credit they refused. In those days it took some courage to resist the Left. Two other ministers in the government, however, David Ennals from the Foreign Office and Albert Booth from Employment, did agree to take part.

My mood at the time was summed up in a speech to engineering shop stewards in Barnsley: 'We must all be aware that extremists, infiltrators and cuckoos in the nest will be using this extremely difficult time for the Labour Party to cause maximum embarrassment to the government,' I warned. 'Democracy is in danger if these people get hold of the reins.' Ostensibly, I was referring to the Trotskyite Militants and to the Communists; but in my view the Tribunites, the unilateralists and Mikardo's committee were just as dangerous. The Reds weren't just under the bed; they were in it. I wasn't impressed that normally sensible people like David Ennals and Albert Booth should agree to give them so much as the time of day.

Quite what they were thinking of, I don't know. Meetings of the group couldn't have been easy, a point summed up Alan Lee Williams, Chairman of the Parliamentary Labour Party's Defence Group and a man who knew defence issues backwards. He had been pondering resigning as a member of Mikardo's outfit and in March 1976 finally did so, with a letter which summed up many of my own feelings.

It is immediately apparent that further reductions . . . must have even greater politico-strategic and economic implications, which would need to examine the fact that the USSR, with a GDP no more than half of the USA, spends rather more on arms in real terms than the USA. Coupled with Mr Brezhnev's reaffirmation that there will be no let-up in the ideological struggle, despite recent moves towards *détente*, we need to be sure that NATO's cohesion would be maintained. . . .

I think the Study Group is in danger of underestimating the manpower implications of a reduction of £1,000 million a year. There will not only be the direct redundancies (and loss of recruitment) arising from the force cuts that would be required. There will also be substantial reductions in military support and in civilian employees.

Alan ended his resignation letter with the suggestion: 'You might give consideration to the eventual publication of all the evidence that has been submitted to the working party, so that members of the Labour Party and the public can form their own opinion.' Well, there was fat chance of that. I knew – and so did Alan – that the last thing Mikardo wanted was an informed debate.

One of the things which most irritated me during that long, debilitating saga was the sheer hypocrisy of many of my opponents. There were many MPs who had made a profession of denouncing me in the

Commons and elsewhere, parading their peace-loving credentials in front of their local constituency parties and demanding deeper and deeper cuts in my budget. All that was for public consumption. In private, they would come weaselling up to me with pleas for more defence spending in their own constituencies – no doubt so that they could go back and tell their admiring locals that they had saved jobs. In the six months after my defence review, I was approached by no fewer than fifty-one Labour MPs seeking my help. Of those, more than half either voted against the government on defence matters or signed Commons motions critical of me for not cutting enough. Two examples: Stan Thorne, the Preston MP, always made a point of sticking like glue to every jot and tittle of the Left's agenda on defence; it didn't stop him begging me privately for more work to be given to the British Aerospace plant in his constituency. And Eric Heffer – admittedly a much more substantial man – wasn't above asking for more work to be diverted to shipyards in his beloved Liverpool.

Such episodes reinforced my opinion that there are no such things as painless defence cuts. They involve real people, with real families and real jobs. If I had had thought that Mikardo and his gang were serious about preserving employment instead of making knee-jerk propaganda I would have had more time for them. In any event, I was determined that they wouldn't make the running on this issue. In June 1976 I wrote to Len Murray, General Secretary of the TUC, pointing out that under my review, some 78,000 jobs in the services and the Ministry of Defence would be directly affected, along with 60,000 jobs in the defence industries. 'This is an inevitable consequence of reductions in defence expenditure, and further defence cuts, particularly if sudden and large, would entail a much more drastic reduction in jobs and job opportunities.'

I made sure that a copy of this letter was sent to every trade union general secretary. Mikardo might have the Left in his pocket; but if I could persuade the unions of the economic consequences of what he proposed, I'd see him off. I was fighting back in any way I could.

Meanwhile, in the face of Treasury pressure for further economies, I had managed to maintain funding for research and development of the maritime Harrier project. I'd always thought the Hawker jump jet one of the most exciting projects with which my department was involved; and if we could make the difficult design transition from a land-based plane to one which could operate at sea, the benefits to the country would be enormous. After all, any flat-decked vessel – including ships in the Merchant Navy – would be able to take a Harrier. That opened up all kinds of exciting possibilities and I was determined we wouldn't just throw them away. This was a British first, after all. Nobody else in the world had developed a vertical take-off plane and many countries were seriously interested in what we were doing, especially the Americans. Potential enemies were just as interested, though for different reasons. Naturally they'd be worried about a plane which could fly anywhere in the world.

So with my defence review out of the way, it was important to win backing for the next stage of the Sea Harrier. I made two presentations, first to the Defence and Overseas Policy Committee and then to the full Cabinet. I wanted around £70 million to develop a more powerful engine for the Harrier, a new seaborne radar system and a new anti-corrosive airframe, so essential for a plane that would be operating over water. I also had to ensure that the design team stayed together.

In the event – and despite all the reports that Denis Healey was breathing fire in his search for ever deeper cuts – things went better than I'd expected. My proposal just rattled through the Committee with no serious challenge over costs. Once that agreement was in the bag, I didn't expect much resistance in Cabinet. So it proved. Perhaps the Treasury understood for once that there is such a thing as false economy. Anyway, the Sea Harrier got the official seal of approval. I was delighted at the time; as I said later in my parliamentary announcement: 'The Russians have an aeroplane called the Bear which can spot ships and then relay instructions to Soviet missiles over the horizon. The Bear must be harried and the Harrier can do it.'

I had no idea then, of course, that the real success of the plane wouldn't come against the Soviet Union at all, but against a more unexpected enemy. Seven years later, Argentina invaded the Falklands. I felt proud then, and still do, at the brilliant part played by the Sea Harrier in that campaign.

The day after the Cabinet meeting, I celebrated the breakthrough by going down to Cotteshall, where the land Harriers were based. I'd arranged for two of the twin-seater aircraft to be jacked up, so that my PPS Pat Duffy and I could experience a flight. We got a very serious briefing – in fact it was more frightening than the flight itself – before taking off for Brough on Humberside, where the major work on the maritime version of the plane was to be undertaken. As we came in to land, I could see all the apprentices at the works lined up with huge cardboard placards: 'WELCOME AND THANK YOU, MR MASON'. It was a great moment. What I didn't know was that they'd just had the grass cut, probably in honour of my visit. A bad move. As we hovered, engines screaming, we whipped up a great whirlwind of cuttings, grass everywhere, covering the lads from head to toe. Still, it didn't spoil their mood. They'd brought some cans of beer out and we sat on the mown lawn drinking and chatting in what was for me one of the happiest moments of the year.

It didn't last. Back at Westminster, the Left was as active as ever, especially over rumours that Britain was considering another underground nuclear test in Nevada. Frank Allaun complained personally to Harold Wilson. Labour's General Secretary Ron Hayward made it clear that he was opposed. The NEC – inevitably – was against it too.

I spelled out my own position in the Commons on 21 October 1975: 'I have stated on many occasions that we intend to maintain the effectiveness of the Polaris deterrent.' And that, of course, was exactly what a new test would be about. If my military advisers thought it necessary, I intended to back them all the way. So when Frank Allaun asked point blank whether there would be another test, I said there may be. That answer drew a very hostile reception from Robin Cook, the present Foreign Secretary, who in those days was making quite a reputation for himself as a clinically clever advocate for the Left, though without the attractive features which made Ian Mikardo such a formidable opponent. Cook wanted to know the current estimate on the future life of the Polaris weapons system.

'Many years yet,' I replied.

Cook flew straight back at me. What did I mean by 'many years yet?' Did my answer 'represent a departure from the view of the previous Conservative government that Polaris had an effective life until the late Eighties? If it represents a departure from that view, what has happened to enable the government to depart from that view?'

'No,' I insisted. 'I cannot be more specific than that.'

Had he but known it, Robin Cook was sniffing around one of the best-kept secrets of this or any other government. The fact is that Britain was engaged in a determined effort to upgrade the whole Polaris system; and at considerable cost too. Yet astonishingly, that effort never provoked the arguments in Cabinet which one might have expected.

The Chevaline project began its life under the Tories, when there was serious concern in military circles over Soviet developments in anti-missile technology. In fact the Russians had made such progress thay they had deployed the GALOSH anti-ballistic missile system all round Moscow. It wouldn't provide an absolute defence; but it was probably enough to destroy a Polaris in flight. It was becoming clear that our deterrent was losing its credibility; and once that happened, there would be little point in having a nuclear capability at all.

The Tory solution, which I inherited, was to upgrade our missiles. In future, Polaris would have not one warhead but three, each of them independently targetable. Such a system would be able to overwhelm the

GALOSH ABM defences, rendering Moscow vulnerable once more and protecting Britain from any possibility of Soviet blackmail.

That was the theory. The practice was something else. When I became Defence Secretary, I was appalled to discover that the whole project was in an utter mess. Victor Macklin, Deputy Chief Scientist at the department and the man in charge of Chevaline, had been trying to run the thing through a very large number of different contracts. The result was that the scheme was way behind schedule, overunning its financial targets and potentially dangerous to the submarine crews who would have to operate the system. This last point was deeply worrying to the Navy Board. Under the scheme as it then stood, the three Chevaline warheads would be propelled from the rocket by a liquid explosive mixture. But we'd been warned by the Americans that liquid propellants aboard a submarine posed an unacceptable risk to safety. Accidents could and probably would happen. In fact their warning was so blunt that our Flag Officer Submarines made it clear that he wouldn't be prepared to order crews to sea with the design as it then stood. In short, Chevaline had the makings of a major shambles.

To be fair, it wasn't entirely Victor Macklin's fault. With the project shrouded in such secrecy, there were arguments for spreading the research and development work around in small packages; and there was less scope for the kind of political and management controls which governed other projects.

But secrecy was essential. One of the features of my defence review was that it was received with very little opposition from our friends in the Commonwealth. Countries like Australia and New Zealand had in fact been very understanding; I doubt if they would have been quite so generous if they had known of the expensive effort we were putting into Chevaline.

Perhaps even more important from the government's point of view was the position of the Left. I'd managed to fend off their demands for swingeing cuts in my budget; but if they had heard so much as a hint that we were updating the deterrent in such a radical way – or indeed that we were updating it at all – there would have been uproar. I think Labour would have been torn apart.

So from the very beginning Chevaline was a programme which hardly had an officially acknowledged existence. It was hardly discussed in Cabinet. Harold Wilson's line was that a bit of updating was going on and that the costs would be modest, in the region of £24 million a year. With that, most of my colleagues seemed content to move on to more pressing concerns. So during my defence review and the various attempts afterwards to cut my budget, no serious suggestion was ever made that

Chevaline should be axed, though it would end up costing the country more than £1 billion. Denis Healey commented long afterwards that one of his mistakes as Chancellor was 'not to get Chevaline cancelled'.

Had that happened, I believe it would have been a real blow to Britain's national interests. Our influence both in the United States and with the Soviet Union would have been diminished. The French would have been left as the only effective nuclear power in Europe. And I think there would have been a serious risk that if Britain pulled out of the deterrence business, the Germans would have been tempted to come in – with potentially grim consequences for stability in the world. I've always been grateful to Harold for the guile and political skill he showed in keeping Chevaline alive. And to colleagues like Jim Callaghan for their unfailing support.

That still left me facing an almighty mess in my own department over the way Chevaline was being managed. It was clear that our whole approach would have to change. On the advice of the admirals, I took control of the project out of Victor Macklin's hands and passed it to the Controller of the Navy. He in turn awarded a contract for the overall management of the scheme to the British Aircraft Corporation. In the event, that change not only led to a stricter watch on costs but helped produce answers to the technical problems too. So Polaris with its Chevaline upgrade remained an effective cornerstone of our nuclear deterrence until the day it was replaced by Trident.

In retrospect, I suppose we were lucky to get away with it. The anti-nuclear sentiment in the party was so ingrained at the time that no fewer than 105 Labour backbenchers signed a Commons motion insisting that Britain 'should not undertake another test'. Heading the list of signatories were the usual suspects: Frank Allaun and Robin Cook, Stan Newens and Jo Richardson.

But there were more immediately pressing problems on the horizon, with persistent reports in the press that another round of defence cuts was on the way. The stories certainly weren't coming from my department. They had to be Treasury inspired. I knew that Denis Healey was using the Public Expenditure Survey Committee (PESC) to examine potential savings throughout Whitehall; and though I'd just conducted an exhaustive review – and been obliged to accept a further cut in my budget only months before – I knew he wouldn't be content to leave me alone. As a former Defence Secretary, Denis understood that there's always a little extra to be squeezed out of the Services. And perhaps after Chevaline – still under Harold Wilson's protection – and the Harrier decision, he thought it time to crack the whip.

My unease deepened when George Younger, the Tory defence

spokesman, sent me a letter which accused me of 'a complete dereliction of duty' if more cuts were imposed. There was talk of an official censure motion against the government. I felt I was being assailed from all sides, with few of my colleagues rushing to support me. Certainly the big spending departments – Health, Environment, Social Security – would do anything to protect their own budgets; and if that meant butchery in my ministry, so be it.

One colleague who did come up trumps was Bill Rodgers, my Minister of State. He actually hinted that he would go if the Defence budget was slashed too far. My own position was being gossiped about too, with press suggestions that I was thinking of resigning.

Matters came to a head at a Cabinet meeting on 5 December, which was held at the unusually early hour of 9.30 a.m. On this occasion I had few friends in the room. The Chancellor was demanding sacrifices from everybody, but especially from me. He wanted savings far in excess of what I was prepared to concede. If push came to shove, I said I would find another £100 million, but not a penny more.

Denis was implacable. It would be wholly unacceptable to the Labour Party if the government were to cut total public expenditure by the huge amount required, but let the Defence budget off with savings of a mere £100 million, he warned.

Of course he had a point. Spending cuts would be bitterly unpopular on the back benches and in the constituencies. If Defence seemed to escape the axe there would be the most bitter reaction. On the other hand, I thought my case was unanswerable. I repeated the warning that I had given months before about the anxieties of our NATO allies and the possibility that further cutbacks in Britain would encourage Germany to become a nuclear power.

But apart from Jim Callaghan, I don't think I had an ally in the room. My colleagues had their own patches to look after. It was a standoff. At this point the tension was so great that Jim, who was sitting two places to my right, slid me a note. It read: 'Roy – compromise.' I scribbled back an immediate reply: 'I'm standing fast.' I felt I was really on the brink. When Harold spoke up in support of the Chancellor I told him, 'If you pursue this further, Prime Minister, I shall have to consider my personal position.'

It was then that the situation changed. After a long silence, Harold went into a semi-private huddle with Denis Healey. The rest of us looked on in an atmosphere which was distinctly uncomfortable. It was a very lonely few minutes.

At length Harold and Denis finished their whispered discussion. Harold said they had a new proposal to put to me. I would still have to make cuts, but this time my ministerial underspend would be taken into consideration. This was an accountancy device really. If a tank factory or aerospace plant went on strike for a week or two, there was bound to be a notional saving, because the money hadn't been spent in the expected timescale. I just looked across at Denis. I could guess where the idea had come from. What he was suggesting was a form of words which might get us both off the hook. He'd get the savings he wanted, though some of them would be on paper. I'd accept cuts which looked greater than they really were. Harold told me he wanted a paper on the consequences of much deeper cuts than the £100 million I had offered. A very large slice of the extra savings, he suggested, could come from 'slippage' on equipment orders. It was still too harsh a demand for me to swallow, but I could see room for manoeuvre. All in all, it was a clever solution to the immediate problem and I jumped at it. I would live to fight another day, though I knew there was still some hard bargaining to be done.

Naturally not everyone was as pleased as I was. Michael Foot, Tony Benn and Barbara Castle were distinctly sniffy about the possibility of a deal. Perhaps they feared their own budgets would suffer in consequence. Or perhaps they just shared Labour's traditional antipathy towards all defence spending. But they were in a minority.

In the New Year, I came up with the paper Harold had suggested. Though I could live with deeper cuts, there wasn't really any military justification for them and I pointed out that there would be industrial and employment consequences. Still, since nearly half the saving was made up of the 'underspend' element, I wasn't too unhappy.

It was then that the haggling really began. Denis wasn't happy with what I had offered. He was holding out for at least £200 million more, if not £225 million. I didn't want to budge. Proposals and counter-proposals bounced back and forth. Eventually, with Harold acting as honest broker, the gap began to narrow. In the and, I agreed savings of £670 million over the next four years. It was more than I wanted to give – especially as my defence review had already lopped £4,700 million off my department's budget for the next decade; but it wasn't nearly as bad as it might have been, especially when the 'underspend' device was taken into consideration. The greatest relief both to the service chiefs and to me was that not a single defence project was seriously affected. Chevaline and the Sea Harrier were still in being. And later I was able to give the go-ahead to the multi-role combat aircraft, which would replace not only our Canberra, Buccaneer and Vulcan bombers, but our Phantom and Lightning fighters too. All in all, I thought it a reasonably encouraging end to a very difficult exercise.

In fact, 1976 began well in another respect too. Like every other ministry, Defence throws an annual Christmas party, though I always preferred to hold ours over until January. There's less chance then of clashing with other shindigs; and besides, a late celebration helps lift the gloom from an otherwise miserable month.

Naturally I was keen to make our party a bit more interesting and different. It so happened that my local Barnsley brewery was closing down that year. I'd fought the closure hard, even going so far as to take part in a public demo in the constituency, but it proved a lost cause. Still, I thought there ought to be a proper wake to mark the demise of Britain's best beer. So I arranged for George Marsh, publican at the White Hart Hotel in the constituency, to get one of the last barrels of Barnsley Bitter off the rack – 36 gallons in all. Friends in the Transport and General Workers' Unionl arranged for it to be brought down to London by lorry.

I sent my car to pick up the barrel from the lorry and bring it to the MoD, where the party was being held. Nowadays, you wouldn't find an official limousine capable of doing the job; but the old Princesses were built especially large; ideal for Defence department purposes, because officers could get into them easily while still wearing their dress swords. Anyway, my car could easily accommodate a barrel and it took no time at all for the beer to be brought up to my office (after the barrel had been electronically swept for bugging devices. Naturally).

George Marsh came down for the occasion to tap the barrel. We had other English beers too, English wines, together with pork pies and black pudding from Albert Hirst's emporium in Barnsley. Albert later became the gold medal winner in Europe for his black puddings. Yorkshire beer and Yorkshire grub: what could be better? At the end of the evening, the Chief of the General Staff, Peter Hunt, came up to me and declared: 'You've introduced a new dimension into my life!'

It was a rare moment of jollity at that time. On Sunday, 4 January five Catholics in Northern Ireland had been murdered by thugs calling themselves loyalists. The following day, Monday the 5th, the IRA took its revenge in the worst single atrocity since the Troubles began. It set up an ambush on a country road near Whitecross in County Armagh, a couple of miles from a textile factory. The gang, armed with machine guns, stopped a minibus full of workers returning home after their day's shift. The victims were ordered to line up. A Catholic youth on the bus was told to stand aside. Then the terorists opened up on the remainder at point-blank range, killing ten men, all of them friends and neighbours from the Bessbrook district.

I was sick with disgust and shock when I heard the news. Murder in

Northern Ireland was nothing new; but this sectarian slaughter of innocent workers seemed especially horrible. I think it affected us all. Everybody in the Ministry. Everybody in the Government. Harold was particularly upset. He wanted a real response to the atrocity, something which might ease tensions in the Province. Northern Ireland then was like a big gas oven ready to explode. We knew that loyalist paramilitaries were preparing to go on to what they called a 'war footing'. Ian Paisley was noisily declaring that the Government had no will to win the battle against terrorism and with typical rabble-rousing dishonesty, claimed that Harold Wilson was committed to a united Ireland. He even threatened action which 'could well involve the workers of the Province' – a clear hint that he and his friends would attempt a re-run of the general strike which had brought down the power-sharing executive in 1974.

So the pressure for an immediate and vigorous response was immense. I got a message from Number Ten saying there would be an urgent meeting of the Northern Ireland group of ministers, which dealt with Ulster matters. It was obvious that we would have to send more troops to contain the crisis; and indeed 600 men of the Spearhead Battalion were already poised to go.

But it seemed to me that we should have something more to put before that meeting. I called in Peter Hunt, head of the Army and Michael Carver, Chief of the Defence Staff and suggested sending a unit of the SAS into a designated area of Northern Ireland – probably into South Armagh, which the Ulster Secretary Merlyn Rees always referred to as 'bandit country'. The service chiefs were rather taken by the idea, so with their approval I took it across to Downing Street. Harold seized on the plan immediately. 'Why not?' he asked. 'Why not?' He seemed genuinely pleased to be doing something with that element of extra drama about it – all the more so because the decision made headlines in the press and led the news bulletins on television.

There were risks, of course. There are many myths about the SAS, and many people who imagine that it has a licence to kill. A number of constitutional Nationalist politicians made no bones about their fears. Gerry Fitt, leader of the SDLP, likened the SAS to the American Central Intelligence Agency – and he didn't mean it as a compliment. His colleague Seamus Mallon said that he was very apprehensive about the 'unconventional and sometimes dubious methods used by this unit'.

But I've no doubt that our decision was right. People in Northern Ireland could see that the government was reacting to the situation with the seriousness it deserved. The Army approved too, because it gave the service day to day access to a highly skilled unit. In fact, only eleven soldiers from the SAS were deployed on this occasion, but their influence had nothing to do with mere numbers. In their covert role, watching and reporting from concealed hides and observation posts, they were invaluable. It was something I remembered when I became Northern Ireland Secretary a year later.

Meanwhile, I found myself embroiled in a much less important dispute. But it revealed some of my Cabinet colleagues in a disappointing new light.

We had just formed a special committee, in anticipation of the great occasion of the Queen's Silver Jubilee the following year. The idea was to put on a bit of a show. All the departments in Whitehall had to be represented, naturally. Nobody wanted to be left out of the planning for what was intended to be a universal celebration. So it was a sizeable group of us – between eleven and thirteen – who met for the first time in the large Ministerial room beneath the House of Commons.

The Chairman was Roy Jenkins, the Home Secretary. I sat next to him. My item on the agenda was to press the committee to agree a Jubilee Medal and when I made my presentation I assumed the idea would rattle through. I stressed that we would be making a national gesture if we offered something tangible to the armed services, voluntary bodies, the police and so on. Most groups in the country, in fact, would have people entitled to receive a commemorative medal. And why not? I spelled out the numbers. I spelled out the costs. Roy Jenkins then went round the room and checked the views of ministers.

I learned something that day. 'Baubles,' sniffed John Morris, now Attorney-General in Tony Blair's Government. Alex Eadie from Scotland was just as dismissive. 'In these days of economic stringency, should we be spending money on medals?' he growled in that impenetrable accent of his. Every minister, without exception, turned my idea down. I didn't get a shred of support from one department in Whitehall or one political colleague. I've often wondered since whether any of the departments had actually briefed their ministers. And whether everybody on that committee was quite as patriotic as he should have been.

Anyway, the experience plunged me into a black mood. I went back to the ministry and told my officials to cut back the content of the proposed medal, cut back the quality and cut back the numbers. If others were so concerned about the cost, I was ready to meet them half way.

Two weeks later, the committee met again. I made a similar presentation, though this time making it clear I was talking about a cheaper product. It didn't make a scrap of difference. Once more, Roy Jenkins went round the room. Once more, every single minister turned it down. By now I was pretty upset. I said I would take the matter up in Cabinet. Roy Jenkins just laughed. So did the committee. They obviously thought

I was being daft. I carried the memory of that laughter all the way back to my department.

There I told my officials that I wanted the Jubilee Medal on the Cabinet agenda and wouldn't take no for an answer. If they thought I was digging a hole for myself, they didn't let it show. They simply did as I asked. All I had to do now was win the final battle.

My chances didn't look very promising. I attended Cabinet a few days later knowing that many of my colleagues had already made up their minds. To make matters worse, my item was towards the end of the agenda, which meant that it wouldn't be reached until late morning. I knew that could mean trouble, because two of my likely supporters would have to leave early.

Sure enough, when 12.30 came the Prime Minister and the Foreign Secretary said they had to go off and receive some foreign dignitary who was visiting the country. I thought then that I'd probably lost my case before I'd even had a chance to present it. Harold Wilson had the common touch and would surely have backed my proposal. Jim Callaghan was an old Navy man and knew the importance of medals. With those two out of the reckoning, my prospects weren't looking good.

Ted Short, the deputy Prime Minister, then took the chair. He wasn't going to waste much time. 'You've got two minutes, Roy,' he barked, like the headmaster he once was. 'There will be no discussion. Afterwards I'll go round the table.'

As usual when I was facing a close vote in Cabinet, I had the initials of all my colleagues written down on a piece of paper, so that I could mark them off as they said yea or nay. I knew the outcome would be particularly tight.

Ted was as good as his word. As soon as I'd finished my presentation, he started collecting the voices.

John Silkin? 'Why not? If we strike medals for war, why can't we have a medal for peace?'

Michael Foot? 'I agree.'

Barbara Castle? 'No.' Well, that didn't surprise me.

So it went on, the ticks and crosses running neck-and-neck on my scrap of paper until the very end. In fact the voting was so close that I wasn't sure of the result until Ted Short said: 'Right you are, Roy. You've got your medal.'

I had, too. By one vote. And when it came to handing the medals out, every Cabinet minister took one. Including I suspect, Barbara Castle.

But I didn't have much time to savour the moment. Three weeks later, completely out of the blue, Harold Wilson announced his resignation. He had just turned sixty – no age at all – and was in the pink of health.

I was sitting almost directly across from him at that Cabinet meeting on 16 March 1976. When he had finished his statement, I could see the expressions all along the other side of the table. They reflected what I felt. Shock, disappointment and surprise. Some were misty-eyed. Ted Short, the deputy actually broke down. He at least couldn't have known what was going to happen. You can't fake that kind of emotion. I discovered later that Harold had confided in only a handful of his closest friends, including Jim Callaghan.

He began his formal statement to the rest of us by saying that he had just returned from the Palace. For a wild moment I wondered if he was about to call a snap election. But he went on: 'I apprised the Queen early in December that in March this year I intend to make way for a successor and I shall resign as Prime Minister as soon as the Parliamentary Party has made the necessary constitutional arrangements for electing a new leader.'

He was speaking in a very matter-of-fact way as he dropped this bombshell. He told us that he had decided in March 1974 that he would go in two years. That time was now up. He'd never wavered in his intention and the decision was irrevocable.

Harold then started to give reasons. He reminded us that he had been leader of the party for what he called 'Thirteen exciting and turbulent years'. Nearly eight of those years had been in government. He had served thirty-one years in Parliament, thirty of them on the front bench and a total of eleven and a half in Cabinet. It was time to make way for others. There were no impending problems, economic or political, facing his successor. 'In all my four administrations, these have been happy Cabinets,' he went on. 'I've presided over 472 Cabinets, thousands of Cabinet committees and answered 12,000 parliamentary questions. I've had to work seven days a week, at least twelve to fourteen hours a day. I've had at least 500 documents and submissions to read every weekend after a busy week.'

So that was that. Harold promised he would play no part whatever in the election of his successor, but intended to stay in Parliament 'as long as my constituents will put up with me'. He added; 'I love Parliament. I'll not go into industry or take paid employment.' Nor would he try to interfere with the way the Government was run in future. 'I'm not going to speak to the man on the bridge. Nor will I spit on the deck.'

It was a magnificent performance and it was impossible not to be affected. Few Prime Ministers ever manage to be both genuinely liked and admired, but Harold Wilson achieved it. Many of us wanted to pay him tribute there and then, but he had decreed that there should be no questions or comments. We had to content ourselves with a press statement afterwards expressing our deep regret and our gratitude for his many services to the country. Every word was sincerely meant.

By the time I got back to my ministry, the word was out. There was a buzz not only in every building in Whitehall but in the Palace of Westminster, in the bars and the tearoom. Harold? Why? What's gone wrong? What's the real reason? Is there sleaze in the background? Some other scandal? There were rumours circulating within minutes, growing more bizarre with the telling and re-telling. But nobody really knew why Harold had decided to go. To be frank, I don't think anybody knows to this day. The best explanation is probably the one he'd given us in Cabinet: he'd done his stint and felt enough was enough.

What started almost as quickly as the rumours was the lobbying for the succession. By that afternoon, the bandwagons were already rolling. There was strong support for Jim Callaghan, but Tony Benn was in the running too. So were Denis Healey. Michael Foot and Tony Crosland. Within a day or two the bars and dining rooms and committee corridors were full of campaign managers for the various hopefuls, all nobbling, pleading, persuading and promising.

Interesting times. All the more so because I was approached too with supporters anxious for me to have a go. Eddie Wainwright, my fellow Yorkshire MP from the Dearne Valley, came to me with a list of mining and trade union MPs who were ready to give me their backing: Alan Fitch from Wigan, Alfred Broughton from Batley and Morley, Geoff Lofthouse from Pontefract, Eric Ogden from Liverpool, Stan Cohen from Leeds and a clutch of others. It was flattering of course and for a long moment I was tempted. Though trying not to be too conceited about it, I felt myself better qualified than some of the candidates who'd declared already. After all, I had been Chairman of the Yorkshire Group of Labour MPs and of the Miners' Group; I had wide experience in office; I was running one of the major departments of state. And some people thought it high time that the Labour Party had a working-class leader. Not bad credentials; but the timing was something else.

The fact is that the idea came too late. There was already a powerful head of steam behind Jim Callaghan and Michael Foot. The campaigns of Benn, Crosland and Healey were in full swing too. If I entered the contest, I'd just be playing catch-up. So I put out a press statement saying that as a large number of my Labour colleagues were already committed to another candidate, I wouldn't be standing. 'To be honest,' I declared, 'I don't think I would get very far.' Harold Wilson sent me a note: 'Have more courage next time.'

Maybe I should have taken a chance, though I doubt very much if I could have won. But it would have been quite something to have taken part in the race. Still, I was now free to throw my full support behind Jim Callaghan and I was genuinely pleased when he won. He was the right man at the right time, and I thought he would do an excellent job. He'd been a good colleague for years and an impressive performer in Cabinet. I thought he was one of the government's greatest assets.

It wasn't long before he made his influence felt in my department. A month after he became leader, I left for an official visit to Hong Kong, in the company of my PPS, Pat Duffy. I was looking forward to the trip, but for him, it was to prove particularly memorable. Towards the end, while we were in the Governor's residence, I was summoned to the phone. It was Number Ten on the other end. I listened for a bit, trying not to let my pleasure show, then summoned Pat over. 'Downing Street,' I told him. 'The Prime Minister wants to talk to you.' He looked a little puzzled, but in a moment or two was beaming. Jim had just offered him the job of Navy Minister. It couldn't have gone to a better man. Pat had achieved a highly distinguished wartime career as a Swordfish pilot, in the course of which held been seriously injured, to such an extent that he needed extensive plastic surgery. He had always been a knowledgeable and loyal colleague and a good friend. I was delighted for him. As it happened, the rest of that night was free of official engagements, so a group of us went out for a celebratory dinner. Next morning, I arranged for him to be piped on board a frigate in the harbour – the first recognition of his new status as boss of the Navy. A great moment.

Then it was back to the old grind of protecting my ministry against the Left. The Tory leader, Margaret Thatcher, had been making quite a splash with attacks on the Soviet Union, so I responded with a fierce speech denouncing her as a 'reactionary imperialist dreamer'. I knew my words wouldn't impress the Frank Allauns and Robin Cooks of this world, but I hoped they might persuade fairer-minded Labour backbenchers that I wasn't an unthinking, gung-ho, cold warrior. On the other hand – just in case anyone thought I'd changed my mind about the Soviet threat – I later challenged the Russians to tear down the Berlin Wall and to reduce the huge arsenals threatening the West. It was imperative, I said, for the Kremlin to demonstrate 'that *détente* is not an empty word or a deceptive peace offensive to cause the West to relax its guard'.

In May that year I followed this up by telling the party's General Secretary, Ron Hayward, that the familiar old Labour demand to cut Defence spending to the bone would 'place at risk' the entire security of Europe. My purpose in all this was to undermine if I could the anti-American, anti-nuclear, anti-NATO tendency in the party.

I was wasting my breath. Robin Cook, for example, assured the

Commons that the Soviet Union had reduced its troop levels in Northern and Central Europe by 65,000 men recently, while NATO's strength had been augmented by another 45,000 man. In naval capability, the Soviets had increased their warships by a mere eighty-four while NATO's strength was up by 151 vessels. And to top it all, the Americans had increased their military budget by a staggering 30 per cent the previous year. The massage was clear enough: the warmongering West was undermining the efforts at *détente* being promoted by a peace-loving Kremlin. It was – and remains – a constant source of amazement to me that the Left could so blithely ignore the facts.

Not that I ever forgot the potential horrors in a policy of nuclear deterrence. How could I? It's a grim business to study the destructive capacity of a single Polaris missile. I was well aware of what would happen if either side in the Cold War made a miscalculation; and there were other risks too, as I discovered early one morning.

I was sitting at my desk, going through some relatively routine papers. Nothing special was happening in the department, no pressing problems demanded my attention. I remember thinking that for once I could look forward to a pretty light day. Then my private secretary, John Mayne, rushed into the room and everything changed. One look at the expression on his face was enough to tell me something dreadful had happened. An RAF bomber carrying a nuclear weapon had just crashed in East Anglia, he told me. There was no further information.

I just stared at him, feeling sick. What about the possibility of an explosion? Or of radiation? What about casualties? He didn't know. Nor could he tell me why the RAF was toting a nuclear bomb over Britain in the first place.

I was sweating at the thought of a national catastrophe. Obviously our nuclear specialists were already on their way to the site; but we needed the police alerted too and all the rescue services. Obviously we had to draw up plans fast for a possible evacuation of the area. All the local hospitals had to be forewarned and the Army put on standby. I wanted someone on the spot who could take overall charge and report back to me, so I orderd the RAF Minister, Brynmor John, to get airborne immediately. Meanwhile I cleared my diary and prepared for an emergency statement in the House that afternoon. Whatever happened, the public had to be given the full facts if a national panic was to be avoided. I wanted an assessment of the dangers, a background briefing on RAF nuclear flights, arrangements for briefing the press, meetings with the military experts. And of course Downing Street had to be kept informed.

One hour passed. Then another. By midday I had established that there had been no explosion, but there was still no news about the risk of radiation. Brynmor John had not yet reported back. For the moment, I'd done everything I could. It was now a question of waiting. I'd been through similar situations before, on those rare occasions when one of our nuclear submarines hadn't signalled headquarters on schedule – usually because it was operating close to the Soviet coast. Such episodes always created tension within the department until the sub made it back to international waters and reported in; but this time our anxiety was very much worse.

By 12.30 I decided I'd wait no longer. If we hadn't got a preliminary assessment from the spot by now, something was obviously very wrong. I summoned John Mayne to demand some answers. He had the grace to look a little embarrassed. 'I'm sorry, Secretary of State,' he said. 'I'm afraid this has all been a training exercise. We were testing the reactions from you and other people down the line.'

I just gaped at him. Part of me just wanted to thank God it was nothing worse; the other part felt an urgent need to kick a few backsides. I didn't do any such thing, of course. An exercise like that has no value unless it's as real as possible; and my military advisers had been taken in too. Besides, it was a sobering reminder of what my job might one day entail. I'd always enjoyed it and still did. But now I had learned what it would be like if things went seriously wrong.

It was a valuable lesson, but I didn't have much time to digest it.

11 Baptism of Fire

I began my last day as Secretary of State for Defence at home in Barnsley, packing my bags for what I thought would be one of the most important overseas visits I was ever likely to make: a major tour of the United States. Like everybody else in the ministry, I was keenly anticipating renewing contacts with our closest and most valued military ally. My RAF VC10 was jacked up and waiting to go. The Chiefs of Staff were all briefed and ready, as were members of the Central Secretariat. Everybody was looking forward to meeting our American hosts.

At 10 a.m. on that Friday, the telephone rang. It was Jim Callaghan, calling from Downing Street. What he had to say knocked all my plans sideways. 'Roy, I'm embarking on a ministerial reshuffle. I want you to go to Northen Ireland.'

It took me a moment to digest the news. When I'd been offered jobs in the past, I had always met Harold Wilson face to face, man to man. I didn't reckon much to being shuffled at the end of a telephone. 'Jim, you'll have to give me an hour to talk to my Missus about that,' I said.

Jim wasn't having any. 'Roy, in an hour's time, your job will be filled.' I wasn't happy with that. But he sounded as though he meant it.

By now, though, I was too used to the ways of government to be easily pushed. 'Then I'll have a word with my Missus now,' I said. 'Hold on, Jim.' So I went into the kitchen to talk to Madge. Throughout our marriage her line had always been: 'Do what you think's best.' Those were her words this time too. She knew perfectly well, of course, that Northern Ireland would be a job full of restrictions and risks, a new departure for both of us. But she's been my rock since the day we married.

I went back to the phone. It doesn't do to keep the Prime Minister hanging on too long. 'My wife says it's all right,' I told him. 'But you're not going to make an announcement until we've talked about this job, policies and ministers. I'm coming down now to see you.'

So that was that. Madge got the car out and drove me to Doncaster, where I caught the train for King's Cross. All the way down to London I was thinking of the new problems I would have to tackle. I suppose I shouldn't have been too surprised at Jim's offer. There had been rumours in the press for months; and anyway, I'd had a sneaking feeling he was thinking of moving me on.

As it happens, I was no stranger to Northern Ireland. As Defence Secretary, I had visited the troops stationed there often enough. Now it seemed I was to see another side of the crisis: the unemployment, poor housing, sectarian bigotry, all the things which gave the terrorists their chance. Maybe I could do something to break that cycle of deprivation and misery. I wasn't so puffed up as to imagine I could solve the problems of centuries; but perhaps I could make a start. Some ideas were beginning to form. By the time I arrived at King's Cross I was not only reconciled to my new job but almost looking forward to it.

There was just time for a quick snack in the Commons cafeteria before I walked across the road to Number Ten where Jim was waiting for me in the Cabinet Room. Our first job, of course, was to look at the policies. You can't even think of taking on a job like Northern Ireland unless you're in full agreement with the Prime Minister on the basics.

I thought this might be a problem. For years, successive governments had desperately tried to reach some kind of political accommodation with the warring factions in Ulster, with little success. Willie Whitelaw and the Tories had actually achieved a power-sharing executive, but that had collapsed under the weight of a Protestant general strike in May 1974. Then my colleague Merlyn Rees had tried valiantly to rescue something from the wreckage, attempting to persuade the two sides to agree between themselves on the kind of devolved rule they wanted in the Province. But despite all his work, he had little luck. Even during the year of a supposed IRA ceasefire, no fewer than 245 innocent victims had been murdered. It seemed to me that no matter how much effort we put into trying to secure agreement, we were getting nowhere.

So I told Jim that my first priority was security. We would never achieve anything in the Province unless we could protect the lives and safety of the people. Next, I wanted to put the emphasis on employment, to bring hope where it was so desperately needed. Meanwhile, I wanted the whole issue of constitutional change put on the back burner. That could wait until we had created the right atmosphere to make progress.

To my relief we agreed on all that very rapidly and moved on to the question of my ministerial team. The first few names Jim put to me were fine. First was Don Concannon from Mansfield, a very tall, very imposing ex-Guardsman and someone I knew I could rely on when the going got rough. Next came Ray Carter, a workaholic with a solid background in local government, utterly trustworthy and the kind of chap who would get on with his job without any fuss. Third there was Jimmy Dunn, a Liverpool Catholic who would certainly help to balance the team and might be able to reach out to the minority community in the Province. I thought myself lucky to be offered such solid support.

Then Jim mentioned a final name which made me sit up. He wanted Lord Melchett on the team. I had never heard of the man, though of course I knew his late father when he was head of the British Steel Corporation. I felt the faintest twinge of doubt, which wasn't helped when I discovered that my new junior minister hadn't even been contacted yet. Jim looked just a little embarrassed at this point. 'He's sailing with his girlfriend somewhere in the Aegean and can't be reached,' he explained. 'But his mother's prepared to accept the job on his behalf!'

I just looked at Jim, not quite knowing what to say. I was to discover that Lord Melchett was young, naïve and – in the environmental sense of the word – very green, not the type I'd personally have chosen to face the terrorists.

Still, I wasn't going to quibble at this stage. I wanted to get off home and spend the rest of the weekend preparing myself for my new role. There were dossiers to read, civil servants to consult by telephone and a fair bit of unpacking and repacking to do. By the Monday morning I was ready to take the plane from Finninglay to Belfast, accompanied not only by Madge, who had decided to come across the water and see for herself, but for the first time by my new Scotland Yard protection team. Of course I couldn't have known then that they would become a central part of my life.

After landing at Aldergrove, we transferred immediately to a helicopter, for the short hop to the grounds of Stormont Castle. In those days, ministers never travelled by road. We would be too tempting a target for the IRA, too easy a mark. Only a few weeks before, my new Permanent Under-Secretary, Brian Cubbon, had come close to death in a bomb attack. He had been in a vehicle on the outskirts of Dublin in the company of his secretary, Judith Cook and Britain's Ambassador to the Republic, Christopher Ewart-Biggs when their vehicle was blown up by a landmine. The Ambassador and Miss Cook, a lass of twenty-six, were killed. Brian Cubbon and the car's driver, Brian O'Driscoll, were badly injured. We had learned a lesson from that terrible cvent. Helicopters obviously weren't a luxury. In fact I was to make ninety-nine such trips by chopper before we reached the stage of being able to use a car again.

As we lifted off and clattered away over the plump green fields, I caught my first glimpse of the welcome awaiting me. From the centre of

Belfast, clearly visible from miles away, flames were leaping into the air, clouds of greasy black smoke coiling and billowing across the city. It didn't take much imagination to understand what it would be like on the ground, the stench and filth, the frantic efforts to contain the damage, the despair of ordinary people whose lives had been so wantonly disrupted yet again. I spent that whole flight staring at what was plainly intended as a terrorist 'spectacular' laid on for my benefit. The paramilitaries were determined to send me a signal I couldn't miss. So that morning they had attacked Belfast bus station and set alight seven double-deckers, destroying them all in the most visible challenge they could devise. They boasted afterwards that it was 'Mason's baptism of fire'.

I landed at Stormont in a sombre mood, too preoccupied to pay much attention to the splendid parliament building on top of the hill. I hurried straight into my office in the turreted Castle, near the bottom of the hill, to be greeted by the officials who would be closest to me in the years ahead. I couldn't know then they would turn out to be the finest team any Minister could possibly wish for. There was Joe Pilling, my private secretary, a man of small physical stature with immense reserves of knowledge and common sense; the ebullient and extroverted David Gilliland, my Press Officer and Tommy Roberts, his deputy; David Ford who represented the Foreign Office input in the Province, a man of immense wisdom and intelligence; Sir Robert Kidd, Northern Ireland's senior civil servant; and Joan Young, a wonderful lass who would run my private office brilliantly. The only one missing was Brian Cubbon, still convalescing after his narrow escape.

What they had to tell me as they crowded into my office took me somewhat by surprise. When I had seen the smoke over Belfast, I'd asssumed it to be the work of the Provisional IRA. Not so. It turned out that the arson had been committed by so-called loyalists from the Ulster Defence Association, in protest at the way Protestant terrorists were supposedly being treated in the Maze Prison. My first crisis was upon me before I'd even had time to unpack my bags.

The problem was that convicted terrorists on both sides of the sectarian divide had been treated as legitimate prisoners of war instead of the criminals they were. Under my Tory predecessor Willie Whitelaw they had been given 'special category' status, which meant that they didn't have to work or abide by the usual jail disciplines. They could wear their own clothes. To a large extent, they controlled their own compounds. That situation hardly said much for our determination to defeat the bombers and gunmen and sent the worst possible signal to the long-suffering people of Ulster; Willie himself later acknowledged that he'd made a mistake. So a few months before I arrived in the Province, Merlyn

Rees had quite rightly decided that enough was enough. There would be no more special treatment for criminals in the Maze or elsewhere for anybody convicted of a terrorist offence after 1 March. 'I must make it clear,' said Merlyn, 'that those who murder, those who shoot, bomb or commit other crimes are criminals and will not get special treatment in the future.' It was a decision which enraged all the gangster groups, whether they called themselves loyalist or republican, because it stripped away their claims to legitimacy. Their anger was deepening by the day, since more and more terrorists were being convicted and jailed according to the new prison regime.

The arson attack in Belfast was just the beginning of a savage reaction from the loyalists. That same day there were no fewer than fifteen bomb hoaxes perpetrated across the Province. Those incidents were rapidly followed up by units of the UDA going on the rampage, with patrols, road blocks, open threats against Catholics and noisy protests against the alleged brutality of prison officers in the Maze.

Meanwhile the IRA was pursuing its more lethal campaign of bombing and shooting, while claiming that its prisoners too were entitled to special category status. In one horrifying November day, these butchers killed a girl of seventeen, Philomena Green, with a bomb in Lurgan. Another Catholic, Frank McConnellogue, was blown up in Derry. He was the father of ten children.

Clearly I had to reassure the people of Ulster that Her Majesty's Government was not going to be pushed around. Almost my first public statement in the Province stressed that I wanted criminals caught by the RUC and punished as criminals, not as 'politicals'. I warned: 'Peace, democracy and personal well-being are being destroyed by these men. They are torturing their own people. The criminals have violence in their souls, so ingrained that they turn on their own kith and kin.'

But I was equally determined that the UDA should be subject to the full rigour of the law. If a mob of masked thugs tried to take over an estate, the security forces would move in to break it up and make what arrests they could. If a barricade went up on a road, it would be cleared by dawn. One thing I was determined to be was even-handed. The government emphatically would not give way to threats, from whichever side they came.

For the moment, however, I wasn't going to rush into dramatic action. At my first press conference I made it clear that I had no new security initiative in mind. My first job, I stressed, was to revive an economy being ruined by violent gangsterism. Thousands upon thousands of people had been forced onto the dole by terrorism. Before the Troubles began, inward investment created 3,000 extra jobs a year in the Province; now that figure was down to a meagre 330. No fewer than seventy-two government-sponsored firms had folded. Sixteen factories had been destroyed and not replaced. Tens of thousands of families had been forced to move house because of violence or intimidation. One in five houses in Belfast was unfit for human habitation – yet housebuilding was at its lowest level since 1962. Unemployment in the Province stood at a miserable 11.4 per cent.

If that cycle of failure, fear, hopelessness and stagnation could be broken, all kinds of things might follow, I hoped. But I thought it futile to barge in with great plans and programmes and proposals for constitutional change. Northern Ireland might have a population of only 1½ million – substantially less than that of South Yorkshire – but its problems were more complex than any I had faced before. I needed to feel my way and do more listening than talking – especially to the local politicians. In spite of the tiny stage on which they operated, they tended to think of themselves as people who had an impact on the world; and as it turned out, they weren't that wide of the mark.

My relations with them were mixed. The most important single figure in the Province at the time – and arguably today too – was Ian Paisley, a big, domineering man, to many a poisonous bigot because of his No Popery rantings, to others a hero of the Protestant cause. I found it difficult to warm to the man, but respected his dedication as a constituency MP. He always did his best for those who needed his help, irrespective of their creed. The problem was that he felt so strongly about loyalism and spoke and behaved so intemperately that he alienated not just the Catholic minority by many in mainland Britain who might otherwise have been sympathetic.

On the Nationalist side they had a much more politically astute figure in John Hume of the Social Democratic and Labour Party. Hume was regarded by many as the great statesman of Northern Ireland; but he was also a politician I could rarely find. He was always away in Dublin or Washington or somewhere in his Derry constituency out of telephone reach. I described him in private as 'the lost leader', but I could see that he was genuinely working for his people and had no real quarrels with him.

I wish the same could be said for Gerry Fitt, the leader of the SDLP. Gerry has always been regarded at Westminster as one of the most genial and warm-hearted politicians around, but we never really got on. He'd not welcomed me to the Province. He thought I was much too close to the Army. I never held that view against him, but it's arguable that had our relations been better, Gerry might not have turned so vehemently against the government, bringing Jim Callaghan down in the process and opening the door for Margaret Thatcher's triumph. Still, that then lay in the future. I've always respected his sincerity and his undoubted personal courage, but I found him difficult.

Oliver Napier of the non-sectarian Alliance Party was much easier. I thought him a good man representing a good cause, but it was obvious that his brand of moderation would never make much headway. I knew it every time he came to see me. And very sadly, the same has to be said for the Peace Women, who emerged as a force in the Province the month I arrived. Horrified by a particularly tragic incident in which a child had been killed, Mairead Corrigan and Betty Williams were passionate in their belief that ordinary, decent citizens could and should learn to live together without fear or hatred, whatever their religion or background. Amen to that. I agreed with their message. But in spite of the huge publicity which attended their cause – and the Nobel Peace Prize which they deservedly won the following year – their movement soon sank from sight, dragged down by internal acrimony and the bitter opposition of the paramilitary gangs. The terrorists just weren't interested in listening. Their interest was in killing and destroying.

And that was my deepest concern. However hard I tried to revive the economy of Northern Ireland, it was becoming clearer by the day that nothing good could ever happen until the IRA and the loyalist gangs were checked. All our resources had to be focused against them, which isn't quite as straightforward as it sounds.

By now we were settling in. Madge, in fact, found herself so busy helping me and developing her own charity work that she now had a social secretary. Meanwhile, I was beginning to make my views felt. I had become just a little concerned about the relationship between the Army and the RUC. I thought there was too much rivalry between them, each side rather too zealous about guarding its own patch of turf. It's a common enough problem when dealing with terrorism, but one which had to be solved. So I arranged meetings with the GOC, General Sir David House and the Chief Constable of the RUC, Kenneth Newman. What I wanted was close, intimate co-operation, not just to deal with the IRA but also to handle the UDA gangs which were trying to take over the streets in Protestant areas. My view – and theirs – was that we had to be absolutely even-handed in cracking down on thuggery, from whichever side of the sectarian divide it came. In the event, I was pushing at an open door. I found David House, who later became Black Rod in the Lords, to be totally reliable, a soldier's soldier if ever there was one. Ken Newman proved equally co-operative. He was strict in his observation of the law and as straight as a die – something I'd find invaluable later on, when the government was under fierce attack over the supposed torture of terrorist prisoners. Anyway, between us I think we did manage to create new and better working relations. It meant that in future, the police, the Army and the Northern Ireland Office should operate at a higher level of efficiency.

But even with an improved level of co-operation, there were limits to what we could do. One of the things which concerned me most in those early months was the black cab racket operated by the IRA in Belfast. It had taken over virtually every taxi in the city, squeezing out all competition by intimidation. Undoubtedly it was a nice little earner for the terrorists. So much so that they were extending their activities to building sites, shops, haulage companies – anywhere, in fact, where they thought they could get away with it.

Of course I was appalled. What was going on amounted to the biggest protection racket in the United Kingdom. The question was what to do. Sure, it would be possible to disrupt this criminal activity through more surveillance, more checks, more raids; but then we would inevitably have to reduce our 'front-line' challenge to the gunmen and the bombers. We simply didn't have enough people on the ground to do everything. So reluctantly I decided to leave the black cabs and their drivers alone. For the time being.

There was another episode at the time which might surprise those critics who accuse me of wading into Northern Ireland with hobnailed boots: the closure of Laneside.

In republican mythology, this heavily-guarded detached villa on the shores of Belfast Lough was the source of all British 'brutality' in the Province. Here was where the SAS was supposed to meet to plan its every nefarious operation. Here was where our dirty tricks were reputedly worked out. It was widely believed that Laneside was a place of skulduggery, murky plots and worse. There were stories that enemies of the British state who were taken there would never emerge alive.

Lurid stuff; but though a few black operations were undoubtedly planned at Laneside, the stories and rumours were largely rubbish. Despite its fearsome reputation, Laneside was an ordinary enough government facility, quite useful but hardly the Lubyanka. It was certainly convenient to have a quiet, private location where sensitive meetings could be held, but that was about the extent of it. The place certainly wasn't worth the negative publicity it attracted, so on that basis I decided to close it down. Of course my action didn't stop all the saloon-bar stories about British treachery, but it may have helped to make our policies a little more transparent.

In what little spare time we had, I was discovering the other side of Northern Ireland, the part that's so often forgotten in the pain and misery and screaming headlines: its tranquil beauty. From the day I arrived, I decided that a Minister should be on duty in the Province, twenty-four hours a day, seven days a week. It really wasn't a hardship to take my turn on weekend duty, including the New Year recess, with all the family. Like the rest of my team, I lived in the old Speaker's residence at Stormont, which was not only handy for the shop but a stone's throw from incomparable countryside. Often on a Sunday I'd walk with Madge in the Antrim Hills and wonder how anybody who lived anywhere near such natural loveliness could be consumed with hatred and murderous intent. We always returned from those excursions feeling better. Even the presence of armed security men couldn't spoil our mood.

And then there was the fishing. From that point of view, Northern Ireland was a paradise. I'll never forget the thrill of landing my first salmon from the River Bann, after a twenty-minute battle which tested my abilities to the limit. On Strangford Lough I did even better, hooking a monster of a tope, all 49 lb of it. If I hadn't been accompanied by a team of very fit and strong security men, I'd never have managed to haul the thing into the boat. Afterwards I received a certificate from the Irish Fish Specimen Society, which is still one of my proudest possessions. In fact it was such an unusual achievement that one of my press friends in Annie's Bar at the Commons wondered whether I hadn't used the underwater skills of the Special Boat Squadron to seize the fish and attach it to my line. Cheek!

I was, however, using our special forces in another way. As Defence Secretary I had sent the first small contingent of SAS soldiers to operate mainly in South Armagh. The quality of their intelligence-gathering was excellent and now I wanted to use the Regiment's skills on a much wider basis. If we wanted to hit the terrorists where it hurt – and that was always my intention, once I had mastered my brief – it was obviously essential to garner as much information as possible about their personal habits, their bolt-holes and their friends. So I steadily began building up the number of SAS operatives. Working in close co-operation with army intelligence and the RUC, they added a formidable new dimension to our security strategy.

Unfortunately, military personnel – even members of the special forces – are as capable of human error as the rest of us. A few weeks before I arrived in the Province, the SAS became involved in an embarrassing border incident which imposed new strains on our relations with Dublin and certainly needed sorting out.

What happened had a touch of the Keystone Cops about it, though it truly wasn't very funny. We had set up a series of hidden observation posts in South Armagh, some of them very close to the line dividing Northern Ireland from the Republic. The rules were that our soldiers should stay at least 100 yd from the border – a restriction which isn't necessarily as easy as it sounds. On this occasion, a couple of SAS men in uniform were given a lift to their observation post by two colleagues in civvies. Having dropped the observers off, the 'civilians' in the vehicle made for their home base. But in the maze of narrow, unmarked country roads they strayed inadvertently into the Republic, where they were stopped and questioned by a member of the Gardai.

If members of the SAS were really the supermen of legend, they would of course have never made that mistake. If they'd been as ruthless and cold-blooded as their critics like to claim, they would have overpowered that policeman and made their escape. As it happened, they took the only rational and responsible course. They handed over their weapons and identity cards, allowing themselves to be taken in.

Back at base, there was obviously concern that the men hadn't returned. Another two cars were sent out to scour the area from which they had last reported. In similar fashion, these cars too strayed over the border – only to be stopped by a local Garda now on full alert. So now a total of four SAS men were in custody, along with their weapons and IDs.

For once, the mystique attached to the SAS proved a handicap. In other cases where soldiers had wandered across the border, they had been promptly returned by the Irish authorities, usually with little fuss. This time it was different. Dublin took the view – perhaps understandably – that the superbly-trained SAS just didn't make mistakes in map-reading. The suspicion was that the border infringement had been committed deliberately and with felonious intent. There was talk of a major trial and lengthy jail sentencs for the 'culprits'.

Jim Callaghan wasted no time getting in touch with the Taioseach, Liam Cosgrave, pressing for the avoidance of a trial. It was too late. Legal proceedings against the SAS men had already started. The only good news was that they were released on bail pending their trial.

It wasn't the happiest of backgrounds for my visit to Dublin in the New Year for talks with Foreign minister Garret Fitzgerald; but in fact the trip wasn't remotely the embarrassment I had feared. Luckily for me, Jim Callaghan and Liam Cosgrave had between them succeeding in calming what might otherwise have turned into an ugly confrontation. The two leaders got on well personally and had put a lot of work into co-operative ventures in things like telecommunications. They weren't about to let a blunder on the border blow them off course. On top of that, Garret Fitzgerald wasn't in the business of petty point-scoring. I found him a charming man, highly intelligent and almost professorial in his approach. That first trip to Dublin, like the many other meetings which followed, proved well worth while. I came away confident that the cross-border co-operation between our security forces and the Gardai – usually pretty good, in spite of the occasional hiccup – would continue as before.

When the SAS men were eventually tried in a heavily-guarded Dublin court they were fined £100 each. Clearly after their initial flurry of excitement the Irish weren't interested in making a meal of the incident. We had suffered some humiliation, but in the end honour was satisfied on both sides.

By now I was more convinced than ever that I needed to take a higher profile in the battle against the IRA and other terrorist gangs. The figures told their own dreadful story. In 1976, Northern Ireland had suffered its highest number of murders in four years: thirteen members of the RUC, ten dead in the police reserves, fourteen from the Army, fifteen from the Ulster Defence Regiment and 243 civilians, many of them victims of sectarian assassination. The New Year promised no better. After its Christmas ceasefire, the IRA promised to 'hot things up' in 1977. It threatened to remove what it called the English presence, even if it meant pulling Belfast down 'brick by brick'. There were killings by the day, booby-trap bombs against the security forces in Derry, stories that the killers were working their way through a list of prominent businessmen. They weren't winning, nor could they hope to win; but they were bleeding the Province dry. It was no accident that unemployment stood at 59,975 – the highest January figure in 37 years.

Such was the background to what later became known as the Second Battle of Culloden, when – according to the subsequent press reports – I was involved in a blazing row with some of the most senior figures in the BBC.

In truth, it wasn't quite as dramatic as all that. But I don't think anybody who was present doubted the strength of my feelings.

One of the things I despised in those early months was the ease with which balaclava-clad terrorists could appear on TV. No doubt programme-makers thought that such dramatic pictures made for riveting television; but wittingly or not, they were certainly helping the IRA with its propaganda campaign. The gangsters interviewed were in my view seldom challenged with the fierceness they deserved. Instead they were allowed to represent themselves as members of a legitimate political grouping and to exaggerate the scale of their success.

All of this was at the back of my mind when the governors of the BBC met me for a private dinner at the Culloden Hotel early in January. Also present were the Lord Chief Justice of Northern Ireland, the GOC, the Chief Constable, the editor of the *Belfast Telegraph* and a number of other prominent locals. It wasn't a formal event. There were to be no speeches. Guests sat in small groups at round tables. It might have been an ordinary social occasion.

At the end of the meal the Chairman of Governors, Sir Michael Swann, suggested that I might like to say a few words about the situation in the Province. Though it wasn't what I had expected, I was happy enough to oblige. Guests brought their chairs up to form a compact audience around me. It seemed to me then that it was time for a few home truths.

There was no point in mincing words. I told the governors of my dismay at the BBC's programming policy in Northern Ireland. I suggested that by giving publicity to the IRA television was making things easier for terrorism and worsening the plight of the Province. By filming Provisional gangs in secret and flashing the pictures all around the world, the BBC was effectively encouraging violence and undermining democracy. What it was doing was irresponsible if not disloyal.

I could see that the governors were deeply shocked – all the more so when my views were echoed by every other guest there. Only the editor of the *Belfast Telegraph* remained more or less neutral in the fierce exchanges which followed.

Of course news of the confrontation leaked at once. How could it not? There was uproar in the newspapers. Among other things, I was accused of demanding a three-month blackout on the reporting of terrorist activity. There were questions in the House. The National Union of Journalists was up in arms. But I didn't regret a word of what I had said. I'm not and never have been in favour of censorship, but I do believe that journalists have a duty to be especially careful when reporting a terrorist campaign which seeks the overthrow of civil society. I hoped that the media, particularly television, would at last wake up to the dangers of being exploited by murderers.

But there were more important things on my mind than the Second Battle of Culloden. The savagery of the IRA was reaching a new pitch of intensity.

Should we simply react to the mayhem, just responding to each crisis as it arose? I thought not. It was time to take the war to the enemy. Using intelligence information supplied by the Army, the RUC and the SAS, the security forces began picking up members of the IRA in sudden raids, usually pre-dawn, in batches of at least fifteen at a time and sometimes thirty or more. Maybe we didn't have sufficient evidence against them to make charges stick in court, but I and my closest advisers were confident of their guilt. Confident enough to want them behind bars, where they could be interrogated. I had the legal power to keep all of these suspects under arrest for three days; and if my intelligence people told me they had particular reason to hold somebody for a couple of days longer, I'd give permission for that too. And when one batch of suspects was finally released, I would give the go-ahead for the next lot to be picked up.

Of course the tactic was controversial. On 2 March, the BBC *Tonight* programme attacked the interrogation methods used by the RUC. Stories about police 'brutality' were being circulated in just about every bar in Northern Ireland, and grew in the telling and re-telling. There were howls of protest from republicans, echoed later by complaints from the Peace Women and Amnesty International. I wasn't much impressed, either then or later on when the attacks on my policy were at their fiercest. The mere fact of dragging suspects into a police station kept some of Northern Ireland's nastiest villains off the street, at least for a few days. Sometimes interrogation produced enough evidence to make a charge stick or enough to provide crucial intelligence information. Even when it didn't, the arrests badly disrupted IRA operations. Terrorists who were picked up couldn't do any damage. Those who escaped the net went on the run across the border for fear of being caught next time. As far as I was concerned, the policy was a winner, inflicting on the IRA just a little of the fear it so cruelly and casually inflicted on others.

All the more frustrating then that some politicians in the Province, people who had the nerve to call themselves loyalists, seemed determined to wreck everything I was trying to do.

12 The Paisley Strike

The most dangerous threat to Northern Ireland in my time came not (as one might suppose) from the IRA, but from people who regarded themselves as loyal and true and pillars of the community. They were led, or at any rate represented, by the Reverend Ian Paisley, Member of Parliament for North Antrim; and in the Spring of 1977, they set out with deliberate intent to undermine the whole structure of British authority in the Province. Had they succeeded, there might have been slaughter in the streets to compare with the worst atrocities of Bosnia. I don't think it an exaggeration to say that Ireland could easily have stumbled into civil war.

I'd been aware, of course, that Paisley and the shadowy figures who supported or used him were growing increasingly restive under direct rule from London. They wanted nothing less than a parliament at Stormont, that old symbol of the Protestant ascendancy. A restoration, they claimed, would not only reflect the democratic will; it would enable Ulster's political leaders, with their special insight and local knowledge, to take on and defeat the republican terrorists.

Of course there wasn't a chance that any British Government would agree. To the resentful and mistrustful Catholic minority, Stormont had become a byword for bigotry and gerrymandering; and it's certainly the case that the revival of the IRA was partly a consequence of the way Stormont so badly mishandled the civil rights protests in the late Sixties. To hand power back to such an institution in the absence of a whole new constitutional settlement would inflame Nationalist passions as nothing else could. It would certainly strengthen the IRA.

Paisley's allies seemed oblivious to this elementary truth. With an ugly combination of recklessness and lying, they began a determined and dangerous campaign of direct action on the streets, citing as their excuse the supposed inadequacy of my efforts to improve security. Masked vigilantes describing themselves as members of the Ulster Service Corps began appearing in loyalist areas, manning roadblocks, checking identities and generally throwing their weight around in a grotesque show of community policing.

I was in no mood to yield to these thuggish gangs. What respect I'd had for Paisley was turning to contempt. Sure, he was the most prominent politician in the Province and the acknowledged spokesman of unyielding Unionist opinion. His views had to be given some weight. But on this occasion, as on so many others, he was behaving more like a wild rabble-rouser than a serious spokesman for his people. He knew perfectly well that I had been harrassing the IRA with as much vigour as was legally acceptable in a liberal democracy. I was being as tough as I could be; and though my policy was undeniably a ruthless business, it at least meant that the level of violence was beginning to come down. I didn't appreciate lectures from the bombastic Paisley – especially when he was giving his noisiest support to the balaclava-clad bullies who were creating such fear and tension in the Province.

His agenda was clear enough. He wanted to outface me and take Westminster out of the equation. Nothing would satisfy him but a demonstration that Protestant Ulstermen called the shots in Northern Ireland, under his leadership, needless to say.

There had to be a confrontation.

It came when eighteen vigilantes going about their thuggish business were arrested in County Armagh by the security forces, an event which provoked Paisley and his Democratic Unionist Party into a rage. They regarded it as an open challenge to their 'authority' on the streets and they weren't the only ones. Paramilitary groups like the Ulster Defence Association, the Ulster Volunteer Force and the Red Hand Commando, not to mention Ernest Baird's United Ulster Unionist Movement, the Apprentice Boys, the Ulster Workers' Council and a whole bunch of other groups all rushed to join his protest.

A crowd of hundreds was waiting to greet the arrested vigilantes when they appeared at the Portadown courthouse for an adjournment hearing on 19 April. Though the atmosphere seemed relatively relaxed – at any rate there was no violence – shops in the town were closed and two local factories came out in support of the demonstration. Paisley was there, of course, boasting to his enthusiastic audience that he too had taken part in vigilante patrols and therefore should be arrested as well. His ally Ernest Baird was just as vehement, promising to outline very soon details of a militant campaign which would end direct rule from Westminster. 'We must ensure that the IRA is destroyed forever,' he roared. 'Those areas where the terrorists breed will have to be "changed".'

Whether or not he was calling for what has now come to be called ethnic cleansing, it was clear that the forces of hard-line Unionism were spoiling for a fight. They thought they could win it, too. Their weapon of choice was to be an all-out strike across the Province, the very same tactic which had humiliated the government when it had been tried before, in 1974.

I knew from the beginning that this would be the toughest test I had ever faced. If the strike proved solid, Northern Ireland would certainly grind to a standstill. The economy would be dangerously undermined. Terrorism would be encouraged. If the pressure intensified to the point where we caved in – not that I or the Cabinet ever considered the possibility – we might be driven to bring back Stormont as the price of a settlement. Paisley's game-plan was obvious; and to make matters worse, our intelligence sources reported that a campaign of intimidation would be mounted across the Six Counties to ensure that nobody dared defy the orders of the strike committee, which was already calling itself the Ulster Union Action Council. In this way, a few hundred toughs might paralyse a whole Province.

Fortunately, we had a few days to prepare. If the events of 1974 were to be repeated, the first target of the strikers would be the power stations, particularly the plant at Ballylumford, just outside Larne. If those could be closed down, industrial production throughout Northern Ireland would cease. There would be roadblocks too, pickets at the docks, determined efforts to stop oil deliveries and public transport, all backed up with the threat of injury or worse to anybody who tried to work. Somehow, we just had to keep the wheels turning.

So began a series of intensive meetings at Stormont with my closest advisers, the key players on the Emergency Committee, set up to see us through the crisis. I couldn't have wished for a more able or supportive team. Apart from my Minister of State, Don Concannon, there was my Permanent Under Secretary, Sir Brian Cubbon and the head of the Northern Ireland Civil Service, Bob Kidd, whose deep knowledge of the Irish scene was invaluable. Other key figures included the GOC, Sir David House and Kenneth Newman the Chief Constable of the RUC, both of them rock-solid in times of trouble. There was John Cradock, regarded by outsiders as a man of mystery and the official who kept us in day-to-day touch with intelligence developments. Dr George Quigley from the Department of Commerce was an important member of the team too, the man who would take charge of all the commercial and industrial problems thrown up by the strike. And finally, I was glad to have David Gilliland, my highly experienced Press Officer, on board. In the coming battle, it was essential to keep public opinion on our side. I think we all understood the consequences if we failed.

Inevitably, one of our first decisions was the necessity of deploying more troops in the Province; but it soon became clear that their impact would probably be limited. Yes, they would send a signal to the local population that the government was serious in its intent. Yes, a strengthened military presence would certainly help in the maintenance of law and order. On the other hand if clumsily used, those same troops could easily hand Paisley and his friends the 'provocation' they craved.

The central question was the attitude of the power workers. Our first reports suggested that men at the generating plants of Coolreagh and Belfast might well support the strike, while at Ballylumford – by far the most important – they felt inclined to go on operating normally. That was a critical advantage, though it could quickly turn against us if the campaign of intimidation succeeded. Or if specialist troops were brought in prematurely to help keep the electricity supply going. The power workers would inevitably resent it if soldiers were used to replace men who hadn't turned up for work. They might well walk out in protest. My private information was that in such an event, the army simply wouldn't be able to keep the generators turning.

It was important then to keep the additional troops in the background as long as possible. Certainly we shouldn't risk stirring the pot by making an early announcement about the arrival of three extra battalions. We would just have to watch how the situation developed on day one, paying the closest attention to what level of power output could be managed and whether the campaign of fear and intimidation was working.

We had some grounds for optimism. The attempt to paralyse the Province was due to start on 3 May, but as the day approached, there were encouraging signs that the people of Northern Ireland were generally unenthusiastic about following Paisley to the brink of the precipice. The Official Unionists were opposed to the strike. Workers at the Harland and Wolff shipyard had voted to carry on working. And among the public at large, there seemed to be considerable confusion about the plans and intentions of the UUAC. It was obviously in our interests to exploit that confusion where we could.

The position of Paisley in all this was crucial. Our estimate at the beginning was that he had gone too far out on a limb, isolating himself from other Ulster politicians. Moreover, it must have been dawning on him that he was relying on paramilitaries who probably didn't have the muscle they claimed. It was an interesting fact that so far he had been relatively cautious in his pronouncements, limiting himself to the suggestion that there would be passive resistance, rent and rate strikes and general non co-operation with the government. On 29 April, for example, he declared that the UUAC was prepared to 'rule Ulster', adding that Loyalists should be prepared to withhold labour, rates, rents and VAT

Greeting Her Majesty the Queen and the Duke of Edinburgh when they visited the Ministry of Defence. Standing to attention is the First Sea Lord, Edward Ashmore

Marshal of the Royal Air Force, Sir Andrew Humphrey, receives Her Majesty the Queen and the Queen Mother at the Air Force Dinner, while Marjorie and I wait our turn

Some of my protectors in the garden at home. South Yorkshire Police firearms teams are on duty round the clock

In my ermine robes on the day of my introduction to the House of Lords, 1987. My sponsors were my old friends, Lord (Harold) Wilson and Lord (Cledwyn) Hughes

The presentation of the Lord Snowdon 'chairmobile' to Andrew Salter. Mr John Salter and his wife Barbara have three sons suffering from multiple sclerosis. In the front row, left to right, are: Barbara Salter, Andrew and his brothers, Ralph and Duncan. The one able-bodied son, Clive, is holding Andrew's chair

A contingent of Bevin Boys, 1997, following their proud march past the Barnsley war memorial – the first time they had paraded since 1945. The following year, the Bevin Boys were received with great acclaim when they joined the national Remembrance Service at the Cenotaph in Whitehall

On picket duty with striking power workers at Battersea in the Seventies. As a miners' MP, I tried to show solidarity with my fellow workers, whenever I could

payments. 'We could,' he declared, 'urge Loyalists to engage in revolution to bring the government down by bombing and violence, but violence will not be used.' It ought to have been encouraging that he was holding back from a call to open insurrection; but in view of the dangerous company he was keeping, his words seemed to me to have a hollow ring.

In a speech at Ballymena the next day, he was more apocalyptic, appearing to stake his whole political future on the success of the strike. 'If it fails, then my voice will no longer be heard,' he declared. 'I didn't choose political life. I went into it because of the call of the people.' He warned that the confrontation would not be short. 'It will be a long, hard climb back. It will continue until we get victory,' he proclaimed.

Uncompromising stuff. No doubt he thought it had to be. What we didn't know then was the personal danger he faced from his supposed allies.

But that information would not reach us for a couple of days. Meanwhile, the threat posed by the strikers was increasing. On that same day – 29 April – I received a special note on how they intended to take over local administration in whole areas of the Province. This document was based on folders which the paramilitaries of the UDA were handing out in Protestant areas and suggested the work of someone with good administrative – or perhaps army – experience.

The details in those folders suggested that the strikers were preparing a fight to the finish. Each area of 400 houses was ordered to appoint a local controller, an assistant controller and a director to take charge of each of the following: food, accommodation, fuel, transport, administration and communication. In addition, medical teams consisting of one doctor and three nurses were to be established, together with local welfare officers, volunteer workers, despatch riders, electricians, plumbers and house maintenance workers. All the elements were in place for a long siege; and of course the UDA and others in the strike were simultaneously encouraging their followers to make a point of picking up their social security benefits. The intention from the start was that the campaign against the government would be largely funded by public money.

Even more disturbing was the line taken by the paramilitaries when distributing details of these arrangements. They began by claiming that the government had demonstrated its weakness both in failing to deal with the Provisional IRA and in caving in to the last Ulster workers' strike. Secondly, they insisted that the strike would break the government. Thirdly, they assured Loyalists that Stormont would be restored, taking over full responsibility for security, law and order.

Then came the truly chilling part of their message. Once the government had been defeated, what they called good Catholics would be 'invited' to leave their homes. After that piece of ethnic cleansing, Loyalist forces would enter the Catholic suburbs, burning them down and killing anyone who dared to remain.

I hardly need dwell on how I and the rest of the Emergency Committee reacted when we learned of this demented scheme. I certainly didn't doubt that the people who had drawn it up meant every word. I only add that the person who provided the report – based on seized documents and other intelligence information – was extraordinarily brave. The anonymity of our source had to be respected absolutely. Had an identity become known, the consequences would have been fatal.

By Sunday, 1 May – seventy-two hours before the beginning of the strike – our contingency plans were laid. The part-timers of the Ulster Defence Regiment had already been called out and the regular troops serving in the Province redeployed. The Spearhead Battalion would be arriving at midday, with an additional two battalions following twenty-four hours later. These new troops would be based in the Loyalist areas where trouble was most likely to erupt – Belfast, County Antrim, North Down, Portadown and Lurgan. Meanwhile, army specialists would start liaising with management and supervisory staff at the power stations and at water and sewerage plants.

The first show of strength by the strike leaders, we thought, would be in throwing up roadblocks wherever they could. These we proposed to deal with as an ordinary matter of law and order, with the police taking the lead and the Army acting as back-up. We wouldn't dignify the UUAC by treating its members as anything other than common lawbreakers.

Similarly, we were ready to declare a state of emergency, which would give us additional powers to keep essential services – especially the distribution of oil – running as normally as possible. I had told Jim Callaghan that it was probable I would have to make the proclamation on 3 May. I already had the power to do it without the need for an order in Council and Jim had explained the position to Buckingham Palace.

In order to keep the UUAC off-balance, I had decided that there would be no mention for the time being of any emergency social security system. Many of my advisers had lived through the strike turmoil of 1974 and told me that nothing did more to undermine the morale of their staff than the fact that welfare benefits were being paid out to all and sundry, on a less restrictive basis than usual. Many people who had struggled into work despite all the difficulties were bitterly resentful at the way strikers – including people manning roadblocks – were blithely picking up their Giro cheques at the same time. Well, it wasn't going to be so easy this time. We'd let the strikers stew in their own juice for a bit.

An important factor in all this was clearly to keep the trade unions on our side. That morning, my Secretary, Robert Ramsay, had spoken by phone to John Lyons, General Secretary of the Electrical Power Engineers' Association, who fortunately had a good understanding of the problems and the government's position. Lyons made it clear that his members were strongly against the strike, but he was understandably concerned about the threat of intimidation.

He also made the point that repeated stories in the press to the effect that 'troops were ready to occupy the power stations' were pretty unhelpful. Well, we couldn't do much about the newspapers, other than urge them to show a bit of restraint; but we did reassure him that troops would be used only as a last resort. As for intimidation, we would be stepping up security across the Province, with more patrols round isolated substations to protect engineers who needed to attend them. We knew, of course, that such lonely plants were ideal for the purposes of sabotage and other acts of terrorism.

John Lyons wasn't the only union official involved. Jim Callaghan had briefed Len Murray of the TUC, and we could expect quiet support from that direction. Terry Carlin, the TUC representative in Northern Ireland, was also kept in the picture and would use his influence to keep the Province working. Barring some disastrous blunder on our side, the UUAC should remain isolated, spurned by the level-headed majority.

My last piece of preparation was to consider whether to use the doomsday weapon of seizing and detaining terrorists during the strike. Internment had come to an end on 5 December 1975, when the last detainee was released. But I still had powers to issue Interim Custody Orders which could be used to lock up – temporarily – anyone suspected of terrorism. We had already examined the prison accommodation available and worked out that we had the capacity to arrest and hold about a hundred suspects in a first batch, with 25 per week thereafter. I should stress that I wasn't contemplating any such drastic action against people who simply refused to work. Nobody could be detained unless I was genuinely satisfied that he was a terrorist. But if I received information that anyone involved with the strike was planning to attack workers or commit acts of sabotage, I was ready to stop it.

We were now as ready as we could be. All that remained was to sow as much doubt and dissension as we could in the ranks of the UUAC. We knew that the strike leaders were very much less confident of a successful outcome than they had been a few days ago. Morale, I was glad to learn, was low. One of the key figures involved, Jim Smyth of the Ulster Workers' Council, was bitterly critical of the fact that the strike had been called without sufficient preparation. Andy Tyrie of the paramilitary UDA had been given a hard time by the wives of his followers.

It was obviously important to deepen those tensions if we could, especially as the paramilitaries seemed determined to ride roughshod over all opposition. Our intelligence sources reported that Tyrie and the UDA intended to start a campaign of intimidation in the Loyalist housing estates from midnight on Monday. He and Paisley, meanwhile, had got the proscribed Ulster Volunteer Force – including the extremely nasty Shankill UVF – to play a prominent part in the strike planning. Clearly, violence and the threat of violence were intended to make up for any lack of popular support.

On the face of it, Paisley's behaviour was baffling. He must have known that the paramilitary groups were not easily controlled and that they were likely to resort to brutal activities outside the law. But as more intelligence information came in, I thought I understood. The man was in fear of his life.

In preparation for a meeting I was due to have with Paisley and his associate Ernest Baird the following day, Monday, 2 May, I had been given extensive briefings on his status within the UUAC. It was clear that he had good reason to be worried. Our assessment was that few of the strike leaders had any time for him at all. They feared he would try to act behind their backs. That was one of the reasons Baird would be turning up at the meeting too: his job was to report back to the UUAC on how Paisley had performed. The man wasn't trusted an inch. Indeed the UDA had told Paisley they would kill him if he deserted them. Our intelligence sources reported that he took this threat extremely seriously and was frightened.

That wasn't the end of Paisley's troubles. According to our sources, he thought he was being pushed to the forefront by a group which couldn't deliver the backing necessary to win the strike and thereby save his political skin. He was trapped, as the Americans say, between a rock and a hard place. It was something I intended to exploit if I could. The need was to deny him as much credibility as possible with the public and to encourage paramilitary doubts about his dependability.

Whatever happened, it would be an interesting encounter. Paisley was cantankerous at the best of times; now he was worried too. And he had a need to show his minder Ernest Baird that he had the stomach to stand up to Mason in private. I found myself remembering how he had tried it on with my predecessor, Merlyn Rees. At the end of one meeting, Paisley simply refused to budge. He just sat in his chair, gripping the arms, his knuckles white with the strain, no doubt hoping to be forcibly ejected. Merlyn just left him to it. That wasn't the only example of Paisley's oafishness. He'd been in the habit of turning up offensively late every time he had an appointment with a minister. Then he would insist on being given his full allotted time, even though it meant a horrible disruption in the official schedule. I'd stopped him pulling that little stunt by warning him before our very first meeting that he had precisely half an hour. If he came late, I'd just knock the time off. Of course he took no notice. When the day came, he turned up fifteen minutes late. He seemed genuinely shocked when after a quarter of an hour I told him his time was up. I had half hoped he might try the chair-hugging routine he'd attempted with Merlyn; but he heaved himself up reluctantly and departed, grumbling. He always managed to be punctual after that.

So it proved this time. Paisley and Baird arrived bang on schedule, but full of reproaches for what they obviously considered my lamentable record as Secretary of State. Paisley was rumbling with indignation over a 'slander' I had apparently perpetrated by describing him and Ernest Baird as paramilitaries. In fact I hadn't been quite so blunt, but by now he was in full flow, claiming that he and his colleague were legitimate party leaders who weren't members of any illegal group. Well, maybe not. But he was certainly in bed with them. And it wasn't so long ago that he'd paraded round the Antrim Hills at 2 a.m. with hundreds of his followers, all waving their gun licences. That display, of course, had been put on for the benefit of the media; but it was an implicit threat to the government too. There was a certain grim humour in his current fears for his own safety, when he had flirted so busily with the forces of thuggery.

I'd already decided that I wasn't going to allow the man to take up the meeting with another harangue. I told him that the stoppage he was threatening would only encourage those on either side of the sectarian divide who wanted to break the union. Didn't he and Baird find it embarrassing to be so closely linked in this damaging exercise with such bodies as the UVF and the Red Hand Commando? I told them I hoped they had condemned violence and intimidation and wondered why they were playing into the hands of the Provisional IRA. The strike might inflict more damage on the Province than anything the terrorists had managed to do in years. To rub the point home, I quoted the improving statistics for killings, woundings, bombings, arrests, charges and convictions. The activities of the SAS had been doubled, I told him. IRA morale was low. On the political front, I added that I was willing to explore new developments, including the possible reform of local government.

They weren't impressed. Paisley claimed (inaccurately) that the number of SAS men in Northern Ireland before the recent doubling was only eighteen which indicated to him that the government had no real will to win aginst the terrorists. As for the damage which might be caused by the strike, the economy was wrecked already. Some 750 businesses had closed in the Province since the Troubles began in 1969. For good measure, he denounced my 'threatening' attitude over the issue of pickets, which he claimed was akin to the 'hounding' of unarmed USC vigilantes.

Ernest Baird then chipped in with an assertion that there was a lot of 'crook talk' about intimidation. What could be more intimidatory than the activities of the IRA, eh?

It was a thoroughly depressing encounter which never had a chance of going anywhere. The visitors left at last, still fulminating against the government in general and me in particular. At least I had seen the whites of their eyes; and Paisley now knew that we just weren't going to cave in. He'd missed his chance of behaving like a proper politician and achieving a face-saving settlement. Whatever doubts he may have had must have deepened. He was still on the hook with his sinister associates. I couldn't feel in the least sorry for him.

Now we could only wait for the inevitable confrontation. There was unease throughout Northern Ireland, deepening as the clock ticked towards the strike; and my own concerns weren't eased when Glenn Barr, a leading Unionist, telephoned my office from Holland on 2 May. He said he had received 'very strong reports' of UDA plans for bloody mayhem against the security forces that very night. On top of that, Paisley and his allies apparently intended to form a 'parliament' to give their actions a spurious kind of legitimacy. Terry Carlin of the TUC also rang, saying that rumours had reached him of intimidation already going on at the Ballylumford power station. The good news was that the bus drivers intended to work, but security forces would need to be in evidence at the depots very early on Tuesday morning, from 4.30 a.m.

In fact none of us was surprised by such reports. Intimidation was a central feature of the strike from the very beginning, as we knew it would be. From the morning of 3 May, our operations room at Stormont Castle – manned round the clock for the duration – was inundated with reports of roadblocks, masked gangs and aggressive picketing. We were aware too that a systematic campaign of threatening phone calls had begun, though these were largely uncheckable by the police. Larne harbour was out of action, while shops in the town had been forced to close by Loyalist gangs. Buses had been sabotaged in Omagh. There were reports too that Loyalist hard-liners from Scotland and Liverpool were crossing by ferry to support the strike.

But there was encouraging news as well. Though industry was badly disrupted and a number of plants and offices had been forced to close early in the day, a majority of people had managed to struggle to work. The power stations in particular were still maintaining more or less a full output. Serious disturbances were fewer than we had expected. And main traffic routes had been kept open, though rail services had been disrupted by a small bomb. On the picket-lines, Paisley's posturing hadn't achieved anything like the impact he must have hoped for. We weren't so foolish as to consider that first day a success for the government; but it hadn't been an unqualified triumph for the strikers either.

Nevertheless an inconclusive first skirmish wouldn't remotely have dismayed the leaders of the UUAC. They were just getting warmed up. Stories in the press were increasingly focusing on the number of stoppages and the activities of the bully-boys; such reports would do nothing for public morale. Meanwhile, Belfast's Downtown Radio was suggesting that the police response to intimidation had so far been less than adequate. That wouldn't help the government's cause either. It was as certain as could be that the campaign of telephone threats would be intensified overnight. As to the outcome, we could only guess. And hope. We were very aware that the oil-tanker drivers were undecided about what to do. In the power stations things weren't much better. John Lyons of the Electrical Engineers reported that workers at Ballylumford and elsewhere were in a state of 'extreme agitation' at the pressures being put on them – and at renewed speculation about the use of troops. He warned that his members would refuse to work with the soldiers, if we tried to bring them in.

It was time to put on a little pressure of our own. I wrote to Paisley in the following terms – making sure, of course, that copies were sent to the press:

You were not in the House of Commons yesterday, when I made a statement on the threatened civil disruption. I thought, therefore, that you would wish to know that the overwhelming view of MPs was that intimidation or the threat of intimidation is the most evil aspect of the situation. The unanimous view of all parties was that everything possible must be done to prevent intimidation and to allow free passage for those who wish to work. It was also pressed upon me from all sides that every possible effort must be made to protect those subject to intimidation and to condemn without equivocation those of your supporters who are responsible.

At our meeting yesterday, you claimed that any action taken today would be entirely passive and that you would not support violence or intimidation. Intimidation has taken place. The RUC has done, and is doing, a first-class job within the limits of its manpower, to protect the ordinary people from thugs and bully-boys. I must emphasize that this will continue with the assistance of all branches of the security forces if required.

I now put it to you again: will you, as leader of the UUAC, instruct your supporters to cease their despicable attempts to prevent ordinary people from earning their living and will you publicly and without equivocation condemn those who in the name of the UUAC are using intimidation and strong-arm tactics to bolster support?

My priority is quite clear. I wish to get on with the job of defeating the Provisional IRA. The RUC, who have been having marked success in the pursuit and capture of these evil men, are now being diverted from their task by the actions of you and your supporters. You are playing the IRA game.

But Paisley couldn't be shamed into disowning the viciousness of his supporters. I quote his reply:

Dear Roy,
Your arrogance is only surpassed by your blatant discourtesy and ready aptitude to excel in misrepresentation and falsehood. To make public the contents of a letter of such a nature as the one you have addressed to me before I received it reveals your true self. . . . You are very well aware that your statement in paragraph 1, that you thought that I would wish to know what happened in the House yesterday, is nothing better than hypocrisy.

When I survey the devastated Province which I love and for whose preservation I will fight to the death and when I think of the blood of my fellow Ulstermen and women for which you and successive British governments and parliaments are responsible, I care very little about the opinion of 'all parties' in the House. Further, when I consider the drunkenness, lewdness, immorality and filthy language of many of those Members, I care absolutely nothing for their opinions. Ulster Protestants are not interested in gaining the good will of such reprobates.

And so on. For the time being at least, we could forget any possibility that Paisley would find the courage or the decency to stand up for law and order. Meanwhile, we could see that the intimidation was getting worse. By the afternoon of Thursday, 4 May, the RUC had received some 400 complaints from people who had been threatened; and of course that was only the tip of the iceberg. Across the Province that day, the majority of shops stayed closed.

There was interference with bread and milk deliveries. Rail and bus services were disrupted, especially in East Belfast and the Shankill. Gangs of youths were roaming the streets, showing more aggression towards the police than hitherto. In one ugly incident, the RUC had to call the Army out in support. Most dangerously of all, the attack on the power-workers was intensifying. That morning at seven o'clock, a bus packed with men on their way to a power station was stopped on the Newtownards Road by a Loyalist mob. A crowd of about a hundred pulled the driver out of his cab, told him he wouldn't be allowed to proceed and stole his pass and driving licence. The demonstrators let down the tyres of the vehicle to ensure that their orders were followed.

It was just as we feared. Public transport was only too vulnerable to that kind of action and our intelligence sources reported that such bullying would become more intense, with the paramilitary UDA taking the lead. Meanwhile we knew that the following day, 5 May, would be difficult, because the vigilantes of the USC were due to appear in court in Armagh. Paisley and his friends certainly wouldn't miss the opportunity to make capital out of the event. It would be their opportunity to whip up the crowds, grab the headlines and perhaps give the strike the real popular momentum it had so far lacked.

I couldn't allow the strikers such an advantage. Somehow I had to blunt the impact of their demonstration. If Paisley succeeded in unleashing the worst instincts of Ulster loyalism, we probably wouldn't be able to hold the line. I was especially concerned about the reaction of the men at Ballylumford, who were due to ballot the following day on whether to join the strike or not. If they were caught up in the emotion of the moment and decided to join the strike, then Paisley would have won. He knew it and so did I.

So I gave the Ballylumford workers something else to think about. While Paisley was preparing for his moment of public glory in the streets of Armagh, I invited all the shop stewards at the power station as well as representatives of the management to a special meeting in the main hall of Stormont Castle that very night. It was a last opportunity to dissuade them from drastic action; and should I succeed in winning them over, I would undermine Paisley's hopes. In fact, it could prove decisive.

Of course it wouldn't be easy. The Ballylumford men came largely from Larne, one of the strongholds of militant Protestantism. Like most Loyalists, they were understandably frustrated and bitter that successive governments had so far failed to secure a decisive victory over the IRA. Many of them had already been subjected to intense and frightening pressure from the UUAC; and we were very aware that at least some had sympathy with the strike and were inclined to throw in their lot with the UUAC.

I could sense their tension as they crowded into Stormont. Many of them had seen the television pictures of how Paisley and his followers had brought Armagh to a virtual standstill that afternoon, the hymn-singing throng of 800 or so augmented by a contingent of Free Presbyterians bussed in from Belfast. Paisley himself had been relatively restrained in his address, simply insisting that the activities of the vigilante USC would continue, whatever the verdict of the court. But neither the hymns nor Paisley's seeming moderation could disguise the edge of hostility in the crowd. Policemen, mainstream Unionist politicians – in fact anybody who wasn't wholeheartedly on the side of vigilantism and the strike – found themselves subjected to verbal abuse, punches and shoving. Journalists were openly threatened with violence. Harold McCusker, an Official Unionist MP, was kicked repeatedly as he left the courthouse and was loud afterwards in his praise of the police, who had managed to deflect many of the blows aimed at him.

My real concern was whether that rage in the streets would find an echo in Ballylumford. The power-workers there knew they were the key to the whole crisis. If they walked out, a whole swathe of industry throughout the Province would be closed down. Would they resist the temptation to give Paisley his victory? They wouldn't be satisfied with mere promises. I had to convince then that I was in deadly earnest about winning the war against terrorism.

So flanked by the GOC and the Chief Constable, I spoke as forcefully as I could of what we had already achieved in making life more difficult for the bombers and the gunmen. I gave them chapter and verse on the number of IRA suspects arrested and jailed, on how the toll of murder and maiming was being reduced and how the security forces were eroding the morale of republican thugs.

The figures told their own story. In 1976, no fewer than 1,276 people had been charged with terrorist offences, including 120 accused of murder and 121 of attempted murder. During the year, 963 terrorists were convicted. As for 1977, 353 suspects had been charged so far, including 20 who faced murder charges and 47 who were up for attempted murder. Overall, there had been a noticeable decline in the number of deaths and injuries. In the first four months of 1976, the death toll nudged 120. For the same period in 1977, that figure had been cut to fewer than 60. Injuries meantime had been halved, down from 900 to 450. Of course conditions were still appalling. It would have been stupid to pretend otherwise. But they were improving.

I repeated the message I had given Paisley: that I would use every means possible within the law to break the will and power of the terrorist godfathers. To reinforce the point, I'd prepared a special security statement which I signed personally and gave to every shop steward there, so they could take it back and show it to their members. These were men, after all, who'd been brought up to distrust politicians' flannel. At least now they had my intentions set down in black and white, backed up by a signature. I prayed it would be enough.

All we could do then was wait. I wasn't particularly optimistic. My judgment of the meeting was that about a third of those present were dyed-in-the-wool Paisleyites who would never really be persuaded by any British Minister. I guessed I could count on the support of another third. As to the undecided remainder, we could only hope for the best. I went to bed that night drained, believing that the fate of the Province was still in the balance.

Thank God for the secret ballot. After the tense hours of waiting and worrying, the result from Ballylumford was all we could have hoped for. Though the campaign of intimidation had reached new depths of ugliness, 286 voted against the strike, with only 171 coming out in favour. We had retained the initiative. The next test would be whether we could hang on over the coming weekend without having to use troops in any high-visibility task.

Still, Paisley was now more isolated than ever. It was clear that the public was disgusted by the tactic of intimidation, which he had so far failed to denounce. Many wondered why he hadn't been arrested. Meanwhile, the official Unionist contingent at Westminster had disowned him and were doing all they could to encourage normal working in the Province. The police and part-time soldiers of the Ulster Defence Regiment ware doing excellent work in maintaining some semblance of order in the streets – to such an extent that the strikers were complaining of their 'brutality'.

But despite those encouraging signs, we had no illusions about the UUAC. The shadowy figures behind Paisley would be desperate to turn the tide. There was no level of violence to which they wouldn't stoop.

Their desperation didn't take long to show. Within hours of the Ballylumford ballot, we had reports that the campaign of intimidation had reached a new pitch, usually in the form of telephoned threats to the wives and children of the workers. There was some bad-tempered picketing outside the power station, though the police generally kept the situation under control. Despite all that, there was a good turnout for the shift beginning at 8 a.m. on 7 May; but tension in the plant increased throughout the day, with many of the men genuinely in fear for their lives. The RUC had to issue a public assurance that they would protect the workers with an increased presence throughout the area.

Paisley, needless to say, did his best to stir the pot by turning up at the power station that morning and trying to gain admittance. Though the management refused to let him in, he did manage to meet representatives of the workers outside the entrance, though he wasn't given a good reception. He finally left after about three hours, telling a radio intervewer that the staff were running down Ballylumford in support of the strike and would be stopping work shortly.

We couldn't dismiss his claim as an idle boast. Despite the ballot, some of the shop stewards made it clear that they were contemplating a rundown. Meanwhile, senior electricity officials phoned to warn us that shop-floor staff were seriously contemplating changing their minds. While the men didn't support the strike, the threats against their families and themselves meant that they couldn't continue operations unless the UUAC stopped the intimidation. They also wanted radio time to make their case to the people of the Province. Unless those demands were met, they warned, the day shift would walk out.

We were caught in a dilemma. My officials were adamant that the Northern Ireland Office could take no direct action on the men's demands. On the other hand, some initiative was essential if Ballylumford was to be kept on stream. So we produced a statement for use by the Chief Executive of the Province's electricity service. It began by stressing the result of the ballot and continued: 'The workers have asked me now to seek, through the media, a public and categorical statement from the UUAC that they and their supporters will not attempt to influence the workers through intimidation and will not condone any such action.'

Those words seemed to clear the air. The 4 p.m. shift changeover took place normally, though many of the workers were clearly still nervous. The midnight shift showed a slight drop in strength, down from thirty-five men to twenty-four. But the management appeared confident that Ballylumford would be able to maintain its output, for the time being at least. It certainly helped that a whole platoon of mainstream Unionist politicians – Roy Bradford, Harold McCusker, Jim Molyneux, Bill Craig and William Carson – turned up shortly before midnight and spoke to men on the shift changeover. They subsequently issued a statement supporting the power men's decision to go on working.

The reaction of the strike leadership was to lash out in all directions. Paisley bitterly condemned as 'black propaganda' any suggestion that he contemplated the strike's failure. Perhaps he was still worried about the possibility of a bullet from his unpleasant allies. Meanwhile the UUAC continued to denounce politicians like Bill Craig and Harry West as 'Unionist backstabbers'. But more significant than any of this was a statement from the Loyalist paramilitaries, including the proscribed Ulster

Freedom Fighters (UFF): 'We strongly advise the working population of Northern Ireland to keep off the streets, as we can no longer can be responsible for their safety,' it declared. The UFF underlined the threat with a message of its own: 'It is with great reluctance that we find ourselves in the position of having to coerce the Loyalist people to support themselves.'

For once, both Paisley and his sidekick Baird condemned the UFF statement, pointing out that the UFF was not affiliated to the UUAC. Weasel words. The term 'Ulster Freedom Fighters' is a cover name adopted by the slightly more 'respectable' UDA when it wants to commit acts of violence. And the UDA, of course, was prominent in organizing the strike leadership. Once again, Paisley was just trying to have his cake and eat it.

But the viciousness of UUAC tactics could not be disguised over that weekend. Two buses were attacked by the mob in Protestant areas of Belfast, with one driver wounded by a gunman. There were bomb-hoaxes in and around the city, disrupting road and rail links. In rural areas, a concerted attempt was made to block roads with farm machinery; a tractor procession from Newtownards to Stormont, other traffic-stopping demonstrations in Belfast, Ballymena, Lisburn, Dungannon and Larne. The strikers were changing tack. Having so far failed to bully and threaten the power stations to a standstill, they were now turning their attention to the transport system in the Province.

From their point of view, it was a shrewd move. Business and industry throughout Northern Ireland were heavily reliant on oil. If the tanker drivers could be forced off the road, the impact could be almost as damaging as a stoppage in the power stations; and of course it would be worse still if buses, trains, milk deliveries and food supplies were also hit.

Our priority was clear. We had to keep the roads open and traffic moving, no matter what. The Chief Constable reported that his officers were already tired and would be further stretched as the strikers' campaign of disruption intensified. We knew that the Army would very probably have to be used in a more visible role – perhaps even in the Shankill, where the UDA was likely to put on a show of force. The possibility of an outright confrontation on the streets was very much on our minds.

Throughout that Monday, 9 May, we played a waiting game. As expected, the UUAC staged tractor cavalcades all over the Province, though our information was that many of the farmers involved were taking part only under duress. Intimidation was still the strikers' main weapon. Ken Newman reported that since the action began, 1,515 cases of illegal threats had been reported; of course they amounted only to the tip of a large and ugly iceberg. Still, intelligence reports were striking a less gloomy note than hitherto. Though the UUAC was pulling out all the stops, thc cconomy of Northern Ireland was still working. People, by and large, were still managing to struggle through to their factories and offices. It seemed to us that the strike leaders would be growing ever more frustrated – a view reinforced that afternoon, when a bomb explosion wrecked a power pylon at Castlereagh. It was hardly the way for the UUAC to win hearts and minds.

The following morning, my private office received a phone call from a shopkeeper in the Shankill, reporting that the area had been completely sealed off by gangs of thugs. He complained that he had only been able to keep his shop open for one full day since the strike began. He was sick of the threats, the constant fear of attack, mob rule and cars burning in the streets. Not unreasonably, he wanted to know why the government and the media didn't take on and expose the bad guys.

My mind was already moving in the same direction. In particular, it seemed to me that we could do more to tackle the problem of telephone intimidation by taping the calls, tracking down the source and using the evidence in court. We might even broadcast some of the calls, in the hope of identifying the culprits. The facility to do this was readily available, though the Post office was dubious about being pushed into such a prominent and sensitive role. Still, the effort would be worth making, if only we could get co-operation from those threatened. We were well aware that Andy Tyrie of the UDA was boasting that he would have Ballylumford closed down by Wednesday. You didn't need to be a security expert to work out how he intended to do it.

Meanwhile it was time to see for myself what the situation was like on the ground. On that day, Tuesday, 10 May, the UUAC was promising a major demonstration of its power in Ballymena, the heart of Paisley territory. This was where sentiment for the strike was at its fiercest. Here was where civil disobedience could easily spill into open insurrection.

I took off in my helicopter from Stormont shortly before noon. I already knew that the town was blockaded, surrounded by tractors, trailers, sprayers, vans and lorries in what was intended to be an impenetrable ring of steel. For the moment, the security forces were doing nothing which might inflame the situation. In fact troops of the Ulster Defence Regiment were deployed round the town, turning back everyone trying to enter. It was important to keep troublemaking outsiders from joining the demo; and just as important to dissuade legitimate travellers from the risk of confrontation on the barricades.

The town itself was choked, scores of tractors stretched in procession along the main streets, clogging every junction, the drivers waving like liberators to the surging crowds. No doubt they were cheering, but of course I couldn't hear. I caught sight of a sprinkling of RUC uniforms in the throng, but the officers would obviously be overwhelmed if the mob turned nasty. Somewhere down there, Ian Paisley was probably exhorting his followers to greater efforts. It hardly bore thinking about. I found myself singing 'Don't cry for me, Ballymena', which in the circumtances may sound a little frivolous; in fact I think it reflected the tension we were under.

I had seen enough. There were another three or four army helicopters hovering over the town and I didn't want a mid-aid collision. Besides, unpleasant though the demonstration was, it showed no sign of developing into a full-scale riot. I learned later that the crowds had dispersed peacefully enough by about 3 p.m.

If I felt relief at the outcome, it was short-lived. At 3.15, bus driver Harry Bradshaw was shot dead in Belfast as he drove his vehicle in Queensland Street. In that instant, all our hopes of outfacing the intimidatory tactics practised so contemptibly by the UUAC seemed undermined.

This was the kind of event we had been dreading. It was a grim meeting of the Emergency Committee that evening. Belfast's City Bus Service had stopped running immediately in reaction to the outrage. The Ulster Bus Company was getting people home that evening. But all services would be stopped the following day for twenty-four hours, in sympathy for the family of the murdered man.

I agreed at once that Don Concannon and I should meet an emergency delegation from the busmen at Stormont Castle. It was a moving experience to learn at first hand of the pressures the drivers had been under: anonymous threats by telephone, wives jostled by strangers in the street, occasional bricks through the window. In spite of all that, they had found the dogged courage to carry on working, but clearly the situation had now changed. The thugs were off the leash. We were told that the men were to hold a mass meeting at noon the next day, when a majority might well vote to turn the 24-hour stoppage into a permanent shutdown. I could only express my admiration for the bravery the men had shown so far and assure the delegation that the most senior officers in the security forces would be having urgent talks with transport managers about increased protection.

In the event, and to my great relief, the busmen kept their nerve. Next day they voted to resume normal working. In the circumtances, it was an extraordinary display of resolution. Not for the first time in Northern Ireland, ordinary citizens were standing firm against the terrorist gangs who sought to rule their lives through fear.

Meanwhile I'd decided that Paisley would have to be arrested, a step which so far I had been reluctant to take. There were obvious risks in such an action; in fact Bill Craig of the Vanguard Unionist Party had privately pleaded with me to leave the man alone, for fear of turning him into a martyr. But I was fed up with Paisley's contempt for the law – and very conscious of the fact that many people in the Province thought that the authorities didn't dare touch him. Throughout the demonstration in Ballymena, RUC officers had negotiated with him at length, publicly calling on him and others under the Public Order Act to cease obstructing the highways. Of course he'd done no such thing. It was time he got his comeuppance. The security forces lifted him and his ally Ernest Baird together with eleven other agitators in the small hours and carted them all off to police cells.

We actually only held them for about half a day before releasing them on police bail. The charges against them were quietly dropped a few months later, when the strike was long over.

But the arrests achieved everything I'd hoped for. The decent majority learned that Paisley wasn't above the law. The man himself achieved no martyrdom from his few hours behind bars; indeed the consensus in the Province seemed to be that he'd asked for everything he got. No doubt the murder of poor Harry Bradshaw had something to do with it. There was a general feeling of revulsion over that crime. Paisley's subsequent denunciation of the murder, however sincere it may have been, didn't seem to impress the public. It wasn't only the members of my advisory team who noticed that he absented himself from Belfast in the immediate aftermath of the shooting.

By now there were clear signs of divergence within the ranks of the UUAC. Our intelligence reports suggested that the campaign of outright violence, probably committed by a handful of vicious UDA and UVF thugs working in concert, was likely to continue for a few more days at least. But with every shooting and bombing, Paisley, Baird and the UUAC 'moderates' would find themselves in greater difficulty. No doubt they would try to continue the strike through the passive resistance of roadblocks in country areas; but with the paramilitaries running out of control, everybody associated with the strike would be increasingly discredited.

Despite the worst the UUAC and its terrorist friends could do, Northern Ireland was working almost normally. Even Larne Harbour, that Paisleyite stronghold, had begun to operate again. Rumours were spreading through the Shankill that the UDA was thinking of pulling out of the strike. Public and political opinion was hardening against Paisley and the rest. Captain Austen Ardill, the Official Unionist Chief Whip, called on them to admit defeat, an appeal echoed by others in the party.

It fell on deaf ears. In a decision which appeared to fly in the face of events and the public mood, the strike leaders voted to continue their campaign. Paisley dug himself into a deeper hole with a ranting speech in Portadown, in which he condemnd both me and the Chief Constable, Kenneth Newman, who had refused to meet him.

The man's unbending truculence seemed hopelessly ill-judged. Brian Cubbon and my other advisers all believed that he must want the violence to subside in order to restore his own political position. He probably wanted to make himself more 'respectable' before the forthcoming local government elections; nailing his banner to the cause of a failing and unpopular strike hardly seemed a clever way of going about it.

But it's always unwise to underestimate Paisley's political resilience. The consensus in my office was that he would try and build a bridge back to majority Protestant opinion by confining his activities in future to the relatively peaceful demonstrations in the countryside. No doubt he'd also claim that more had been achieved for the security of Ulster in the last six days than in the previous six months; and it was obvious that he would stress the need for more Paisleyite councillors as a means of keeping the government up to the mark.

The last thing I wanted was for the man to re-emerge as a strong figure in the Province. I'd come to see him for what he was – a bully and a bigot, a man who seldom touched on a political problem without making it worse. Some of my advisers thought that a substantial majority of voters would be relieved and pleased if he was eclipsed. Those who had behaved responsibly throughout the strike – not least mainstream Unionist politicians – would probably feel badly let down if the government tamely allowed Paisley to regain his influence.

Of course there were strict limits to what we could usefully do to prevent it. We could try and reduce his status by paying more attention to other political leaders in the Province, but such a policy would take months or years to make itself felt. More contentiously, we considered excluding him from high-level meetings with Ministers, but he would certainly make a propaganda meal out of that. In fact any overt government action to hammer Paisley would probably rebound. Until the final, messy stages of the strike were over, I thought it best if we stuck to the line of implicitly condemning him by focusing in our public statements on intimidation, lawbreaking and disorder in the streets. In the end, only the voters could decide Paisley's future.

We were by now in an increasingly confident mood. So much so that the Commander of Land Forces was already pressing for troop reductions. We were all aware of the undesirability of keeping extra soldiers in Ulster for a day longer than was strictly necessary. On the other hand, it was important not to send the wrong signal by moving too soon. I wanted to see a full day and a full night of tranquillity in the streets – and normal economic activity – before giving the go-ahead. Even then, I was anxious for the Spearhead Battalion to remain. I knew that the Provisional IRA had been given time to regroup, and restore their capability because of the strike and feared an imminent upsurge of terrorist activity. The police, who had been at full stretch for more than a week now, would welcome a measure of additional army support.

Those fears were brutally confirmed on Thursday 12 May. On that day, the IRA staged a shooting incident – not fatal – in Rosslea and mounted a bomb attack on a shop in Belfast's city centre.

But by then I was grappling with a far greater crisis. With one act of savagery, the militants had probably given the strike a new lease of life. That same day in Daphne Street, Belfast, an oil-tanker driver called William Hughes was shot by Loyalists while driving his vehicle. Fortunately, he escaped with his life. That was the only glimmer of comfort in what was a desperately dangerous development.

To begin with, it was immediately clear that the attack wasn't the work of some lone maverick. A whole mob of thugs had been involved in the ambush. Afterwards, the police rounded up nineteen UDA men suspected of complicity in the shooting. If the Association was thinking of pulling out of the strike, as rumour suggested, it nevertheless seemed clear that the hard-liners were determined to carry on.

Worse still was the impact the attempted murder might have on the tanker drivers themselves. Like the Ballylumford men, their attitude had been crucial since the strike began. Had they allowed themselves to be bullied into withdrawing their labour, the life would have been choked out of Northern Ireland's economy. Though we of course had contingency plans to use troops for essential deliveries of oil and petrol, everybody in my office knew that a stoppage of even a few days would have a devasatating impact on public transport and goods lorries, not to mention the private motorist.

So far, despite some worrying moments for my officials and me, the drivers had worked more or less normally. Now everything was at risk. In Belfast, not surprisingly, the men had already embarked on a 24-hour stoppage in protest at the attack. According to reports they were in a bitter mood and fearful for their own safety. The drivers' liaison committee had already met to consider either making the stoppage permanent or restricting fuel deliveries to the list of essential services drawn up by the UUAC.

It was the worst possible news, coming at the worst possible time. Throughout the Loyalist heartlands – including the Paisleyite strongholds

– I had seen a growing acceptance that the confrontation with the government had failed. I had serious hopes that the UUAC would officially concede defeat and end the strike within the next twenty-four hours. Now we could be pushed back to square one. Whether the tanker drivers extended their stoppage or merely decided to work according to the instructions of the UUAC, the consequences would be the same: encouragement for the strike leadership, more disruption and probably the need to call out the troops to make deliveries. Paisley and his friends would be in their element.

Somehow, we absolutely had to keep the drivers on side. If we could prevent them making an announcement the next day, it might well be enough. It seemed to me that the UUAC was about to crumble. Its supporters were already disillusioned and coming under intense pressure from the Loyalist community to call off their campaign. Only the tanker drivers could change that situation now. The next few hours would be critical.

How could we buy the time we so desperately needed? It was at this point that my deputy, Don Concannon, came into his own. He knew the unions well. He was on good terms with the management. He had a commanding physical presence and great political skills. If anyone could keep the drivers from rushing into a damaging decision, it was Don.

We agreed there and then that we would invite the men's representatives and their managers to a meeting at Stormont the following day. It was just too bad that the gathering would be held on Friday the 13th. It was likely to prove unlucky for somebody; I just hoped it would be the Paisleyites.

Don's task sounded simple. In fact it was anything but. The job was to keep the drivers talking and talking all day and into the night, keeping them closeted while he listened and explained the government's point of view in great detail. The men couldn't be allowed to leave the building and go back to their depots and branches. If that happened, they might well recommend a continuation of the tanker stoppage and give the UUAC a last-minute reprieve. Every hour he kept the talks going was another hour of pressure on Paisley and his allies.

Don's handling of that meeting was masterly. It needed to be. It was 9.15 a.m. when the drivers' representatives and union officials trooped into Stormont Castle, to be confronted not just by the Minister of State, but by the Army Chief of Staff, the Deputy Chief Constable John Hermon, Chief Superintendent MacChesney of the RUC and a clutch of other senior Northern Ireland officials. Don had also arranged for John Freeman of the Transport Workers' Union to be present. It was a first-division turnout, demonstrating to the tanker men that their concerns were being treated very seriously indeed. Of course it was also true that a large team on our side of the table meant that the proceedings would tend to be lengthy, since everybody would have to be allowed a say.

The meeting began with Don stating our intention to provide more effective security for the drivers. They in turn warned that they couldn't recommend their members to return to work when there was every prospect of more shootings. They urged Don and me to pay an early call on Paisley and his sidekick Baird, to achieve an early end to UUAC action.

Plenty of meat there to be going on with. At 10.15 the meeting was adjourned so that the drivers' representatives could have private talks among themselves. At eleven o'clock, senior members of the security forces joined them to discuss how better protection might be provided. It was 11.45 before Don and his officials returned to the talks. There was then a break for lunch. In the afternoon, it was agreed, the tanker management would be brought into the discussions.

The talks should have resumed at 2 p.m. In fact it was 2.15 before all the drivers' representatives returned, but on this occasion nobody on the government side was in the least concerned about punctuality. There was still no word of capitulation from the UUAC. It was necessary to keep going. At 4.10 a short recess was called, to allow drivers and management to have private exchanges.

Still no word from the Paisleyites – but at least the tanker men were showing no inclination to leave. At 5.15, copies of a draft paper on improved security were distributed, which gave everyone something to chew on for a while longer.

Then came the first sign of a breakthrough. At 5.35, John Freeman of the TGWU took Don to one side and told him that new rumours were circulating about the UUAC. Apparently the strike was to be called off officially at 10 p.m. That wasn't the end of the good news. The drivers' representatives had abandoned their plans to recommend an all-out stoppage; but they were insistent that Paisley and Baird should be called in for urgent talks.

We just had to keep hanging in there. I was of course being kept closely in touch with events both in the meeting and outside. I too had heard rumours of an imminent end to the UUAC strike; I knew equally that things could still go wrong. I was disturbed when half a dozen of the drivers' representatives left Stormont at eight o'clock, ostensibly to get themselves some fish and chips. Would they be in touch with the UUAC? Might they yet be got at? We could only hope. Don meanwhile was plugging gamely on with those who remained. At 9.10 he began a plenary session to clarify outstanding points on the security paper. At 9.35 he held a private meeting with the tanker men only. He gave them his assurance that he – and I – would use all our endeavours to end the UUAC strike as soon as possible. After all, that's what we'd been doing from the beginning. He also pledged that if needs be any new security arrangements would be reviewed at ministerial level.

It was 9.45 when the visitors at last left the building. Don and the rest of the official team were drained, but they had good reason to be satisfied. Not only had they succeeded in reassuring the tanker men; they'd effectively kept them out of circulation for more than twelve hours, on a day when a rash word or an emotional gesture could have reignited the flames of protest. Now we could only wait to see what happened at ten o'clock.

And this time, thank God, the rumours proved accurate. Paisley announced: 'The stoppage has been halted.' He and his followers had suffered a shattering defeat. They had failed to repeat their triumph of 1974, when they'd brought the Province to a standstill and forced the collapse of power-sharing between Loyalist and nationalist Ulster.

I think we were all too exhausted to feel much elation. At any moment during the ten days of crisis, the balance could so easily have tilted against the government: intimidation might have worked. Paisley might have succeeded in rallying the great mass of Protestants. There could have been the kind of incident between the security force and the strikers which would have inflamed public opinion. Yes, we had won; but I was very conscious of the fact that last time we had lost.

When I attended Cabinet on 17 May, Jim Callaghan sent me this minute, which was also circulated to Ministerial colleagues:

> You have displayed courage and firmness against these dangerous men; and by your successful appeal to the good sense and loyalty of the people of Ulster, you have achieved a signal victory over those whose unconstitutional actions would have destroyed the economic recovery you have done so much to promote.

I can't pretend that I wasn't pleased and flattered. But in truth, the victory didn't belong to me, or to my team of ministers and officials, superb though they were throughout. It didn't even belong to the RUC and the security forces, whose competence and sheer professionalism had once again proved exemplary. No, the real heroes of the confrontation were the ordinary men and women of Northern Ireland, people who had braved the blackmailers and the thugs, people who stood up for themselves, their families and the wider community. They had refused to see their homeland slide into anarchy; and in doing so they'd kept alive a hope for Ulster that might otherwise have been crushed beneath the hobnailed boots of Ian Paisley and the forces behind him.

From my point of view, there was one depressing little footnote. Less than a week after the strike was called off, Northern Ireland went to the polls in the dictrict council elections. Contrary to what so many of us had hoped, Paisley didn't suffer at all for his irresponsibility and hypocrisy. His DUP won no less that 12.7 per cent of the vote and took a total of 74 council seats. He was still a force to be reckoned with.

So when he asked for a meeting with me after those elections, I readily agreed. I was curious to see what position he would take, now that his attempt to seize power by unconstitutional means had failed.

It turned out to be a complete waste of time. He blustered into my office, ostentatiously refused to shake hands and began a harangue. It was the same old story: he wanted the return of rule by Stormont, accused me of not doing enough to defeat the IRA and insisted that he and his friends could do a far better job. I reminded him, none too gently, that he had promised to abandon politics if the strike failed. I spoke of the thugs who had wreaked such misery under his banner. At that he grew more red-faced and angry than ever. When he'd bellowed for a bit I asked if he intended to try the stunt he'd pulled on Merlyn Rees, by clinging to his chair and refusing to budge. It wasn't what you would call a meeting of minds. Still, almost to my disappointment, he didn't try it on. He stamped off at last, not in the best of tempers. Like the Bourbons of old, he had learned nothing and forgotten nothing.

13 A Most Distressful Country

With the strikers defeated. we were able to resume the real job in hand: making life difficult for the IRA and other criminal gangs. They'd had an easy time of it for the past ten days. With the pressure off because of the lunacy of the UUAC they'd been given time to recover and regroup. Now I was anxious to turn the heat up once again.

One tragedy in particular affected me. On 17 May, the very day I'd received that handsome memo from Jim Callaghan, a young officer in army intelligence had been abducted from the car park of the Three Steps pub in Drumintee, South Armagh. Captain Robert Nairac had been drinking in the pub – a known haunt of terrorists – in plain clothes but without the back-up which is so essential in such operations. Clearly he'd been spotted as an undercover officer. In the circumstances, he had no chance. Though the locals professed not to have seen any sign of a struggle in the car park, Robert Nairac was forcibly seized and driven away. It was later established that the terrorists tortured him before killing him.

Of course the security forces threw everything into finding Captain Nairac. Sadly, they failed. His body has never been recovered. It was as part of this response that a well-known Republican, Gerry Adams, was picked up and questioned at Castlreagh, on suspicion of being a member of the IRA. But the police were soon satisfied that he had nothing to do with Nairac's abduction and murder.

Before Paisley and his friends stuck their oar in, we'd been having considerable success in our campaign of picking up suspected terrorists in batches and subjecting them to hard questions. Though we had to release most of them after a few days, some did confess and were charged. Other gave us information – wittingly or unwittingly – which had proved of immense value. By March that year I had been able to talk publicly of the inroads being made by the RUC against senior paramilitaries.

Inevitably, of course, there was a reaction. By that summer hundreds of suspects had been through Castlereagh Interrogation Centre – some of them emerging with tales of beatings and other forms of ill treatment. Naturally enough, IRA/Sinn Fein exploited these stories for all they were worth as yet another example of British 'brutality'. It was a line taken up by the BBC *Tonight* programme, which broadcast an attack on RUC interrogation methods. Evidently my words to the Corporation's governors hadn't really changed anything.

Now I wasn't so naïve as to believe that each and every one of those allegations was automatically untrue. Just before I arrived in Northern Ireland, the European Commission on Human Rights published a report which showed that back in 1971 prisoners in Northern Ireland had been subjected to unacceptably harsh treatment, involving hooding, prolonged standing with fingers pressed against the wall, electronic noise, sleep deprivation and a bread and water diet. Those abuses had been corrected – and rightly so.

Had they now crept back on a systematic scale? I just didn't believe it. I don't think I was being blind or blimpish. I knew the Chief Constable Kenneth Newman to be a man of utter integrity. He wouldn't tolerate such methods for a moment. Then there was the fact that suspects had the right to a medical examination – by their own GP if desired – when they were picked up and again when they were released. That hardly left much scope for 'torturers'. And finally, everyone in the RUC knew that a confession extracted under duress would be thrown out by the no-jury Diplock courts if ill-treatment could be established. No officer wants to see a case collapse in such circumstances – or to face the disciplinary consequences afterwards.

So if there were cases of ill-treatment, I believed (and still believe) that they were very much the exception. I couldn't know then that the issue would later blow up into a national and international row; perhaps I should have remembered that a lie can be halfway round the world before the truth has got its boots on.

That wasn't the only area in which the propagandists were active. The whole question of special category status for convicted terrorists was slowly coming to the boil. The original protests by the UDA were taken up with equal enthusiasm by the IRA. Both Catholic and Protestant prisoners in the Maze were increasingly refusing to work, to wear prison clothes or to take exercise. So far they were all still conforming to the extent that they would sweep out their cells, empty their own night-time chamber pots and collect their own meals; and they all took a shower twice a week. But sooner or later, I feared, the paramilitaries would launch a really major effort. After all, there would be plenty of publicity in a campaign for the restoration of special category status. It would be irritating for the authorities. It would certainly strike a chord with the sentimentalists, particuarly in the Irish–American community. And if the protesters won and were treated virtually as prisoners-of-war their cause would take on a spurious legitimacy. So I wasn't particularly surprised that summer to receive evidence that some prisoners were being intimidated into joining the protest. By July, the number of convicted terrorists refusing to co-operate had risen to 143.

It wasn't yet a major problem, but I suspected that it would eventually dawn on the godfathers of the IRA that they had a situation which could be profitably exploited. So I asked to be kept in regular and detailed touch with what was going on in the Maze. Whatever happened, I was determined not to budge. The prisoners were criminals and as far as I was concerned would always be treated as criminals. But I didn't want to be caught napping when they stepped up their campaign, as they probably would. For the moment, it was a waiting game; but it wouldn't be long before the Maze and the people in it became an international cause célèbre.

The one genuinely happy event in that summer of 1977 promised to be the Queen's visit to the Province. I can still hardly bear to think of how close it came to going tragically wrong.

I knew the risks. Thanks to the breathing space afforded by the UUAC strike, the IRA was well on the way towards regaining the initiative. Full operations were being resumed. No target was regarded as too ambitious. None of my security advisers doubted that the terrorists would kill the Queen, if they could. Only a week before she was due to arrive, searchers had discovered a bomb with a ten-day timing device hidden at Coleraine University. It was there, in one of the most important engagements of the whole visit, that the royal party was due to have lunch before strolling through the grounds to meet local people. Had that device exploded while the Queen was in the vicinity, it would at the very least have presented the IRA with a propaganda triumph. The worst-case scenario hardly needs describing.

Though relieved that we had thwarted one attack, I couldn't rest easy. After examining the bomb, our technical experts reported that the terrorists had well and truly mastered the difficult art of setting such long-delay timing mechanisms. Deeply worrying news. A small explosive package could be so easily concealed weeks in advance: in a desk, a lavatory cistern, even buried beneath a shrub. It meant that the threat to the Queen's safety might be even greater than we feared.

Yet the thought of cancelling the visit or changing the arrangements never crossed my mind. The Queen's presence in Northern Ireland was an essential part of her Jubilee Year tour round the United Kingdom. It mattered very much to her, just as it mattered to me and to so many others. For the vast majority in the Province, decent people who had endured years of terrorist atrocity, her presence would be an event of huge symbolic importance. I was especially encouraged by the fact that she and her advisers agreed with me that there should be no question of scurrying in and out, wrapping up all her engagements in a few hours. Instead, I'm pleased to say, she wanted to do us proud by staying for two days.

I was delighted with that, though it afforded a wider window of opportunity for the IRA. Clearly we had to redouble our security efforts and redouble them again. We would check and recheck, leaving nothing to chance. At Coleraine, for example, troops and police officers went back to search every cupboard and desk and locker, every ventilator duct and wiring shaft, every inch of the path the royal party would be taking through the grounds. Even the books in the university library were taken out and carefully examined, one by one.

After putting the same intensive effort into every point on her itinerary, I was confident we'd done all that was humanly possible to protect the Queen's safety. That still left the problem of how she would travel round the Province. Her overnight stay would be on board the Royal Yacht *Britannia*, where security would pose no difficulty; but how would she get to Hillsborough or Coleraine or any of her other engagements?

Journeys by road, I thought, were out of the question. However much the Queen wanted to be seen by her subjects, her car would be too tempting a target. It wasn't a question of being over-cautious; my Permanent Under-Secretary, Brian Cubbon, had been badly injured years before, when his vehicle was bombed by terrorists. I myself never travelled anywhere except by helicopter. I was adamant that the Queen would have to do the same.

As the visit approached, I was in touch with the Palace virtually every hour of every day. We agreed – to my relief without any real argument – that the Queen would be ferried everywhere by chopper. From her base on *Britannia*, she would cross by barge to the accompanying Naval warship, HMS *Fyfe*, where a helicopter would be waiting to whisk her from one engagement to the next. To the best of my knowledge, it would be the first time the Queen had carried out a visit in her own country by such means.

The great day dawned at last. Nervous but excited, I boarded *Britannia* to welcome the Queen, Prince Philip, Prince Andrew and the rest of the royal entourage. It was a proud moment, marred only by the faintest twinge of anxiety. I was sure that every possible security angle had been covered, but in a crowded schedule there could be all kinds of administrative hitches. And what if Republican extremists staged a hostile demonstration?

In the event, I needn't have worried. That day at least passed off with clockwork precision. We crossed to HMS *Fife* by barge without mishap. Our helicopter took off exactly on time. As we whirled away from the impossibly tiny postage-stamp of the destroyer's landing-pad, the Queen seemed genuinely thrilled, leaving her seat to peer though the windows as the hills and fields of Ulster slid past underneath. It was a good start to an excellent day; warm and welcoming crowds, plenty of cheers, not a sign of trouble. At Hillsborough, the Queen planted a tree before giving a very pleasant garden party. We returned to *Britannia* for the evening cocktail party in high good humour. The reception itself was as jolly as anyone could have wished. Afterwards, Madge and I dined informally with the Queen before staying on board overnight. In that relaxed atmosphere, I couldn't have guessed what the morrow would bring.

The crisis began with an urgent telephone call from my private office, just as we were preparing to leave for Coleraine. In fact the advance party was already *en route*. The message was the one I had been dreading; we'd had a warning from the IRA that another bomb was waiting for the Queen at the university. I would have to give a ruling almost immediately on whether the engagement could go ahead.

I phoned my Permanent Under-Secretary, Brian Cubbon, who was already at the university. There was one piece of information I had to double-check: was the warning genuine? 'Yes,' he replied. 'The validation code checked out.' Well, that was it. I was on my own, with none of my security experts available for consultation. The Chief Constable was on his way to Coleraine. So was the GOC. I simply didn't have time to ring Jim Callaghan at Number Ten. We were already running late. I thought of all the precautions we had taken and of the troops who were still probing the ground with their bayonets. I thought too of the crowds waiting to greet their Queen. And of the terrorists' delight if they could be seen dictating the royal agenda. To call off the visit now would be a defeat for Britain and the monarchy, celebrated in IRA song and legend for years to come. Unthinkable. I knew I would just have to trust in the thoroughness of our security operation. Taking a deep breath, I said that the engagement would go ahead as planned. And no, I didn't intend to tell Her Majesty of the threat. My responsibility.

It was only when I turned round that I saw that Prince Philip had been listening to the entire conversation. He had come down from the royal stateroom above, no doubt wondering what the delay was all about, and had been standing behind me. We stared at each other for a long moment, unspeaking. I thought that he was going to reproach me for wanting to keep the bad news to myself; but then he nodded and left, without a word.

He must have reported it all to the Queen, however. When she came down to embark for the short trip to HMS *Fife*, she seemed preoccupied. On the helicopter trip to Coleraine, she showed none of the excitement and interest that had been so evident the day before. I don't know whether it was because she was on edge, or because she didn't appreciate being kept in the dark over a threat to her life. But it was too late then for me to make amends.

The morning's tour of the university was conducted with commendable briskness. In fact we more than made up for our delay in starting out. It seemed to me that the Queen was eager to get this part of her tour over and done with, though I doubt whether her university hosts detected any signs of nervousness or strain. By this time, inevitably, key people in the royal entourage knew that something was up. Over pre-lunch drinks, the Queen's Private Secretary, Martin Charteris, tried to lighten the atmosphere with a bit of clowning, balancing Polo mints on the end of his tongue.

I couldn't stay to see whether his efforts succeeded. I had to go into a huddle with the Chief Constable and the GOC to discuss the afternoon's planned walkabout. Once again we reviewed the precautions. Every square yard on the route had been examined and examined again. If there was a bomb, we agreed that it would be too far away from the royal party to do any damage. It was also agreed that Prince Andrew could join the party.

That didn't ease my tension as Madge and I set out after lunch with the Queen, Prince Philip and Prince Andrew to meet the people. I made a point of staying as close as I possibly could to the main target. I suppose I was feeling somewhat guilty over my determination to keep quiet about the threat; but at least the Queen would know that her Northern Ireland Secretary was sharing whatever risks there might be.

In spite of everything, it was a happy afternoon. The crowds were enthusiastic and obviously delighted to see the royals. The Queen responded with all her usual charm. Best of all, there were no incidents. As we helicoptered back to *Britannia* afterwards, I think we all felt relieved at how well the day had gone.

Prince Andrew had gone on ahead and was waiting to greet us, casual now in slacks and sweater, looking forward to watching cricket on TV. 'Come on, Mr Mason,' he urged. 'We'll just see Boycott get his century then maybe we'll catch ourselves on the news.'

It seemed an excellent plan to me. What could be better for any

Yorkshireman than to enjoy the incomparable Boycott doing his stuff? It would be the perfect end to what had turned out, in spite of everything, to be the perfect day.

Until the news came through. A bomb had just exploded. In the grounds of Coleraine University.

A vigorous security policy is certainly necessary in the war against terrorism; but it isn't enough. I never believed that normality could be restored to Northern Ireland simply through more arrests, more roadblocks, more army patrols and the rest. If we were to wean people – particularly the impressionable young – away from the culture of violence, we absolutely had to provide them with some hope for the future. Hard experience taught me long ago what it's like to be without a job, without money, without decent housing, without a purpose in life. In Northern Ireland I saw too many people who had none of these things.

On 1 August 1977, I tried to do something about it, announcing a substantial new package of grants and incentives for the Province. There would be a write-off of debts incurred by the Electricity Service, bigger subsidies for new factory building, selective assistance for key employers, new efforts to attract internationally known companies to locate in unemployment black spots and a campaign to attract more investment from overseas. What I was proposing was expensive, running into hundreds of millions of pounds, but essential if progress was to be made.

The trouble was that it could take years for this initiative to make an impact. In the meantime, the terrorists would be trying to dictate the agenda not just by acts of violence but by an increasing understanding of the value of propaganda. In the Maze, more and more prisoners were refusing to work or wear prison clothes, with men 'on the blanket' beginning to win sympathy in the Republic and the United States. But for the moment that seemed containable. Rather more pressing was the IRA's campaign against British 'brutality' at the Castlereagh Interrogation Centre, a campaign already winning support in respectable quarters. In June, the Northern Ireland Civil Rights Association called for an inquiry into RUC methods of questioning suspects. In July, the Strasbourg-based European Human Rights Commission began hearings into the treatment of Irish prisoners in English jails. In October, the SDLP condemned the 'public scandal' of police interrogation methods and Thames TV broadcast a controversial documentary on the same subject. And the following month a team from Amnesty International arrived in the Province to begin an investigation into alleged brutality.

All this was a consequence of the number of people being picked up. We were without question hurting the IRA and hindering its ability to conduct operations. The reports which I saw daily established that; so it didn't surprise me that the terrorists were squealing. Still, it was disappointing to see their complaints taken so seriously, when by definition any evidence from the IRA had to be tainted. Nevertheless, I saw to it that my officials and the police gave Amnesty every co-operation.

Of course I suspected that the investigation would pose problems for us later on. It would be a pretty poor politician who didn't see the potential for embarrassment. But I hoped that Amnesty would understand the immense difficulties which liberal democracy faces when it is subjected to savage and sustained assault by people who despise each and every democratic principle. I doubted then as I doubt now whether any other country in such circumstances would have treated its enemies in as decent a manner as we were attempting.

I can illustrate the point by listing some of the worst terrorist outrages before and after the Amnesty team arrived. On 7 October, the Chairman of the Northern Ireland Prison Officers' Association, Desmond Irvine, was shot dead in Belfast. The next day a woman officer in the Ulster Defence Regiment was shot dead in County Armagh. On 12 October, a Catholic driver of a school bus was shot and killed. The Provisionals admitted later that they had mistaken him for the regular driver, a part-time sergeant in the UDR. On 18 October, a retired police reservist was killed by gunmen at Girvan's Bridge. On 11 November, a man was killed and several injured when a car bomb went off in central Belfast. On 13 December, shops in Belfast and Derry were wrecked by fire bombs. On 21 December, more bombs damaged five hotels in the Province. The New Year offered no relief. On 12 January, a part-time member of the UDR was shot and killed. The next day, the Provisional IRA boasted that it had perpetrated forty-six bombings and shootings since the beginning of the month. On 19 January, six people, including five policemen were injured in a car bomb attack at Cookstown, County Tyrone. On 23 January, eight soldiers and three policemen were injured in a combined mortar and booby-trap bomb attack on a security base at Forkhill. On 7 February, a part-time member of the UDR who worked as a postman was shot dead while delivering letters near Pomeroy. The next day another part-timer in the UDR and his 10-year-old daughter were killed by a booby-trap bomb outside their home in Maghera. And these were only the low spots. In this same period there were also countless acts of lesser thuggery, beatings, maimings, threats and robberies all perpetrated in the Republican cause. This was the everyday reality of life in Northern Ireland. Words can't express the disgust I felt when the people responsible for such evils bleated about the alleged erosion of their human rights.

14 Downfall of a Government

The worst weekend of my political life began on the night of Friday, 17 February 1978, while I was the guest at a dinner given by Yorkshire TV. I wasn't in an especially sociable mood to begin with. Earlier that day, Lieutenant-Colonel Iain Corden-Lloyd, commanding the 2nd Battalion, the Royal Green Jackets, had been killed when his military helicopter crashed near the border with the Republic. It still wasn't clear if that tragedy was just the result of an accident or whether the chopper had been brought down by an M60 machine gun. There had been intelligence warnings that the Provisionals might have got hold of these fearsome weapons – a deeply worrying development, if true.

But that concern was swept to one side with the message I received as dinner was ending. A bomb or bombs had gone off at the La Mon House restaurant at Comber, 14 miles from Belfast. The place was now a charnel house. Many were dead. Dozens were injured. Bodies were burned and charred beyond recognition as flames gutted the building. The voice telling me these dreadful things was shaking with emotion. Understandably. What had happened was one of the worst acts of terrorist savagery since the Troubles began.

I left the table at once and arranged for my HS125 to be jacked up and ready to go from Finningley first thing in the morning. I hated to think of the horrors which awaited over the water. I knew La Mon to be a complex of bars and restaurants, one of the most popular spots in the Province and a place never before seriously troubled by violence. At weekends it was always packed with hundreds of happy, innocent revellers. Among the people who had been present when the bombs went off were members of a junior motor cycle club, a group from the Irish Collie Club, families enjoying a treat with their children, young couples, pensioners, ordinary folk with no more in mind that a good night out. They were the easiest of targets for the IRA.

By the time I flew in the next morning I knew the worst. Twelve people were dead, children among them. Some thirty others were seriously injured. La Mon itself was a smoking ruin. Rescuers were distraught at what they had seen. One witness said: 'I have never experienced such a ghastly sight in all my life. Small, charred bundles of what had been people were being dragged out and there seemed no way of knowing how many were still inside.'

All of Northern Ireland was shocked by the carnage, the more so because evidence of what had happened was being shown in ghastly detail on television. The IRA had planted two large petrol bombs, designed to cause the maximum damage, at La Mon's windows. The explosion created a firestorm which gave the victims little chance. With their usual hypocrisy, the terrorists had given a telephoned warning; but as was so often the case the 'warning' had been hopelessly inadequate and much too late.

Already it was being claimed that the Provisionals had staged such an atrocity in response to all the claims I had been making about having the terrorists on the run. Peter Robinson, one of Ian Paisley's acolytes, described the bombing as a direct result of my 'muddling, fiddling and hollow boasting'.

Poisonous stuff, but I didn't want to get into a slanging match. Of course I'd talked up the successes we had been having against the IRA: that's part of any Northern Ireland Secretary's job. Still, this wasn't the time for self-justification. My critics could wait. Instead I spent much of that awful weekend in consultations with my security advisers. And writing to the relatives of the dead.

One other task remained before I returned to make a statement in the House. We had already stepped up the process of picking up IRA suspects and hauling them off for questioning in Castlereagh. Now I wanted to increase the pressure on them even further. Every decent person in the Province wanted the perpetrators of the La Mon atrocity caught. In fact the mood was so fierce – stronger than anything I had known before – that I hoped ordinary citizens would at last turn on the terrorists who were making their lives a misery. With my blessing, the RUC began preparing a leaflet which would be distributed throughout Northern Ireland, showing photographs of the charred bodies at La Mon. It wasn't an easy decision, expecially as some of the victims were children. We had never before presented the public with such horrific material. But I thought it time that the ugly reality behind IRA propaganda was revealed. I hoped people would be so shocked and disgusted that they would overcome their traditional antipathy towards 'informing' and provide us with hard evidence against the bombers and gunmen.

In the Commons that Monday I appealed to everybody in Northern

Ireland to show restraint. It would play into the hands of the IRA if there was a violent reaction against Catholic communities or people suspected of republican sympathies. I repeated that there would be no change in our policy of treating jailed terrorists as anything but common criminals. There could be no amnesty for such people.

No amnesty. No concessions to prisoners. It wasn't just stubbornness or a desire to appear macho which prompted such a hard line. Special category status for convicted terrorists undermined our effort to defeat the IRA and the Loyalist gangs. That was why my predecessor Merlyn Rees had abandoned it. He always regarded the move as an important link in a chain of mutually reinforcing positions. Other links in that chain included helping the RUC to be seen more and more as a non-sectarian force; the increasing use of terrorist confessions to produce convictions; the continuing use of the Diplock courts to ensure that such evidence could be used without fear of jury-tampering; and no possibility of amnesty. By such means we were able to confront the IRA with great effectiveness while staying within the rule of law. It was proving an effective strategy, which of course was why the IRA was so desperate to undermine it.

A couple of weeks after the La Mon bombing, the penny finally dropped for the terrorists. In March 1978, a number of Provo prisoners already on the 'blanket' protest in H-Blocks H3 and H5 at the Maze began to intensify their campaign. I had long expected such a development and thought it would probably take the form of a hunger strike; but in the event, the IRA men proved somewhat more imaginative. They began refusing to clean their cells, to wash or use their showers or to empty their chamber pots. That wasn't the end of it. They started to foul their cells by systematically smearing their own excrement all over the walls, doors, ceilings, light-fittings and windows.

From their point of view, it was a brilliant stroke. Before the 'dirty strike' began, the IRA protest had been getting nowhere. Messages passed between prisoners in the Maze showed signs of increasing depression at the lack of support from outside. Now in their desperation to be noticed they'd hit the jackpot; and at last started to believe that they might actually win.

The publicity breakthrough they craved wasn't long in coming. On 12 April BBC Radio reported that the H-Blocks were stinking. 'War of nerves amid the stench' screamed a headline in the *Irish Times* three days later. And as the media fell with enthusiasm on what was admittedly an unusual story, the humanitarian lobby wasn't far behind. Lord Brockway, the Howard League for Penal Reform and the National Council for Civil Liberties all demanded action. Lord Longford requested and was finally granted a visit to the Maze. With the support of Bishop Daly of Derry, the Peace People called for the introduction of 'emergency status' – undefined – for convicted terrorists. Amnesty International and several Labour MPs called for an independent inquiry.

I couldn't be under any illusions about the effect the dirty strike was having. The image of prisoners naked in their cells with nothing for company but their own filth is undeniably potent; and it was being trumpeted round the world. But despite the adverse publicity, I couldn't give way. To do so would give the IRA its biggest victory in years. It would appal the law-abiding majority in Northern Ireland. It would dismay the security forces. It would mean the abandonment of the policy of police primacy and the rule of law. It would in the end lead to more death and misery.

Our only course, it seemed to me, was to explain the facts as patiently as we could. Sooner or later, I hoped, the message would get through. So Don Concannon, who had day-to-day charge of prisons, robustly informed Parliament that conditions in the H-Blocks were among the best of any prison in the United Kingdom. He pointed out that of the 300 terrorists fouling their own cells, 74 had been convicted of murder or attempted murder, 80 of firearms offences and 82 of crimes involving explosives. I followed this up with a comprehensive memorandum to MPs and others pointing out that the prisoners themselves were responsible for the conditions under which they were living and making it clear that neither I nor the government would budge in the face of their self-degradation. We also made clear the efforts we were making to clean up the squalor: a weekly use of high-pressure steam hoses in the cells, with operators covered from head to foot in protective clothing.

Up to that point, I'd believed that the situation, though certainly embarrassing, was containable. What changed all that was a visit to the Maze on 30 July by Dr Thomas O Fiaich, Archbishop of Armagh and Roman Catholic Primate of All Ireland.

For us, that visit was a disaster. The scale of the damage started becoming apparent the next day, when he issued a statement describing conditions in the C Blocks as 'unfit for animals', comparing them unfavourably with the sewers of Calcutta. Well, in view of what the prisoners had done to their own cells, this could be construed as fair comment. What appalled me was the argument which the Archbishop then proceeded to advance. He claimed that the protesters weren't ordinary criminals; they'd been sentenced by special criminal courts without juries, mainly on the basis of voluntary confessions. In a few emotive and grossly biased sentences he seemed to be undermining the legitimacy of our entire struggle against terrorism. In fact his words could have been written by any propagandist from Sinn Fein. I was appalled that such a prominent churchman could appear so indulgent towards gangsters who had caused such pain to so many innocent people over the years, including members of his own flock. I was just as sickened by the irresponsibility of his remark that the protesters 'would prefer death to being classified as criminals'. From such an authoritative source, those words amounted to a self-fulfilling prophecy. After I left office, the IRA stepped up its campaign another notch with the weapon of the hunger strike. The whole world knows what happened then.

I came back at the Archbishop at once, with a statement expressing my surprise that he hadn't mentioned the fact that the prisoners themselves had made conditions as they were. But however strongly I hinted at the man's hypocrisy, I knew it was too late. His partisan words had far more impact in the world than anything I could possibly say. From that point on, publicity began to move decisively against us, particularly in the United States. As John Hume of the SDLP told us in September, the Provisional IRA was 'winning the propaganda battle hands down'.

His warning was fully borne out the following month, when Jack Anderson's widely syndicated column in the *Washington Post* asserted: 'Human rights violations, reported to us by a number of reliable sources, have put Northern Ireland on an unenviable par with some of the most barbarous regimes of the Communist Commissars or tin-horn Latin American dictators.'

And it wasn't just the Americans who were succumbing to hysteria. In Northern Ireland a pair of Catholic priests not noted for their sympathies with Britain, Father Denis Faul and Father Raymond Murray, produced a pre-Christmas document under the headline 'The caves of Long Kesh'. I think it worth quoting the front page in full:

Jesus, our Saviour, was born in a cave at Bethlehem because there was no room for Mary and Joseph in the Inn. The cave was a stable for animals where their shepherds sheltered with them from rough weather in winter and the sun in summer. It was dark and dirty on that first Christmas night, a silent night, a holy night in a squalid cave.

The cells in H Block, Long Kesh, are like caves. The heavy door opens. A dark hole appears before one's eyes. Dirty floor. Filthy walls. A dark and dreary atmosphere. Figures squat on damp and foul greasy mattresses. Blankets draped round their waists and towels over their shoulders. They remind one of the cave at Bethlehem which was the only place men would allow their Lord and Saviour to come into the world. There is no room for 363 young Irishmen and 33 young women at the Inn of Decency and Human Rights.

Maybe Bethlehem has more meaning for the prisoners on protest than for the rich rulers in their homes of luxury. We pray that God will protect the prisoners and their families and bring about a just and peaceful solution of their problems caused in the Irish community by people from outside.

There were many, many such attacks on British policy. Some were motivated by malice, others by ignorance; but the majority, I would say, were inspired by a soft-headed romanticism which saw IRA butchery through rose-tinted lenses. In that perverted vision, any attempt by a democratic government to protect the lives and liberty of ordinary people had of course to be damned as brutality. It was contemptible stuff; but it was undeniably having an impact.

Naturally I wasn't passive under such onslaughts. Throughout the year and into 1979 I saw to it that our position was spelled out repeatedly, both in Britain and overseas. There were visits to the Maze by MPs, visits by journalists and members of the European Commission of Human Rights, pamphlets and television appearances by my colleagues and me; but it was an uphill struggle and would obviously remain so until we showed 'flexibility'.

But if anything I had become even more determined not to budge. My original reasons for continuing to deny the gangsters special category status remained as valid as ever. Besides, there had been a series of savage attacks on prison officers. On 27 November, Deputy Governor Miles of the Maze was shot dead by the IRA. In December there was a spate of letter-bomb attacks against other officers. The killings and maimings went on until the day I left office and beyond. I never forgot the advice Mr Miles had given me before he was murdered: any face-saving formula to end the dirty strike would be seen as an insult to the memory of his six colleagues in the prison service who had already been killed.

In this battle of wills there could be no compromise. Indeed the words of an intercepted letter which a Maze inmate had tried to smuggle out summed up the point: 'It is no longer a status issue. Whoever wins this has the war won.'

I simply wasn't going to give the IRA a victory. Nor was I about to forget the honest politicians like Gerry Fitt, who had risked everything to stand up to the terrorists. Whatever our personal differences. I had always admired his almost reckless courage. Unlike one or two English backbenchers on the Labour side, he had no shred of sympathy for the criminals locked up in the Maze. He flatly refused to support their protest, even though he knew the IRA would try to kill him in retaliation. His house in Belfast had already been attacked on occasion by mobs whipped up by Sinn Fein and the IRA and had recently been stoned again by supporters of the Maze prisoners. It was obvious to me that if we made concessions now, Gerry and every other Nationalist politician who agreed with him would be finished. We'd have pulled the rug from under the very people who could give the Catholic community a legitimate political voice. Of course I couldn't know then that Gerry would later turn against the government, with devastating consequences; but it wouldn't have made any difference to my attitude.

Meanwhile a second front had opened in the propaganda war. In June, Amnesty International published its report into the treatment of suspects at the Castleragh Interrogation Centre, seventy depressing pages claiming that RUC officers in plain clothes had inflicted physical and mental maltreatment on prisoners. Nineteen people said they had been beaten about the head with an open hand or closed fist; the same number complained of being subjected to physically exhausting procedures, such as being made to stand at a wall for long periods. There were allegations of choking, wrist bending, sleep deprivation, hooding and cigarette burns.

Some complained of humiliating treatment, such as being forced to remove their clothing. Three women said they'd been threatened with rape.

At least none of Amnesty's findings amounted to outright torture; but that was no comfort. Not only would the findings be greeted with ecstasy by the IRA as 'proof' of British brutality; if true, they suggested a pattern of mistreatment which was wholly unacceptable – not only because it was wrong in itself, but because it would call into question our entire strategy for getting terrorist suspects into court and behind bars.

Yet the more I studied what Amnesty had to say, the less persuaded I became that it had made a compelling case. In the first eleven months of 1977, after all, some 3,444 suspects had been picked up and interrogated. Yet the Amnesty team had spent just eight days in Northern Ireland.

In that period it examined seventy-eight complaints – a remarkably high figure for the limited time available, even if very low in relation to the total number of suspects questioned. How could Amnesty possibly have tested the allegations against the police with the rigour they merited?

My doubts deepened. Where was the solid evidence? Of the seventy-eight people who alleged mistreatment, thirty-nine could produce no medical corroboration at all. In twenty-six cases such corroboration was apparently available – but Amnesty was unable to question the individuals concerned. In fact the overwhelming bulk of the report seemed to me a catalogue of unsubstantiated allegations against unnamed police officers.

I wasn't impressed by that. Or by Amnesty's demand for a public inquiry into the methods of the RUC. That would certainly become a propaganda circus for the IRA; in fact I found it quite baffling that anybody in his sane senses should seriously expect named policemen to answer allegations made by anonymous complainants. That was one recommendation I would certainly reject.

Yet I obviously couldn't just shrug off the report. Whatever my doubts about this particular investigation, Amnesty International had a reputation which deserved respect. To suggest otherwise would only deepen the suspicion in which British policy was held. And anyway, if members of the RUC were indeed mistreating suspects in the way claimed, I wanted to know about it and put a stop to it. I wouldn't be part of any attempt at a cover-up.

There was only one way to sift truth from propaganda. I ordered an independent inquiry into the practices and procedures of the RUC. It would conduct its hearings in private, after which I would issue a public report. In this way we should be able to get at the facts without presenting the terrorists with a propaganda gift.

I wasn't in the least surprised to be attacked from all sides for that decision. Jim Kilfedder, the Unionist MP for North Down, claimed that the inquiry would play into the hands of the IRA and prolong its campaign of violence. On the other side of the argument, Patrick McClean, Chairman of the Northern Ireland Civil Rights Association, said he would approach other groups with a view to boycotting the inquiry. In Dublin, some ministers in the Irish government wasted no time in running to the newspapers to complain at my refusal to have public hearings. The *Irish Times* suggested that all I wanted was to ensure 'that disquiet be allayed for sufficient time to allow Labour to win the approaching general election'.

But I was sure I had done the right thing. The inquiry would be headed by Judge Harry Bennett QC, a lawyer of impeccable credentials. Sitting with him would be the Professor of Clinical Neurology at the University of London, John Marshall and Sir James Haughton, a former Chief Inspector of Constabulary. Anybody who seriously thought that such a team could be nobbled or bullied into producing a whitewash wasn't living on the same planet as me.

Meanwhile I'd been pressing Amnesty for more and better information. If that body had evidence that policemen had broken the law, I wanted it given in confidence to the Director of Public Prosecutions. But to my dismay, Amnesty refused, claiming that it had promised confidentiality to its informants.

Well, I understood that. What I didn't understand was Amnesty's flat refusal to go back to those informants to seek their permission. That seemed a shoddy attitude. This group was quite willing to blackguard members of a police force which had suffered appalling casualties over the years; but it seemed strangely reluctant to take any steps which might lead to its allegations being tested in a court of law. In fact, despite my best efforts, Amnesty didn't come up with usable evidence against a single police officer or substantiate a single one of its allegations. Not one.

In fact it wasn't until Judge Bennett finally reported, in March 1979, that some of the allegations against the RUC seemed to gain weight. He found evidence that suspects had been injured while in police custody, adding that whatever the precise explanations for such injuries, there was no doubt that they were not self-inflicted. It was a pointed reminder that however disciplined the RUC might be, there was still room for improvement.

But in general the Bennett inquiry took a much more realistic and grown-up view of policing in Northern Ireland than anything suggested by Amnesty. If the RUC wasn't perfect, it was still the case that existing police safeguards in Northern Ireland went further than in any other police force in the United Kingdom. And the report went on:

> Up to 31 December 1978, 117 members of the RUC, including the Reserve, had been killed and 3,251 injured. We have in the course of our inquiry seen abundant evidence of a co-ordinated and extensive campaign to discredit the police. We have been shown literature in which the intemperate nature of the language and the character of the illustrations leaves no doubt that it was designed to destroy the reputation of the police at home and abroad. This propaganda is principally concerned with allegations of ill treatment of prisoners in the course of their interrogation.

None of this, of course, would prevent Republican opinion believing the worst. In fact when Judge Bennett formally presented his report to me, he said that an improvement in interrogation standards was essential if public opinion in the Province – particularly on the Catholic side – was to swing in our direction. The key to this improvement was for senior RUC officers to be more willing to lean on their juniors when they overstepped the mark. The judge thought that in the short term, the RUC should put up with more failures to press cases to a conviction, in return for improved support from the nationalist community. This advice corresponded with what I had been hearing from senior policemen in Northern Ireland. Jack Hermon, who later became Chief Constable, had privately told my officials that he wanted a shift in the emphasis of intelligence work; there should be more effort in getting independent evidence and less reliance on confessions.

It was certainly clear to me that under the current system the police were wide open to allegations of brutality – allegations which if believed would make it far harder to tackle the IRA. So I was more than happy to accept the key recommendations in Judge Bennett's report, which included closed-circuit TVs in interrogation rooms, better access for prisoners to their solicitors, regular visits by medical officers to prisoners on a 24-hour basis and a better complaints procedure. Such safeguards might make life a little harder for interrogators, but they should improve the reputation of the RUC and take the wind out of the IRA's sails.

All in all, I thought the Bennett Inquiry an excellent piece of work, marred only by an extraordinary and distasteful row before its publication.

On 11 March – more than a week before I was due to make my statement in the Commons – the London Weekend TV programme *Weekend World* featured the police surgeon Dr Robert Irwin, who was explaining his continued concern about interrogation methods at Castlereagh. He spoke of 150 cases of ill-treatment he had witnessed and claimed a hard core of around twenty thuggish detectives was involved. The programme had obviously been in preparation for some time, and appeared to have been deliberately brought forward to pre-empt my statement to the Commons.

Dr Irwin's allegations had a huge impact. The story was of course seized on by the press and all the old stories about RUC 'brutality' were trotted out once again. There was genuine anger both on the Labour Left and in the United States. To make matters worse, it soon became clear that some newspapers had got hold of the critical passages in the Bennett report – lifted out of context – and were preparing to publish. It no longer mattered that the police had already cast serious doubts on Dr Irwin's allegations or that they had been strongly and openly contested by the Chief Constable. We had a public-relations disaster in the making. In the circumstances I had no option but to make my official statement much earlier than I'd intended, in an attempt to regain the initiative.

Luck wasn't with me. On the very morning I was due to speak, the *Daily Telegraph* published a sensational claim – said to be based on official sources – that Dr Irwin's judgement had been adversely affected because his wife had allegedly been raped by two former members of the RUC.

I knew that the report meant trouble as soon as I saw it. It appeared that somebody was trying to smear Dr Irwin in the crudest way possible; and clearly the finger of suspicion would be pointed at my department or the RUC. So I immediately ordered the most urgent inquiries to be made into any possible source for the story. By the time I stood up in the House that afternoon I had been assured that there were no traces of Northern Ireland office involvement.

That didn't satisfy Gerry Fitt. As soon as the Speaker called me to make my statement, he intervened on a point of order to complain about 'a vicious smear' and demanding an emergency debate. Kevin McNamara, the Labour Member for Hull, joined in with the comment that the affair 'has implications for the Northern Ireland Office which throw doubt upon the quality of what we may hear later'. It was the beginning of quite a bumpy ride. Though the Bennett report was received well and my acceptance of it welcomed, there was an unmistakable undercurrent of suspicion that the Northern Ireland Office had been playing dirty tricks. Whoever planted that nasty little story in the *Telegraph* had done me no favours at all; but we never managed to track the culprit down.

I received the impression later on, after conversations with some of my advisers, that Dr Irwin had in fact been intimidated by the Provisional IRA.

Still, there was in the end a relatively happy outcome. On 28 March, in one of my last engagements as Secretary of State, I had a meeting with the Association of Forensic and Police Surgeons, among whom was Dr Irwin. In the circumstances the atmosphere was surpisingly harmonious; and the Association made it clear that it would be closely involved with the way the government implemented the Bennett report. At least some fences had been mended.

And we had succeeded in blunting the edge of Republican propaganda. From that point on, allegations of police brutality never had quite the same impact. How could they, when so many scrupulous safeguards were in place? It wasn't until the hunger strikes of 1981, when IRA prisoners began starving themselves to death, that the issue of British 'cruelty' again became such a prominent feature of terrorist mythology.

Meanwhile I had never lost sight of the need to confront terrorism by other means. However necessary the public-relations battle, however important it was to support the police and use every weapon the law allowed to harry the gunmen and bombers, I knew it wasn't enough. The violence might be the work of a few hundred gangsters; but it was encouraged and sustained by unemployment, poverty and despair. People were growing from youth to adulthood in the mean ghettos of Northern Ireland without hope of a job, a decent house, a proper holiday, a car or any of the comforts which the majority on the mainland had learned to take for granted. There were worse pockets of hardship in Belfast, Londonderry and a dozen other towns than anything I'd seen in my native Barnsley since the hungry Thirties.

In 1978, unemployment throughout the United Kingdom averaged 5.7 per cent. In Northern Ireland it stood at 11 per cent; but that statistic concealed the worst of it. In some areas, like Catholic West Belfast, somewhere between 35 and 40 per cent of all adult men were without a job. Youth unemployment stood at 50 per cent. Up to 30 per cent of all households were badly overcrowded; and in some parts up to 90 per cent of all properties lacked basic amenities. Here was the pool of misery on which the IRA could draw. Here was where it found its recruits, its safe houses and its political support. Here was where it could pose as a defender of the nationalist cause. The terrorists needed unhappiness and hopelessness as fish need water.

Something had to be done about it. Not just because it was morally wrong that our fellow citizens should live out their lives on the scrapheap, but because the heaviest blow we could inflict on the Provisionals would be to bring jobs, hope and self-respect to the ghettos.

It was easier said than done. The chances of a political settlement in the Province were in my view nil, for the moment at least. I'd had many meetings with the individual constitutional parties, but had never felt that they were ready or seriously willing to co-operate with each other for the common good. The collapse of the Sunningdale Agreement in 1974 was fresh in my mind. Sinn Fein meanwhile remained obdurately beyond the pale, actively supporting and applauding every act of murder and mayhem by its friends in the IRA. Though I wouldn't rule out talks with that party – a wise politician never says never – there didn't seem much point. Sinn Fein's political support at the time was derisory, after all.

If progress was to be made, it seemed to me, it had to start on the basis of stability. That not only meant reducing the level of terrorism, but somehow reviving the economy of Northern Ireland. The Troubles had choked off inward investment and even with a generous package of incentives it was difficult to persuade firms to come in. Nevertheless in 1978 and 1979 we did manage to attract seven American companies to Northern Ireland, bringing job prospects for 4,100 people.

Among those firms was a Chicago-based manufacturer, the DeLorean Motor Company. As far as I was concerned, our success in this deal was a tremendous achievement, something to be celebrated without reservation. It involved building a vast new factory on a greenfield site which would provide jobs for 2,500 people from West Belfast. For the first time in years, the people of that beleaguered area had a chance to be trained and employed, earn themselves a decent living and take pride in themselves. Moreover, they would be producing a futuristic, gull-winged sports car which I hoped and believed would spread the reputation of Northern Ireland as a centre of engineering excellence. Bringing John DeLorean to the Province promised to be one of the best things I ever did; and it is still among the most bitter disappointments of my life that the whole project would one day be damned by the Commons Public Accounts Committee as 'one of the gravest cases of the misuse of public resources to come before us for many years'.

Well, there was a misuse of public resources right enough. There was also a lamentable failure of the imagination too. But neither of those things came from my department or from the Labour government.

I was enthusiastic for the deal from the very beginning. I knew that DeLorean was in detailed negotiations with both Puerto Rico and the Republic of Ireland to find a location for his new plant, but I was determined to get it for Ulster if I could. John DeLorean had been in charge of the Chevrolet division of General Motors. He had an impressive track record and when he left the company he'd taken a number of senior managers with him to start his own firm. He struck me as just the kind of entrepreneur we needed in the Province, provided the financing could be arranged.

Throughout June and July 1978 my Department engaged in a whole series of hectic negotiations. We knew the risks, just as we knew the need for a rapid decision. We were dealing with a small, aggressive and ambitious American company which was already half committed to locating in Puerto Rico. There were some doubts about whether sufficient private finance would be forthcoming. My own Department of Commerce admitted that it was unable to take a realistic view of the project's viability in the limited time available. It regarded DeLorean as a high-risk but potentially very rewarding project which in the end would have to be decided not just on the grounds of pure economics but on the basis of a political judgement too. But my key advisers believed that the proposed new factory would meet its production targets, even if there was less certainty about market penetration. Would the new car really sell in large numbers in the United States?

Such concerns began to multiply. We commissioned an American firm of business consultants, McKinsey's, to examine the project and its preliminary report described the DeLorean Motor Company's balance-sheet projections as 'ambitious – even unrealistic'. In subsequent discussions with my officials, McKinsey's softened its tone somewhat, but remained extremely cautious. Meanwhile, the Chief Secretary to the Treasury, Joel Barnet was pressing for more private money to be invested in the project. And Edmund Dell, the Trade Secretary was worried whether the Americans would impose crippling import duties on the new car.

One by one, the worst of the doubts were overcome. Right at the start of our negotiations a lurid series of articles had appeared in the *New York Times* about the Troubles in Northern Ireland, upsetting potential investors. So my deputy, Don Concannon, flew to America to beat the drum for the Province and explain the business opportunities on offer. Meanwhile I got the Cabinet Office to tip off key Irish–Americans like Senator Ted Kennedy and Speaker Tip O'Neill about the possibility of DeLorean coming to the Province; through such contacts it became clear that the new car could be imported into the States without suffering heavy customs duties. While this was going on, a team of my officials was in intensive discussions with DeLorean to ensure that it could deliver what it promised. I in turn was pressing for more private investment to balance the public funds which would be committed to the project. As it turned, out, no fewer than 120 investors each subscribed a minimum of $150,000 and 206 car dealers entered a sales agreement with DeLorean to purchase 26,000 cars over two years.

Frantic activity; but we were getting there. By now the Department of Commerce and the Northern Ireland Development Association were backing the project, though adding that it was primarily a political decision. Top consultancy advice had been obtained which pointed out the risks but did not warn us off. The expert legal and political advice from the United States was that the new car could be imported without serious problems. So when a message came from Jim Callaghan that the whole project would now have to go before the Cabinet's Economic and Industry Committee, I was ready.

There were thirteen ministers present when the EIC met on 26 July, with the Trade and Industry Secretary Eric Varley in the chair. Not one voice was raised in opposition to my going ahead with the scheme. Though it wasn't a copper-bottomed investment, the most serious of the objections had been met. I concluded the deal on 28 July and made the announcement on 3 August 1978. I believed then that I had won a glittering prize. In the words of one trade union official, 'The factory would do more to destroy the IRA than deploying the entire British Army.'

So it would have. So it should have. What happened afterwards with the collapse of the company in recriminations and bitterness was a tragedy for the people of Northern Ireland.

What went wrong? One answer came out in a Manhattan courtroom in March 1998, when the accountancy firm Arthur Andersen was orderer to pay $46 million to creditors and investors in the DeLorean plant.

Plaintiffs in the case accused DeLorean of siphoning off millions of dollars into a front Panamanian company set up by two of his associates in 1978. The jury found that Arthur Andersen had been negligent and in breach of contract for giving DeLorean a clean bill of financial health, despite evidence of possible fraud.

Clearly, it appears that there was some shady dealing right from the beginning, but even so, the final disaster could have been avoided. I left office long before DeLorean's factory was built. By the end of April 1979, only £17.7 million of public money had been handed over. The really big spending came as the project got into its stride – something, unfortunately, which coincided with a change of government. My successors as Northern Ireland Secretary, Humphrey Atkins and Jim Prior, gave further loans to the project. But the problem was that they – or more accurately their boss, Margaret Thatcher – didn't really believe in industrial intervention and therefore failed to ensure that the money was controlled and spent carefully. They seemed lethargic. Certainly there was none of the detailed, hands-on supervision which Don Concannon and I would have insisted on. I believe that was their fatal mistake.

When recession began to bite and the prospects for DeLorean sales started to wane, the Tories came close to panic. They saw only the financial black hole which their own lack of involvement had helped create. They lacked the political will to rescue the plant and the future of all the people who so desperately needed the hope it offered. For a mere £20 million the DeLorean company could have been financially restructured, production adjusted to take account of the changed economic outlook and new market opportunities explored. One year's savings on unemployment benefits together with the tax revenue generated by DeLorean could have saved the company and at the same time helped to tackle the terrible social deprivation in West Belfast. If only a tiny percentage of the public money poured into the British motor industry had been committed to Northern Ireland's fledgling car plant, it would certainly have survived. What happened was a tragedy created not just by John DeLorean and his associates but by a lack of political will among Tory ministers.

Do I accept any responsibility at all for the débâcle? Only to this extent. The original master agreement which Don Concannon and I concluded could certainly have had tighter safeguards. We were determined to secure the deal. But then, we were equally determined to watch over the project carefully. We expected to be involved at every stage of its development. With that kind of supervision, cash couldn't have been squandered behind our backs for very long. It was only later, when we had left office, that John DeLorean came back to ask for yet more aid.

There were several occasions then when Tory ministers could have insisted on altering the master agreement to include more effective monitoring of the spending. They didn't take those opportunities.

That is my lasting regret. Had Don and I still been in Northern Ireland when the factory was built and the product launched we would have kept a much tighter grip, because the project mattered passionately to both of us and we had the political will to make it succeed. I believe DeLorean motor cars would be coming off the production line in West Belfast to this day if we'd only had another couple of years' grace. But the election denied us those years and denied thousands of people – people who were universally acknowledged to have been a superb workforce – their best hope of a decent future.

It's always seemed to me a particularly bitter irony that the advent of the Tories and Thatcherism was hastened by the man whose own people had so much to lose from the new Government: the SDLP Member for West Belfast, Gerry Fitt.

At that time, Labour had no overall parliamentary majority and we had to rely for survival on whatever support we could find from the minority parties. It never was a comfortable position; and after the adverse results of two devolution referenda in Scotland and Wales it became even trickier. Both the Welsh and Scottish Nationalists were bitterly disappointed at the way things had turned out; and though the outcome certainly wasn't our fault, they were ready to turn on us the moment the opportunity presented itself. That couldn't be long delayed. Margaret Thatcher had the scent of victory in her nostrils. Labour's reputation for being able to handle the unions was taking a terrible battering with the Winter of Discontent. Even Jim Callaghan's formidable skills couldn't overcome the raging militancy which had so much of industry in its grip. With picket lines forming outside hospitals, rubbish piled in rotting heaps and the dead unburied because gravediggers were on strike, I thought our chances of winning a general election were slim. Evidently Thatcher thought so too. On 28 March 1979, she pounced, with a motion of no confidence in the government.

Our parliamentary position was desperate. Not only were the Tories ranged against us, but at least eight of the Ulster Unionists too, not to mention the Liberals and the Scottish and Welsh Nationalists. On top of that, one of our own backbenchers, Alfred Broughton, was desperately ill. It would have been theoretically possible to drag him in by ambulance from his sickbed to be nodded through; but there is some decency in politics, even when the situation is critical. Jim wasn't going to save himself at the expense of a dying man. So when all the frantic arithmetic had been done, it was clear that his future and the fate of the entire government would depend on the votes of two Irish members: Gerry Fitt and the seldom-seen (and never heard) Independent MP for Fermanagh and South Tyrone, Frank Maguire.

None of us had much faith in Frank. He was a publican by trade, an amiable boozer whose contribution in Parliament was roughly nil. That he'd managed to get himself elected at all was a mystery. Still, a vote's a vote. Though the word was that he would only turn up in order to abstain in person, there was certainly some possibility that in the end he would support the government. So the party whips saw to it that he was cosseted, flattered and given a drink in the hope of persuading him to our side.

That left Gerry Fitt, a far more formidable and forceful character. He had been rock solid in our support many times before, proudly proclaimed himself a socialist and would certainly have noted that most Ulster Unionists were going with the Tories. All that gave us some hope that he might ride to our rescue once again. Certainly many Labour Members spent that day trying to persuade him.

But Gerry had been growing increasingly unhappy with the government. The previous year, an all-party Speaker's conference had recommended an increase in the number of Northern Ireland seats, since the Province was heavily under-represented in Parliament. But Gerry believed that a change would only benefit the Unionists and resented the fact that the government was willing to contemplate such a change. He was equally bitter about the Bennett Report, which he claimed revealed that men had been brutally 'ill-treated' in the holding centres in Northern Ireland.

His speech that night in a tense, packed House was a *tour de force*. It all came pouring out; his anger over the decision to increase the number of Ulster seats, his conviction that the Bennett report revealed a scandal comparable with Watergate, even his frankly bizarre belief that I and the government hadn't stood up to Unionist extremists as we should have done. Evidently he had already forgotten about Paisley's failed strike.

'Some journalists and others,' he declared, 'have said that there is a personality conflict between the present Secretary of State for Northern Ireland and me. That is totally untrue. The Right Honourable gentleman is only implementing Labour Government policies in Northern Ireland. If I criticize him, I criticize this government.' I supposed I could take a little personal comfort in that, but not for long. A couple of minutes later he really let fly.

If there is a Conservative government I warn them not to get carried away with the belief that somewhere around the corner there is a military solution. Unfortunately, that is the tune we have heard from the Secretary of State for Northern Ireland. Every Monday morning at ten o'clock he sees the Chief Constable. Every Monday at 1 p.m. we hear on the news that so many IRA men have been caught and so many have been sent to jail. Every Monday the Secretary of State looks for a military solution. But there will be Mondays and Mondays and more Mondays when there will be no military solution and there will be no solution at all until we start to grapple with the political problem of Northern Ireland.

Powerful stuff. There was no gainsaying the impact of what Gerry was saying, though I disagreed with every single word. Of course there wasn't a military solution pure and simple; I'd never pretended there was. But to achieve any hope of agreement in the Province there had to be a measure of stability, which is why I had used all the constitutional means at my disposal – and used them to the limit – to harrass the IRA and cause it as many problems as possible. Hope had to be brought to the ghettos too, which is why I had put such effort into new factories and new jobs, especially in Catholic areas such as West Belfast. I couldn't turn to look at Gerry. I'd only have scowled at him. Did he really expect his constituents to do better under the Thatcherite free market than under Labour?

It was clear by now that there was no chance of winning his support in the crucial vote. Everything depended on the way Frank Maguire would jump. I could only hope that the whips had jollied him into a co-operative mood. But if that was ever a serious possibility, it was blown apart by Gerry's next words.

The Honourable Member for Fermanagh and South Tyrone – I cannot really call him my honourable friend – is very rarely in this House and has yet to make his maiden speech. On all the Northern Ireland issues we have had in recent months – the Bennett report, the Prevention of Terrorism Bill, the Bill on the redistribution of seats – we would have liked to have had the benefit of his opinions. We would have liked to hear whether he accepted or rejected the Government's view on such matters. But he did not appear when such issues were discussed. There is a rumour circulating today – and if it is true it is despicable – that he is somewhere within the building talking to someone from the government whips' office. He cannot talk to me, in case I persuade him to do as I am doing tonight. I shall be watching very carefully, and if he goes through the Government lobby tonight it will be in opposition to everything that his constituents sent him here to do. Such an action would be completely dishonest and he has not given us the benefit of his opinion or his vote on any of the issues that affect Northern Ireland. If this government has to depend on such a representative to get support tonight, it is a very sad day for the Labour Party and the Labour government. It is terrible to think that they have descended to such a level.

It was terribly wrong-headed stuff. In view of what happened afterwards in Northern Ireland and the rest of the United Kingdom, it was tragic too. But I have to admit that it was a great parliamentary speech. There was no way now that Frank Maguire would support us. It would take a better man than he to brave Gerry's scorn. He was publicly shaming Maguire into abstaining.

Ans so it proved. When the vote was announced, the Liberals, the Welsh Nationalists, the Scottish Nationalists and eight Ulster Unionists trooped into the division lobbies with the Tories. Gerry Fitt abstained. So did Frank Maguire. We lost the motion of confidence by 311 votes to 310. If either one of them had voted, the government would have survived – and then been able to choose its own timing for the general election.

Jim Callaghan stood to face the explosion of Tory cheers.

Now that the House of Commons has declared itself, we shall take our case to the country. Tomorrow I shall propose to Her Majesty that Parliament be dissolved as soon as essential business can be cleared up and I shall then announce as soon as may be – and that will be as soon as possible – the date of dissolution, the date of the election and the date of meeting of the new Parliament.

It was over. I had no great expectation that Labour could win. The public mood had moved against us and barring something totally unexpected the country was about to be led by its first woman prime minister.

Would it have made a difference if I had got on better with Gerry Fitt, if I'd flattered his opinions? Maybe it would. Maybe the government would have been able to go into an election on a date of its own choosing. Who can say what might have happened then?

But for all that, I won't apologize for what I did in Northern Ireland. Nor would I change my approach if I had my time all over again. These figures for deaths and injuries may explain why. I served in the Province from September 1976 until May 1979.

	Deaths	Injuries
1976	297	2,729
1977	112	1,387
1978	81	985
1979	113	975

It is difficult to grasp the pain and grief behind those figures; but at least the trend was beginning to come down. I wanted to carry on if I could, harrying the terrorists until their ability to kill and destroy was reduced still further. But the voters seemed likely to remove Labour from office. I had at least the consolation of knowing that my probable successor would be Airey Neave. He was a good man, with robust views about the IRA. I had no doubt that he would do an excellent job in Northern Ireland.

I was in my office at Stormont that dreadful day, Friday 30 March. Though the country was gearing up for the general election, the business of government still had to go on. In fact I had so much on my plate that I wasn't due to leave the Province until that evening.

My paperwork was interrupted by an urgent message from the House of Commons. It appeared that my Parliamentary Private Secretary, Alan Lee Williams, had been killed in a terrorist attack within the precincts of Westminster. I just sat there, stunned. I had often been brought news of murders, of course; but never before when the victim was a friend and close political colleague. People were crowding into the room, but I couldn't take in what they ware saying. Then another message was thrust in front of me. The victim wasn't Alan after all, but another MP as yet unidentified. The poor man had been driving his car up the ramp from the underground car park at the Commons when a bomb had exploded. The blast was so powerful that the body was beyond recognition.

All I could do was wait for further news, trying not to think of who the murdered man might be. Friend or enemy, party colleague or political opponent, the petty distinctions we make for ourselves no longer mattered. A human being was dead, somebody's husband, somebody's father, murdered because he happened to be a democratically elected politician. It was a long, miserable wait before we learned that the victim was my Tory opposite number, Airey Neave.

I was terribly sad. Airey had worked with me on a bipartisan basis and was always solidly supportive of what I was trying to do. In private, he had used very tough language about the Provisional IRA and I'd been confident that he would maintain the pressure on the terrorists if and when he took over my job. Now he was dead – killed not as it turned out by the Provisionals, but by a pseudo-Marxist breakaway gang, the Irish National Liberation Army (INLA).

Perhaps it was his own undoubted courage which gave the murderers their chance. Airey's wartime exploits had become the stuff of legend and I suspect he wasn't the kind of man who would welcome round-the-clock protection wherever he went. I know he had guards in his Abingdon constituency and whenever he visited Northern Ireland; but when in London he did without them.

That was his tragic mistake. There was nobody watching when his killers attached a trembler bomb to the underside of his car, together with a timing device which would make it active. He could have driven anywhere that day; through crowded London streets, to his constituency, anywhere at all. In the event, he went and parked underground at the Commons. While he was away, the timer activated the bomb. The slightest movement now might trigger it off. It exploded as he drove up the incline to the surface.

In the perverted minds of the terrorists, that murder of a decent and honourable man certainly counted as a triumph. They would be encouraged now to seek other triumphs with attacks on public figures, which made it all the more important that protection for possible targets should be stepped up. We could no longer make it easy for the gunmen and the bombers. In future, those of us most at risk would have to accept armed guards, whatever the inconvenience; but even in the shock of Airey's death, I never imagined that I would still be a target for assassination, so many years on.

15 Tearing Ourselves to Pieces

Oddly enough, it wasn't the news that I had been targeted for assassination which made the 1979 election and its aftermath such a grim experience. I'd grown used to a certain level of threat and had been looked after by protection officers ever since I'd been Secretary of State for Defence. A few months more – maybe even a year or two – in the presence of armed guards was a burden I could accept. What had happened to Airey Neave couldn't be forgotten; and a well-attended 'Stuff Mason' march arranged by Sinn Fein in February suggested that I would stay high on the IRA hit-list for some time to come.

What depressed me far more was the state to which the Labour Party was being reduced. The Winter of Discontent had exposed a side of the movement I'd never thought to see: a bullying, threatening use of union power which didn't scruple to harrass people when they were at their weakest and most vulnerable, including hospital patients and families mourning their loved ones. On top of that, the Left in Parliament, led by Tony Benn under the banner of the Labour Co-Ordinating Committee, had been displaying the kind of intolerance we hadn't seen since the heyday of the Bevanites. It wasn't a surprise to me when Margaret Thatcher and the Tories wiped the floor with us. On election day we suffered the biggest adverse swing recorded against a government since the war. And Labour's 37 per cent of the vote was the lowest we had achieved since 1931.

I took some consolation from my 22,000 majority in Barnsley, but not much. What was happening in my own constituency under the malign influence of Arthur Scargill was even worse than the blight suffered by the party nationally. For a year and more before the election he'd been building up Labour's membership in his native Worsborough ward, giving himself an increasingly powerful voice on the constituency General Management Committee. Increasingly at party meetings I had begun to spot people I knew to be members of the Trotskyite Militant Tendency or former members of the Marxist Socialist Workers' Party, most of them now dancing to Scargill's tune. Worse still from my point of view, he'd started using his position as President of the Yorkshire NUM to ensure even more influence on the GMC by paying his supporters.

There was nothing illegal or unconstitutional about it. Ward delegates are of course never paid for attending party meetings. But delegates who happened to be members of the NUM could be paid for attending a union caucus held immediately before the GMC in the same building. So every month, delegates from the mines in the constituency would assemble under Scargill's chairmanship to go through the agenda for the subsequent Labour Party meeting. Then they would all troop into the GMC, well instructed on how to vote on every issue coming up. It could be a nice little earner. Under the NUM's Rule 74, everyone attending a caucus meeting was entitled to expenses of around £4. Anyone who missed a shift down the pit in order to attend could claim up to £20. The man doling out the cash was Scargill's factotum, Eric Illsley, who later became my successor as MP for Barnsley.

Not surprisingly, Scargill's influence in the constituency had been growing by leaps and bounds. Every month at the beginning of party meetings, NUM delegates would troop in *en masse*, sitting in a block at the back of the hall. All except for Scargill. He would take his place at the front, a convenient spot from which to move resolutions calling for a unilateral defence policy, withdrawal from the Common Market, import controls, all the usual left-wing stuff. Invariably his supporters at the back would raise their hands to vote precisely as he wanted. With a few honourable exceptions, they were puppets, their opinions and votes bought and paid for. It was a grotesque misuse of a system originally intended to allow working men the opportunity to take an active part in politics. Of course it caused resentment among 'ordinary' party members. My friend and ally Ron Fisher – later deposed as party chairman in favour of a Scargill placeman – described it as 'political prostitution'.

That was no exaggeration, as I discovered during the election campaign with a quite extraordinary act of treachery against the party.

Right from the beginning, I'd been aware that Irish republicans were planning a stunt. Their intention was to put up a candidate against me for propaganda purposes; and to this end a group calling itself Troops Out of Ireland, backed by the Socialist Workers' Party, submitted the name of one Brendan Gallagher. This man had a son who had been convicted of terrorism who was currently serving his sentence in the Maze. As it happened, Gallagher junior had been arrested, tried, found guilty and sent to prison during my time in Northern Ireland.

Well, Gallagher's candidacy was no great concern in itself. I certainly wouldn't give him any publicity by appearing with him on a public platform. It was obvious he'd lose his deposit and in fact he ended up with 638 votes. But what genuinely shocked me was that his nomination paper was signed by two members of Barnsley Labour Party, Michael Clapham and someone rather inappropriately called Dan Paisley.

The political offence could not be more serious. In Labour circles, the one unforgivable sin is to lend support to another party during an election. The penalty is virtually automatic: expulsion. On this issue there had never been any difference in view between Left and Right. Party discipline absolutely has to be upheld.

And so it proved for the hapless Paisley. Once the election was out of the way, he was summoned to appear before the next party meeting to explain himself. Clapham was summoned too, but sent apologies as he was attending an NUM conference – as indeed were Arthur Scargill and other miners' delegates. For once the 'political prostitutes' weren't in control. Paisley made a speech attempting to justify himself, answered a few questions and was then formally expelled, by a majority of two to one.

It was what happened next time which revealed how deeply the rot had set in. The following month, Clapham appeared for his own drumhead court-martial, but now the Scargill caucus was back in full strength. It made all the difference. In spite of his undeniable guilt – and I still have a copy of the nomination paper with Clapham's signature on it – the man escaped the penalty which should have been inevitable. He was reprieved and allowed to stay a party member as though his act of treachery had never taken place. Today Michael Clapham sits as Member of Parliament for Barnsley West in Tony Blair's New Labour Party.

I like to think of myself as quite a resilient character, always capable of bouncing back. But this time I couldn't entirely shake off my gloom. Events in Barnsley were making a mockery both of the party rules and the principles in which I believed. And I wasn't particularly happy at Westminster either. After the election, Jim Callaghan had asked me to take on the job of Shadow Agriculture Minister, not a post I wanted. Though I love the countryside and must have spent hundreds if not thousands of hours walking the hills and fishing in remote streams and lakes for trout or salmon, the business of farming doesn't appeal. Try as I might, I can't get excited about sheepmeat regimes, fatstock prices and the vagaries of the green pound. So I had tried to resist Jim's offer. Couldn't I take on the Foreign Office portfolio instead, even as deputy? But I was in a weak position. I'd done indifferently in the elections for the Shadow Cabinet coming in about tenth. Jim had other obligations to honour. In the end I accepted, trying not to be grudging about it. But though I quite enjoyed parts of my new job, such as visits to agricultural shows (always with a couple of armed protection officers in tow), it never gave me real satisfaction.

In the wider party meanwhile, things were going from bad to worse. Labour's conference in October was a nightmare, with Tony Benn and his friends railing at Jim Callaghan and Denis Healey for losing to Margaret Thatcher. In their view, the Winter of Discontent only happened because the party leadership had ignored conference and TUC Congress decisions. It wasn't just the Labour Co-Ordinating Committee which peddled this dishonest line; the wider Left proclaimed it too. People like Harold Wilson and Jim Callaghan, men who had served the party honourably and well all their adult lives, were now routinely denounced as traitors. Members of Parliament too were held up to hatred and contempt. The enclosure in which we sat in the conference hall became a daily target for insults and abuse. I wasn't alone in thinking that it resembled the dock at Nuremburg. The Labour Party seemed to be having a collective nervous breakdown.

In all this hysteria there wasn't the slightest hope that anything sane or sensible would emerge. This was the conference in which the likes of Benn and Scargill were fêted as heroes, while better men than them by far were scorned. If anyone these days complains about Tony Blair's stage management, they should remember the venomous shambles of the 1979 conference and those which followed. This was when decisions were taken which would help keep Labour out of power for nearly a generation: the agreement that the NEC should control future election manifestos and that there should be compulsory reselection of MPs. The 1980 conference went further still, enthusiastically endorsing the reselection of MPs and deciding to elect the party leader on a wider franchise, details of which were to be agreed at a special conference at Wembley in January 1981.

All this was bad news for me. By 1980, Arthur Scargill controlled 110 of the 185 delegates to the Barnsley GMC. His supporters now occupied every single constituency office. I was as sure as could be that he would move on to dump me as the Member of Parliament if he could; and thanks to the influence of the rabid Left in the party nationally, he now had every opportunity. Why not? I'd seen him off to humiliating defeat years before, when he tried to stir up trouble for me with the NUM. I'd seen him off again when he tried to dictate the way I should vote over Europe. His loathing for me was obvious. Already he was taking petty revenge. Sometimes, for example, I would be unable to deliver my monthly parliamentary report because the GMC devoted so much time to other business that the meeting dragged on past nine o'clock. Under party rules, I couldn't then take the platform. But then, Scargill hated debate, unless he could control the outcome. He even stopped discussion of how the Barnsley delegate should vote at Labour's 1980 Conference. In every previous year, the constituency had argued over the conference agenda point by point. Not this time. Scargill suddenly moved that the Barnsley delegate should simply vote in accordance with recommendations put forward by the left-wing Campaign for Labour Democracy – and needless to say his puppets at the back of the hall all put their hands up in agreement.

I couldn't conceal my disgust. Scargill was behaving like a Communist dictator. But then, I shouldn't have been surprised. He had a hatred of anybody who tried to stand up to him. It couldn't be too long before he came gunning for me.

The attack came when Jim Callaghan announced his resignation as party leader, shortly after the 1980 conference. For me, that decision was another blow. I'd always liked and admired Jim; I thought nobody could be better qualified to hold the party together in the hard times ahead. Still, I couldn't blame him. He'd wanted to go immediately after the Election defeat, only to be told that the Parliamentary Labour Party was ready to re-elect him unanimously. Since then, he'd been regularly accused of betrayal by people who weren't fit to tie his shoelaces. Small wonder he didn't feel any great temptation to hang on.

And so we were plunged into a leadership election, the last that would ever take place under the old system, in which only MPs voted. There were four candidates: Michael Foot, Denis Healey, John Silkin and Peter Shore. For me, there simply wasn't a choice. Peter Shore was an old-fashioned patriot, but his bitter opposition to Britain's involvement in the European Community ruled him out as far as I was concerned. I had little in common with John Silkin, a member of the sensible soft Left. Michael Foot, that veteran dissenter and unilateralist wasn't an option either. So it had to be Denis, a man with whom I had had many differences but a brilliant mind, a brave politician and someone who generally spoke my language.

Scargill, needless to say, knew exactly which way I would jump and didn't waste a moment before trying to put me – and others of my persuasion – on the spot. On 27 October, a week before the first leadership ballot, he chaired a meeting of the Yorkshire Miners' Council which passed an emergency resolution calling on all mining MPs to support Michael Foot. It went further. NUM delegates to every Labour constituency in the county were told to make sure that GMCs held special meetings 'in order to win support for Mr Foot'. And the clincher came at the end: 'This Area Council makes it clear that any mining MP who acts contrary to the policy of his GMC on this issue cannot expect the support of the union in any future reselection process.' The resolution was passed overwhelmingly, only eight people daring to vote against.

So there it was, Scargill had obviously learned nothing from his previous attempt to bully MPs, when he had tried and failed to force us into voting his way over Europe. Now he was at it again. He'd even ensured that we couldn't take refuge in the secrecy of the ballot. Here's how the Yorkshire Area Council put it: 'In order that there should be no misunderstandings, we should ask the MP to show the constituency party officials the way in which his vote is cast.'

Four days later, my own Barnsley GMC echoed the same message, in precisely the same words, by 92 votes to 22. I had to do as I was told. Or else.

But there would be no 'misunderstandings' as far as I was concerned. I wouldn't vote for Foot and I'd be blowed if I showed my ballot paper to Scargill and his caucus.

So I publicly stated:

> I will not submit to Arthur Scargill's dictates, no matter what he threatens to do. My honour, principles and personal conscience will never allow me to bend before intimidation and threats. He is using his position as President of the Yorkshire Miners to browbeat MPs into a cowed submission to his known political views. But he isn't succeeding. Men of mettle do not kowtow.

Of course the Left didn't like it. Norman West, Chairman of Barnsley Labour Party said of me: 'He must make up his mind to conform.' A letter in the local paper, obviously from one of Scargill's cronies, demanded that I should 'compromise'. In fact the pressure building up against me was so great that my old friend Geoff Lofthouse, MP for Pontefract, publicly urged more people in Barnsley to join the Labour Party and 'turn back this ruthless tide'. It was brave of Geoff to stick his head above the parapet, but it would take time to stop the Scargill juggernaut; and time was something I didn't have. Still, if I was going to be dumped by the Left – as seemed highly likely – at least I'd go out with a bang.

In the event, Denis Healey lost the leadership battle by the narrowest of margins, 139 to 129. I couldn't have been more disappointed, even though Michael Foot was a superb orator and an attractive human being. He'd proven his loyalty as one of Jim Callaghan's most valued ministers, but his appeal to the wider country was minimal. One poll showed that he had only 19 per cent support among the voters, compared with 75 per cent for Healey. In fact Denis was far more popular in the country than the Tory leader, Margaret Thatcher. It seemed crazy to saddle ourselves with a man who had such slight public appeal; but then, my parliamentary colleagues had been stunned by the hatred showered on them at the last party conference. Many of them were under severe pressure from the Left in their own constituencies. Perhaps they thought a Foot leadership would bring them a quieter life. Or maybe they thought a man in his late sixties would be just a caretaker leader.

I wasn't particularly surprised when Michael asked me to stay on as Shadow Agriculture Minister. Obviously he needed balance in his parliamentary team. But though I was happy enough to stay on for a bit, I couldn't help feeling that the political outlook was bleak. That mood wasn't helped by Labour's special conference at Wembley in the New Year. Here was the Left rampant and triumphant in all its viciousness. Once again, anybody who dared to take a moderate line was denounced as a class traitor. The atmosphere was so poisonous that Harold Wilson felt moved to describe the new breed of young Labour activists as 'fascists'.

I was desperately depressed to see the party I had always associated with brotherhood, justice and comradeship taken over by this mob. It was a horrible experience, made worse when the Left so easily won the vital decision. In future leadership elections, 40 per cent of the votes would be cast by the unions – which were still bitterly unpopular with the voters after the Winter of Discontent – 30 per cent by the constituency parties, now heavily influenced by the Left, and 30 per cent by Labour MPs. It was arguably the most disatrous single decision ever taken by a Labour conference. We never won an election with a leader elected under this harebrained system. It was a gift to the Tories and a betrayal of our own people.

To some on the Right of the party it was the last straw. Later that week, the so-called Gang of Four, Roy Jenkins, David Owen, Shirley Williams and Bill Rodgers issued their Limehouse Declaration and formed the Social Democratic Party. It was a disastrous split in the Labour ranks, involving some of the best-known names in the party. Opinion polls in March showed the new SDP with a formidable rating of 30 per cent.

I'd been approached to see if I would consider joining. No doubt members of the Gang thought my views on NATO, Europe and the Left chimed in nicely with theirs. They also lacked a trade unionist in their number. But I turned them down flat. I had some time for Bill Rodgers, who had once been my deputy at Defence, but the others I couldn't abide. I'd always found Jenkins snobbish, David Owen was extraordinarily arrogant. And I never shared Harold Wilson's view that Shirley Williams was a potential leader of the party. Moreover I despised what they were doing. They were running away instead of standing and fighting their corner. They were abandoning the great mass of honest, decent Labour supporters to the likes of Scargill and Benn. I made my feelings plain in a speech urging my fellow MPs to 'stand fast'.

Back in Barnsley, meanwhile, the atmosphere was growing ever more venomous, to the extent that Scargill's cronies began making life as difficult as possible for my protection team. At the regular monthly party meetings, they flatly refused to allow security officers to stand in the passageway *en route* to the Miners' Hall. There were repeated calls to 'get rid of Mason's men'. Ironically, sellers of the Trotskyite paper *Militant* had no such obstacles put in their way, and were allowed to peddle their wares in the passageway without the slightest hindrance.

Among those responsible for whipping up feeling against my protectors was Scargill's right-hand man, Eric Illsley. He was also prominent at the time in supporting emergency resolutions calling for the removal of British troops from Ireland. As I have said, Illsley became my successor as MP for Barnsley Central. I'd always understood that NUM sponsored MPs should have worked in or around a coal mine, but Illsley never had. As far as I was concerned, he was Scargill's placeman (rather like the local MEP, Norman West, who was described in the Lightman Report on the miners' strike as 'Scargill's puppet'). Placemen in South Yorkshire tended to do rather well. When Illsley came up for selection, for example, he only had the NUM nomination, together with the support of just two other branches. Not even his own Labour ward nominated him. His main rival, Councillor Ron Fisher, had no fewer than seventeen nominations from trades union and Labour Party branches. It didn't do him much good. The Chairman at the selection meeting ruled his candidature out of order because he didn't live in the constituency. It was all quite unconstitutional, of course. But then, Ron Fisher had two disadvantages. He was an ally of mine. And he wasn't a member of the NUM.

In the event, Eric Illsley not only won the parliamentary nomination and the seat. Until the last election, he was one of Tony Blair's official spokesmen on Ulster. He has not, however, found a place in the Government. Yet. It will be interesting to see if he does.

Perhaps I can sum up the awful atmosphere by recounting what happened at the election count in 1979. A local Labour councillor approached me and I went to shake hands. His response: 'I would rather stick a knife in your belly than shake your hand.' On another occasion, just before a Labour Party meeting, I was standing near the bar of the King George Hotel in Barnsley with members of my protection squad. The same man came up and snarled: 'I wish I had known you were all here. A bomb would have finished you all off.'

In the wider world, meanwhile, the impact of Thatcherite Toryism was wreaking immense damage in the country. Recession was biting deep, with lengthening dole queues and a growing sense of alienation and despair. There had already been riots in Bristol and Brixton, in West London and Manchester, in Liverpool, Birmingham, Hull, Preston and Wolverhampton, not to mention lesser disturbances elsewhere. The old core industries of Britain, coal, steel and the railways were particularly vulnerable to the Thatcherite challenge, because they desperately needed state-sponsored investment if they were to modernise and thrive. So in February 1981 I formed the so-called Triple Alliance, involving the unions and sponsored MPs. My hope was that by presenting a united front we might persuade the government of the need to protect and regenerate a whole swathe of the economy on which many jobs depended.

Through the Westminster grapevine, meanwhile, I'd learned that the Energy Secretary, Nigel Lawson, was considering appointing me as the next Chairman of the Coal Board, in succession to Derek Ezra. Would I be interested if such an offer was made? Would I? I'd jump at the chance. The word was that Nigel wanted to see me soon, possibly within the next couple of weeks. It was hard to suppress a twinge of excitement, though I'd been in politics long enough to know that you must never rely on nods and winks. I had grown up in the coal industry, knew how it worked from the pitface to the boardroom. It would be an honour and a privilege to end up running it. But as the days dragged on, no word came from Nigel Lawson's office. My initial enthusiasm began to evaporate. I knew that something had gone wrong, but had no idea what. Later on I heard that Margaret Thatcher had frowned when my name was put forward: 'Is he one of us?' Well, the answer to that was simple enough. Obviously I wasn't. So the job was given to the Scottish-born American industrialist Ian MacGregor instead. He it was who'd be in charge during the Scargill-inspired strike of 1984, probably the greatest tragedy ever to have overcome the coal industry. I sometimes wonder whether that calamity could have been avoided if I had been running the NCB. Probably not, since Scargill was determined on an all-out confrontation, no matter what. But the dispute, I believe, would never have been so bitter or prolonged if I'd been in charge.

Meanwhile I hoped the Triple Alliance might help both to revive Labour's effectiveness and give industry some protection. But this attempt at unity and coherence was soon overtaken by other events. Within weeks, Tony Benn announced his decision to challenge Denis Healey for the deputy leadership later that year, under the party's new rules. It was an utterly irresponsible and selfish decision. It guaranteed that for months, until Labour's annual conference, the whole party would be plunged into more division and turmoil. It was yet another political gift to Margaret Thatcher and I wasn't the only one appalled by the sheer stupidity of it. Even Neil Kinnock felt moved to attack Benn for what he was doing.

Scargill, needless to say, was soon up to his old tricks. In June he accused those of us who supported Denis Healey of 'sabotaging not only the candidature of Tony Benn but the principles of socialism which are basic to our movement'. By now the party was in utter disarray. I know that some on the Right were in such despair that they were beginning to regret not joining the Gang of Four. On the Left the mood wasn't much better. Key members of the Tribune Group led by Neil Kinnock were now united in a determined 'stop Benn' campaign. Unfortunately, the 'sensible' Left couldn't bring itself to support Denis Healey either, because of his robust opposition to unilateral nuclear disarmament – so it tried to promote the candidature of John Silkin instead. It meant that the picture was more confused than ever, with three candidates and three mutually hostile campaigns all snarling and snapping at each other. The Scargillite bloc in Barnsley, of course, was loud in its support of Benn, but this time I wasn't the only MP in the firing line. In dozens of constituencies, there was a bitter falling out over this issue between the Member of Parliament and the local activists. Neil Kinnock, for example, found himself in the unusual position of having to defy his own party membership in Bedwellty.

In the end, Denis Healey won, but by the merest whisker. Though it was a tremendous relief to those of us who believed Benn would wreck the party, it wasn't anything like the decisive victory we had wanted. The hard Left had shown the extent of its power and was still in a position to create havoc. Kinnock himself now discovered what it was like to be hated by his former allies. At the Tribune rally traditionally held in the middle of conference week he was angrily heckled. Someone presented him with thirty pieces of silver. In the lavatory of Brighton's Grand Hotel he was kicked by a disappointed Bennite supporter – a bad mistake. Neil's an old rugby player, well used to rucks and mauls. He turned on his attacker and taught him the error of his ways.

But by now the Labour Party seemed beyond saving. Our standing in the opinion polls was at its lowest for thirty-five years, despite the harshness of Thatcherite rule. Some in the Centre and on the Right were growing more and more concerned at Michael Foot's lack of leadership qualities, underlined when he turned up for the annual Remembrance Day ceremony at the Cenotaph in a donkey jacket. It certainly wasn't intended as an insult to the war dead; Michael was incapable of such a thing. He just wanted to wrap up warmly on a cold day. But there were plenty of people, including some Labour MPs, who chose to paint the incident in its blackest colours.

Yet the outlook wasn't entirely bleak. Back in Yorkshire, Arthur Scargill's attempt to impose a Stalinist control over the Labour Party was meeting some resistance. The unthinkable was beginning to happen. Local constituencies which had traditionally supported someone nominated by the NUM as their parliamentary candidate were beginning to kick over the traces. Scargill's Yorkshire Miners' Council had started choosing their sponsored candidates for MP whenever a miners' seat became vacant. But at Normanton and Pontefract, local Labour General Management Committees simply spurned the Miners' Council choice and plumped for their own runner instead. That meant two fewer NUM sponsored MPs at Westminster and a reduction in the strength of the Parliamentary Miners' Group – another example of the way Scargill was damaging the very cause he was paid to represent.

I didn't really expect that these stirrings of rebellion would help me. Scargill regarded Barnsley as his fiefdom and would move heaven and earth to get me out. It seemed that nothing could stop him. But then fate intervened. In November 1981, he won the national Presidency of the NUM, by an overwhelming majority. I thought even then that it was a disastrous decision by my union, but I knew that it offered me an opportunity too. Now that he had wider responsibilities, his grip in Yorkshire was bound to be weaker. He'd no longer have the time to campaign so meticulously against me. His puppets of course would do their best; but without Scargill on the spot to pull the strings maybe I could see them off.

But it proved a damned close run thing. At least ten NUM branches in the area failed to submit a nomination for me in the run-up to the reselection meeting on 22 March. I suppose I should have been relieved that they didn't go the whole hog and offer open support to my left-wing challenger, County Councillor Jack Brown; but their lack of enthusiasm for my cause was undeniably a blow. Still, I did pick up forty-five of the possible seventy-six nominations from party wards and trades unions, including eight from the NUM. Jack Brown managed only four. On paper, I seemed in a strong position, but appearances can be deceptive. The Scargillites, the militants, the unilateralists, the anti-Europeans – all those, in fact, who considered themselves on the Left – would vote against me, no matter what the membership in the wards and union branches thought. And so it turned out. After an unusually tense meeting, with speeches followed by questions, I just managed to beat off Jack Brown's challenge, by sixty-one votes to fifty-three. A majority of eight wasn't much to shout about, when I'd been the local MP for twenty-nine years, but as Winston Churchill observed, one is enough. I tried to be content with what I had, hoping – perhaps optimistically – that the Scargillite tide had reached its peak.

There was another reason for optimism too. Though the voters deeply mistrusted the Labour Party, Margaret Thatcher had managed to make herself the most unpopular prime minister in living memory – hardly surprisingly, since her policies had created a dole queue of 3 million people. Support for the government in the polls had plunged to a mere 30 per cent. That didn't necessarily benefit us, since our support was also a miserable 30 per cent. But it seemed to me that at least we might be in with a fighting chance next time – if only we could get our act together.

What happened next is part of legend. On Friday, 2 April 1982, Argentina invaded the Falkland Islands in a piece of unprovoked aggression which united the nation in outrage. The House of Commons met in emergency session the following morning, when Michael Foot delivered one of the finest speeches of his career with a major attack on the government for 'betraying' the Falklanders. Margaret Thatcher, in contrast, seemed feeble and unconvincing. Hers was a depressing performance and I wondered if she was really up to the challenge. I thought her government had woefully miscalculated the nature of the Argentinian threat. It certainly blundered badly with its decision to withdraw the ice patrol vessel HMS *Endurance* from the South Atlantic – a mistake which persuaded the junta in Buenos Aires that Britain would never fight to protect its own far-flung citizens. An apparently minor decision on the defence budget like that – and I think the sum involved was a paltry £15 million – can have devastating consequences.

But as most would acknowledge, the ten desperate weeks which followed proved to be Thatcher's finest hour. When all her original errors have been acknowledged, nothing can detract from her courage in the crisis or the brilliant performance of our fighting forces. By the time the conflict was won, she and the Tories were unstoppable.

Back in Barnsley I was embroiled in more conflicts of my own. As our fleet was sailing down to the South Atlantic, the Scargillites on the General Management Committee passed a resolution demanding a British withdrawal from the war. I could hardly contain myself. Not only was the constituency party stabbing our forces in the back, but it was contemptuously rejecting the overwhelming opinion of the constituency. But nothing I could say made a jot of difference. Most of the people in that meeting seemed to have a hatred of their own country, even when it was conspicuously in the right.

I wasn't prepared to take it lying down. So afterwards I approached the mayor, Councillor Ken Rispin, to see what could be done to repair the damage. Ken was a D-Day veteran and shared my disgust at the local party's attitude. He agreed with my suggestion that Barnsley should put on an official civic reception for all those from the area who were fighting in the Falklands campaign. The idea was then put before the Labour Group on the council and to my elation rattled through by a two to one majority.

It took some time in negotiations with the Ministry of Defence to fix up the details. Every local serviceman and servicewoman who had served in the South Atlantic had to be given leave for the same day. And I had to get official agreement for the memorial scroll I wanted presented to each of them. But the effort was worth it. The hall that day was full, men and women in uniform marching proudly forward to receive their scrolls while wives and families, mums and dads applauded till their hands were hot. There were tears too for those who never came home. This was the real Barnsley, my Barnsley, the only town in Britain, I believe, which arranged such an occasion.

For me, the circumstances surrounding that event were another reminder of the gaping chasm between the decent heart of the Labour movement and some of the people who led it in Barnsley. Though I still had friends and allies in the constituency party, people like Jim Hammill, Jack Wilde, Jack Wood and Ron Fisher – stalwarts all – they were increasingly feeling the strain of the endless bickering and petty point-scoring. I at least could get away to Westminster every week – though even there the atmosphere of unhappiness and apprehension couldn't really be escaped. Many of my fellow MPs had problems with their own activists. Quite a few were genuinely fearful that they would be kicked out to make way for some crypto-Communist or perhaps an undercover member of Militant. Yet again, we seemed to be spending more of our energies fighting among ourselves than in confronting the Tories.

I felt one brief moment of optimism at the party conference in Blackpool that September, when the Centre and Right staged something of a comeback, winning a clutch of seats on the National Executive Committee. That led to Tony Benn being removed as Chairman of the powerful Home Policy Committee, after an eighteen-year reign which had done absolutely nothing for the party's credibility. But it proved a false dawn. Within months the Left had won its greatest victory in years, very nearly destroying the party in the process.

It was obvious to everybody that Margaret Thatcher would call an early election, in the wake of her Falklands triumph. That probability became a rock-solid certainty when the Tories did well in the local elections, in Spring, 1983. Yet when she finally took the plunge and announced the general election for 9 June, it took us utterly by surprise. We had no plans, no strategy, no money and no manifesto. We had only 34 per cent support in the polls – against 47 per cent for the Tories and 19 per cent for the Liberal–SDP Alliance – and not the faintest idea of what to do about it.

It was then that we really paid the price for all the left-wing idiocy of the past. A hastily-arranged meeting between the Shadow Cabinet and the NEC agreed a manifesto which embraced just about every half-baked idea which had been peddled for so long by Benn and his friends: a huge rise in public spending and therefore taxes; massive renationalization; exchange controls; the abolition of charitable status for private schools; an incoherent stance on nuclear weapons; a ban on council house sales, which would reverse one of the few genuinely popular policies which Thatcher had introduced; the end of mortgage tax relief, thereby enraging the middle classes; and withdrawal from the European Community. As Gerald Kaufman bitterly observed, it amounted to 'the longest suicide note in history'.

I wasn't present at that disastrous meeting. Months before I had resigned my front-bench post and gone with some relief to the back benches. But my presence wouldn't have made a scrap of difference. The party seemed determined to learn its lesson the hard way.

I think it was then I decided than enough was enough. I was fed up with defending major parts of manifestos with which I didn't agree. There was less and less satisfaction in constituency work, when many of my local 'supporters' in the GMC openly despised the things in which I believed. I'd achieved most of my ambitions in politics and hadn't the slightest expectation that I would ever serve in government again. Moreover I was sixty years old and by the time of the next election would be entitled to a bus pass. So I determined to fight and win Barnsley this one last time. I'd stay on long enough to beat off the inevitable reselection challenge – I certainly wasn't about to let Scargill chase me out before I was ready to hand in my cards – and then announce my retirement, effective from the following general election, which I thought would probably be in 1986.

With that decision under my belt, I found the 1983 campaign far less of a strain than it might have been. There was a certain poignancy in knocking on doors, bellowing through a loudspeaker and addressing meetings in the knowledge that next time somebody else would be doing these things. But even in a Barnsley which has never wavered in its loyalty to the Labour cause I could sense the unhappiness. People wished me well, as always, shook my hand, promised me their votes. They delivered too, though not as handsomely as usual. My majority was down to

14,000. It was a bit of a disappointment; but I knew that many of our traditional supporters all over the country felt in their hearts that Labour was letting them down.

Just how badly became only too apparent on election night. Once again I sat up late with Madge, watching the results come in. But there was no excitement or anticipation this time. Only gloom. The figures told their own miserable story: Tories 397 seats; Labour 209; the Alliance 23. And that wasn't the worst of it. Our share of the vote was down to a wretched 27.6 per cent, only a whisker ahead of the Alliance on 25.4 per cent. But for the brutal arithmetic of Britain's first-past-the-post system, we would have done even worse in terms of parliamentary representation. It was our most humiliating electoral setback in sixty years.

Yet still the Labour Party wouldn't face the truth. In September the NEC held an election post-mortem and came to the conclusion that the party's main problems lay in disunity and poor presentational style. Evidently nobody was prepared to consider the possibility that our policies might be wrong. I wasn't impressed either when Neil Kinnock won the leadership contest in the Autumn, with Roy Hattersley as his deputy. I liked Neil personally, but was deeply suspicious of his unilateralist and anti-European background. My vote had gone to Roy Hattersley and the fact that he had to play second fiddle like Denis Healey before him seemed to me another example of the party's refusal to sort itself out. Well, as it turns out, I was wrong about Neil. He grew into the job and became a real leader; if the Labour Party is transformed today it's largely because of the foundations he laid.

But my political concerns were soon overtaken by real industrial tragedy, the worst I'd seen in all my years of public life. On 1 March 1984, the National Coal Board announced that it intended to close Cortonwood Colliery in Yorkshire. It sparked the beginning of the most damaging and futile dispute in British industrial history, a strike which sucked the life out of the pits, virtually destroyed the NUM and wreaked miseries in the coalfields the like of which I had never known since the hungry Thirties. For me, the year of the miners' strike was utter misery. But I was lucky. For hundreds and thousands of honest, decent families it meant ruin and despair.

Scargill had been aching for a confrontation ever since he became National President of the NUM. In his inaugural speech he'd uttered the sinister words: 'Every trade unionist has to be determined to defy the law and render it ineffective.' That just about summed up his approach. I think he saw his own members as cannon fodder who could be hurled over the top in pursuit of some socialist vision of his own. He'd already had one success against the Tory government in 1981, when the threat of a walkout in the coalfields had persuaded Margaret Thatcher to keep some uneconomic pits open. He obviously thought he could go on winning, no matter what. In fact various efforts to call a national pit strike had been frustrated by Scargill's failure to get the minimum 55 per cent majority of miners on his side. Now he would seize on the decision over Cortonwood to have another go.

He still didn't have his 55 per cent majority. But since Yorkshire and Scottish miners had already decided to come out if more pit closures were announced, he had what he obviously thought was the next best thing. On 6 March, the NUM Excutive met to call all the coalfields out on strike.

It was a crazily irresponsible decision. It's an unhappy fact of life that pits sometimes have to close, either because they are exhausted or because it is uneconomic or because of geological difficulties. In my own time as Minister of Power, the NCB closed thirty mines, since there was no real choice in the matter. But I also saw to it that other pits were opened or expanded, discouraged coal imports, cut back on opencast mining and promoted a coal-fired power station. This, it seemed to me, was the only way to maintain a thriving industry and preserve long-term jobs. I was appalled that Scargill preferred the path of confrontation instead, especially as it was obvious that Thatcher and the Coal Board Chairman Ian MacGregor were themselves spoiling for a fight – and well prepared for it, too.

What made matters worse was that Scargill, with unforgivable tactical ineptitude was starting his strike in the Spring. Demand for coal would be low for at least six months, which meant that miners and their families were committed to a long, painful dispute before their action could even begin to bite.

That wasn't just irresponsible. It was downright bad tactics. But I thought there was still some hope. The NUM called a special delegate conference at Easter and it seemed obvious that it had no choice but to order a national ballot on the dispute. The miners certainly had their grievances, but I believed most of them would take the opportunity to pull back from the brink.

Scargill had other ideas. He refused to call a vote on the question of a national ballot. I suppose he knew that his members would give him the thumbs-down. And with that shoddy exploitation of his position he doomed the members he was paid to represent. Without a national ballot, miners in the booming and profitable Nottinghamshire pits could keep on working with a clear conscience. Without a ballot, the Tories could claim the moral high ground. Without a ballot the Labour Party was hamstrung in its efforts to defend the NUM. Margaret Thatcher must have thanked her lucky stars that a once formidable union was now led by such a man. The only thing Scargill had on his side was the traditional loyalty of the mining communities. And he exploited that loyalty with the ruthlessness of a First World War general sending his troops into the barbed wire and machine guns.

It was heartbreaking to see what families had to endure. Even the overtime ban imposed back in October 1983 meant a loss in wages of around £30 a week – a modest sum by today's standards but enough then for miners to dip into their meagre savings, default on their gas bills or be forced to borrow from relatives. But with a full-blown strike there was no money coming in at all. As weeks dragged on into months you could see the desperation growing in men's eyes. There was no unemployment pay from the government. Thatcher was as ruthless as Scargill in her determination to win at any cost. Families were reduced to scavenging for coal, going hungry so that their children could eat. They defaulted on their mortgages, allowed insurance policies to lapse and suffered additional hardship when their electricity was cut off. Sometimes they managed to run up debts at the local grocery store, until the shopkeeper could no longer carry the burden. Sometimes they tried to borrow, but banks are not noted for their generosity. Sometimes they tried to sell their cars, or TVs or bits and pieces of furniture, but few could afford to buy. Once again, the soup kitchens appeared in Barnsley as in so many other towns. Soup kitchens, in Britain, in 1984. It was as though half a century of social progress had been wiped away.

Like many others who still had an income, Madge and I made up food parcels for the people who were destitute: a few tins, some tea and sugar, odds and ends. It was never enough. No matter how many parcels we prepared, there were always hundreds still in need. We helped arrange a trip to the seaside for the strikers' children, with ice cream, free rides at the funfair and a bite to eat; but we had to deliver them back to households without electricity, some where the larder was empty.

At least they had a drop of milk. From the beginning of the dispute, a local farmer, Hector Buckley, had been delivering free supplies to the town, day after day, with clockwork regularity. Hector is the best-hearted of men and couldn't bear to see his friends and neighbours go short. But after six months it simply became too much for him. He came to me and said he couldn't afford to continue. He was already stretched beyond his financial limits. It was a bleak moment, because we both knew that his supplies would be seriously missed. I thought for a moment of my own good fortune and told him to keep the milk coming. Somehow I'd manage to pay for it. In that way I would share some of my constituents' hardships; after all, they were sacrificing far more.

Meanwhile the dispute itself was becoming nastier. The Tories were clearly intent on grinding the miners into the dirt, presumably in revenge for the humiliating defeat inflicted on Ted Heath in 1974. Ministers couldn't care less about the hardship in the coalfields; and Thatcher even had the nerve to talk about 'the enemy within'. Some enemy. These were among the best and most decent people in Britain, men who spent their lives deep underground, cutting coal for the kind of money the Prime Minister and her friends would regard as small change. But then, as far as they were concerned, this was no longer an industrial dispute. It was a political vendetta, being run not by the Coal Board but by Margaret Thatcher and her sidekick, the Energy Secretary Peter Walker. Ian MacGregor, the Chairman of the NCB, was just their errand-boy.

And as usual, Arthur Scargill was their greatest ally. If he had an overall strategy in the dispute it remained a mystery to me and to everyone else. His answer to everything seemed to be mass picketing and never mind if it turned violent. The TUC guidelines that disputes should be conducted peacefully, with never more than six pickets at any one site, were contemptuously ignored. And of course with every act of bullying intimidation the miners' cause was diminished.

Not that the violence was one-sided. At a mass picket of the Orgreave coking plant in South Yorkshire, the police seemed to lose control and charged on horseback against the miners, flailing their victims with batons. Many men had broken bones that day, and there were too many other incidents when the forces of law and order behaved like a private army for the Tories. They certainly didn't scruple to arrest people without a shred of evidence, scooping them up in their hundreds, only to release them later without charge.

At times like that I would find my mind turning back to the hints from Nigel Lawson in 1981. Might it have made a difference if I'd become Chairman of the Coal Board? I certainly wouldn't have knuckled under to Scargill, so I don't doubt that he would have found some excuse to engineer his strike anyway. But I wouldn't have been a pushover for the government either. Unlike Ian MacGregor I'd have searched for a sensible accommodation. In fact I would have insisted on it, because the government's determination on absolute victory was as damaging to the industry as Scargill's intransigence. The facts couldn't be denied. Quite apart from the misery imposed on the miners themselves, the cost to the nation had to be counted in billions of pounds in lost coal production, lost electricity production, lost steel production, lost tax payments, lost markets and extra government borrowing. It was bitterly frustrating to think that I might have been in a position to influence events – and for the better, I believe. Could I possibly have done worse than Ian MacGregor?

Instead I had to do what I could from the opposition backbenches. In months of speeches and parliamentary questions I returned again and again to the way ordinary miners, men who'd been found guilty of no offence, were being treated. Some, for example, had been declared redundant before the strike was called on 6 March and had played no part whatever in the dispute. Why were they being denied their unemployment benefits? And what about the miners who had been arrested and then released without charge? Would ministers ensure that their future job prospects did not suffer? Would their fingerprints and photographs be expunged from the criminal records? Would chief constables be advised to call in those miners to witness their files being destroyed? Would the Coal Board be discouraged from discriminating against men who had stood on the picket-lines?

I never received a satisfactory answer to any of these questions while the strike continued. Ministers seemed more interested in keeping up the pressure against the strikers than in ensuring elementary justice for men who had done no wrong. It wasn't until I arranged an adjournment debate on 7 March 1985, a few days after the dispute was called off, that the Home Office minister Giles Shaw at last made it clear that the photographs and fingerprints of the innocent would be removed from the records. By then, of course, there was no further need for ministers to engage in what amounted to psychological warfare.

But if the government's behaviour was shoddy throughout, it has to be said that Arthur Scargill's tactics played into its hands. The sight of pickets with bludgeons, the television pictures of attempted intimidation against working miners, arson attacks against Coal Board buses and the tragic death of a taxi driver, killed when concrete blocks were dropped on his cab as he took working miners to the pit, all helped move public opinion against the strikers, as did the deaths of two miners' pickets, killed on the road. Against that background, Ministers could be as harsh and unreasonable as they liked.

Scargill was losing the public-relations battle in other ways too. Desperate for extra money to keep the dispute going, he sought assistance from Soviet miners and then from Libyan trade unions. It was a disastrous blow to what was left of the NUM's reputation, because the money from both sources was tainted. Everybody but Scargill knew that the Communist regime was a brutal tyranny. As for Libya, the regime of Colonel Gaddafi was notorious throughout the world for its sponsorship of terrorism. The prospect of help from a man who provided Semtex to the IRA turned the stomachs even of people who were well disposed to the NUM. And though Scargill eventually said that he wouldn't accept Gaddafi's money, the damage was done.

There was an even more unpleasant sequel. Years later, in March 1990, press stories began to circulate, claiming that some in the NUM leadership had their fingers in the till during the strike. The main allegations were that Scargill received £163,00 in support from Libya, that he had used some £70,000 of the money to repay personal debts for himself, his General Secretary Peter Heathfield and his Chief Executive Officer Roger Windsor and that the NUM had received £1 million in 'secret funds' from the Soviet Union. The impression these claims left was that while rank-and-file miners had been suffering dreadful privation, their leaders were living well. And on union money too.

I found it difficult to believe such lurid claims. I despised Scargill and his cronies for their political extremism, their bullying of anyone who disagreed with them and their ineptitude, but I didn't think them venal. Still, it was obviously important that the matter should be cleared up as quickly as possible. When an inquiry was set up under Gavin Lightman QC to investigate the affair I was reasonably confident that it would show no wrong-doing.

But it didn't turn out quite like that. True, nothing criminal had been done. After the Lightman Report was published in July 1990, the *Yorkshire Miner* magazine brought out a special edition under the screaming headline 'Lightman and the lies'. Inside were other headlines claiming that the report had rejected the 'slurs' and reporting Arthur Scargill's complaints of 'Lies, smears and character assassination'.

But in truth Gavin Lightman's findings were shocking. If Scargill and his cronies hadn't engaged in embezzlement or stealing, they had certainly played fast and loose with the elementary principles of financial control. For example, the report could reach 'no concluded view' on whether the union received money from Gaddafi. One of the reasons for this, said Mr Lightman, was that 'It has been my strong impression that Mr Scargill's story on a number of points has changed as it suits him throughout the conduct of this inquiry.' He virtually accused Scargill of lying over money from the Soviet miners. In addition there was 'a degree of irregularity regarding authorization' over the money spent on Scargill's house. Peter Heathfield, meanwhile, was accused of misleading the union over the nature of work done on his home, with the help of NUM cash. Mr Lightman said:

In my view as a matter of law, there have been a number of misapplications of funds and breaches of duty . . . The great problem is that Mr Scargill has acted throughout without the benefit of properly informed legal or accountancy advice. I regret that I am of the view that was in part because Mr Scargill was unwilling to accept the constraints which such advice would have placed upon him. Indeed when I put this view to Mr Scargill, he accepted that this was the case.

In most unions, officials accused in such language would be made to resign. Not in the NUM. Far from accepting the findings of the Lightman Report, a special one-day conference of the union agreed merely that the document should be 'noted'. Nor were there any plans to publish the outcome of an inquiry which had been made at such expense. The report only won general circulation when it was printed by Penguin Books, without the NUM's permission. One of the people fully aware of Penguin's plans for publication was the Chairman of the Miners' Group in the Commons, the MP for Rother Valley, Kevin Barron. He soon paid the price. For his temerity in insisting on plain dealing and publicity, Kevin was promptly removed from his chairmanship. No doubt Scargill was delighted.

By then, of course, the strike was long over, the miners driven back to work by deprivation and despair. Their industry is now but a shadow of what is was, the pits closed, the traditional mining communities no more. Thousands of families who suffered so badly in Scargill's strike are still paying the price. Men who once wrenched a living from the ground today find what work they can in shops and factories – if they're lucky enough to escape the dole queue. The union which commanded their loyalty has become a feeble creature, utterly without the influence it once took for granted. Of all the damage done by extremism in the labour movement, none has been so permanent or left such scars as Scargill's reckless militancy.

With the failure of the strike, I expected that the man's venom would once again be turned on those of us who didn't offer him uncritical and toadying support. But his ability to get at me through my own General Management Committee was now diminished. Because of boundary changes, his stronghold in the Worsborough ward was no longer in my constituency. It made a real difference. At the Barnsley reselection meeting in May 1985 I easily beat off my left-wing challenger, Joe Power by fifty-nine votes to eighteen. It was quite a relief after my narrow squeak on the previous occasion; but it didn't alter my determination to retire at the next election.

It would be a wrench, of course. In spite of all the frustrations and disappointments, there were still worthwhile things a backbench MP could do. That year, for example, I led an all-party delegation to Moscow to meet refuseniks, Jewish people who desperately wanted to leave a hostile Soviet Union to be with their families in Israel and elsewhere. It was the strangest and at the same time most moving trip I had ever made.

We were officially booked on a weekend charter tour, but took the first opportunity to slip away to make the necessary contacts. It was all somewhat cloak and dagger. We split into small groups, travelling desperately in taxis, trolleybuses and the metro. Between us, we met no fewer than thirty-seven refuseniks in one weekend, taking care at each meeting that we weren't under observation before we knocked on a door.

To anybody brought up in the freedom of the West, it was a sobering experience to see the plight of these brave, defiant Jews. Most of them lived in poor conditions, were condemned to miserably menial jobs, were denied decent education and faced harassment by the police if they dared to speak openly about human rights. But nothing could quench their spirit. They positively welcomed our promise to give publicity to their plight, even though it might mean more trouble for them. I think every member of the delegation returned to London in a reflective frame of mind, grateful for the democracy at home which we so often take for granted.

Such experiences could, I suppose, have changed my mind about retirement. But I was pretty sure that this battle at least was being won. Mikhail Gorbachev's government was changing Russia, albeit too slowly. People like Nathan Sharansky were being freed after years of incarceration in Soviet prisons. At home, the government clearly took the plight of the refuseniks as seriously as I did, as became clear when I arranged an adjournment debate on the issue in 1986. It was one of the very few occasions when a minister has actually thanked me for initiating a debate. I knew then that the pressure on the Kremlin would be kept up, whether I stayed or not.

And I had hopes that there would be some political life after the Commons. When I confided my retirement plans to Neil Kinnock, he told me that he would like me as a working peer in the House of Lords. Well, we'd see. In the meantime I had to inform my party colleagues in Barnsley, before anything appeared in the press. Some of them would certainly be glad to see the back of me. Others – the majority, I hoped – would be sorry. But the people who really mattered were my constituents. We would have been together nearly thirty-five years, come the election, through good times and bad. I'd miss being their MP, no doubt about it. But at least I could look them in the eye when I met them. I would always have the satisfaction of knowing that I never gave anything less than my best. If an MP can honestly say that at the end of his Commons career, he hasn't done too badly.

16 In Harm's Way

These were the television pictures I had never expected to see. Even in the frenzied speculation of the preceding days, I'd never quite believed that it would happen. But there were Gerry Adams and Martin McGuinness of Sinn Fein/IRA sitting down in apparent agreement with constitutional politicians like David Trimble, John Hume and Seamus Mallon. They were all beyond exhaustion after days and nights of argument and hard compromise; but they had done a deal at last. Good Friday, 1998, promised a new beginning for Northern Ireland. I looked at Madge, hardly daring to hope that it might mean a new beginning for us too.

It was then twenty-one years since Inspector Pat Thomas had come into our dining room with the news that the IRA had targeted me for assassination. Even before then, ever since I had become Secretary of State for Northern Ireland in 1976, the threat had been there. Madge and I had not spent a single day together without armed guards around us or a panic-button within easy reach. We hadn't been able to take a spontaneous walk or travel by train, or go into a pub by ourselves or have a restaurant meal without advance security planning. We'd seen our home in Barnsley turned into a fortress. When in London we had to live in safe-houses, our address kept secret from all but close members of our family. Now all that could change. Perhaps. I didn't want either of us to hope too much. We'd been disappointed before.

A few days later I was in London for an appointment with an official from the Home Office, who for the sake of discretion I'll call Mr Smith. He was – and still is – my case officer. In liaison with the Joint Intelligence Services Committee, he runs the protection programme which at varying levels of intensity looks after a range of potential victims. Salman Rushdie would be well acquainted with him, though I hope there aren't many others who require his level of security – or mine. If Madge and I had any prospects of being able to resume a normal life, Mr Smith was the man who would know.

Madge was waiting for me in the safe-house when I returned. One look at my expression told her the answer. The peace deal notwithstanding, our protection would remain. It is with us to this day. For all the hopes inspired by the peace process, the intelligence services and the police are still keeping up their guard.

Over the years, I'd never asked for a detailed analysis of the threat. Nor did I this time. The people who guard my family and me know their business. I trust their judgement and accept their decisions. If some gunman is on the loose and actively seeking me out, I don't want to know. It seems to me that a refusal to worry unduly counts as a small victory against terrorism, though I certainly wouldn't make life easier for the IRA by refusing the protection on offer. Even now, after all these years, there may be Republicans who passionately want me dead.

There's no great mystery why. They'd managed to convince themselves that I had treated them unfairly and with undue harshness. It's a curious fact that terrorists who think it perfectly all right to plant bombs and shoot off-duty policemen in the back are often genuinely astonished when anyone takes them on.

So the IRA and its friends in Sinn Fein were noisily outraged when I sent the SAS into Northern Ireland during my time as Secretary of State for Defence. They were even more hostile when I expanded the role of the special forces during my time in the Province. The policy of picking up terrorist suspects in batches seriously disrupted IRA operations and added to Republican venom against me. But my real offence, I think, was in refusing to allow prisoners in the Maze special category status. The complaint was that I had 'criminalized' the IRA, a thought the terrorists couldn't abide. On top of that I obviously hadn't given a sufficiently sympathetic hearing to complaints of 'police brutality' against terrorist suspects held in the Castlereagh Interrogation Centre. According to intelligence reports, some Provo commanders were for the first time contemplating the possibility that their campaign might be defeated. The Republican movement wasn't going to forget that. As late as September 1993, Martin McGuinness was telling the *Guardian* newspaper that no Secretary of State for Northern Ireland had been impressive. 'The only one who impressed anybody was Roy Mason. He impressed some of the Unionists, because he beat the shit out of us.'

Even before I left Northern Ireland, I was aware of my place in Republican demonology. That had been made clear in the 'Stuff Mason' march mounted by Sinn Fein in February 1978 and in the slogans on the walls and gable ends in West Belfast: 'Stonemason will not crack us' and 'Mason the mad midget'. The assassination attempt against me was planned the following year. By January 1980 *An Phoblacht*, the

Republican newspaper, was positively glorying in the threat, with a boast that a former British GOC in the Province 'will be wearing a permanent flak jacket the rest of his life along with Airey . . . sorry, Roy Mason and Kenneth Newman'. That sick gloating over the murder of Airey Neave was another reminder of the need to heed security advice.

My growing suspicion that the IRA wouldn't easily let go was reinforced that September with two articles in the Irish current affairs magazine *Magill*. One was a well-informed analysis of IRA tactics which contained the following words:

> Such was the success of the 'criminalization policy', as it was called, that the then Secretary of State Roy Mason and his security chiefs at one time thought that they had actually pulled it off and defeated the IRA. 'We WERE almost defeated,' admits one present Provo leader.

But it was the second article which really caught my eye, a piece written by Ed Moloney after an interview with 'a leading member of the Provisionals who has been authorized to speak on behalf of the IRA Army Council'.

Moloney put it to this terrorist godfather that after the killing of Lord Mountbatten, the IRA threatened to kill more prominent personalities. Did that threat still exist? Here's the IRA man's reply:

> Yes. As I've explained, the importance of these people, like British ambassadors abroad, is that they put out false propaganda. They are part of the British military machine. It would be stupid and morally wrong for us to attack an ordinary British person, but for us to attack a pillar of the British establishment like Mountbatten or Quintin Hogg or for us to attack the likes of Roy Mason, who we will never forgive for what he did to the Irish people, gains us more attention and political effect. Yes, we do intend to carry out more of those attacks.

Well, that was clear enough. I hardly needed an expert analyst to draw a conclusion for me; and in the years which followed I had plenty of reminders of what the terrorists were capable of doing on the mainland. In July 1982 they bombed a squadron of the Queen's Household Cavalry in Hyde Park, slaughtering men and horses indiscriminately. They killed and maimed again when they bombed the bandstand in Regent's Park, an attack which they no doubt justified on the grounds that the musicians were part of the 'British military machine'. And in the October 1984 they came close to murdering the Prime Minister and half her Cabinet with the explosion at the Grand Hotel, Brighton.

More recently, the threat has come closer to home. In 1991, Scotland Yard and senior officers in the South Yorkshire Police suddenly decided that my protectors should adopt a higher profile. From that moment on, the men protecting my home began wearing full uniform, with flak jackets, pistols and sub-machine guns clearly visible at all times. Presumably – I didn't ask – word had come down that the threat had increased. The higher profile, I guessed, was designed to frighten off anyone tempted to have a go. I don't suppose it was a coincidence that shortly afterwards, during a terrorist trial at the Old Bailey, my name was read out as being on the IRA's very latest list of targets.

The terrorists' sheer persistence in the determination to attack politicians was again demonstrated the following year, when they tried to murder one of my successors as Northern Ireland Secretary, Jim Prior. A so-called 'active service unit' bombed the block of flats in London where he lived with his wife. The explosion blew out doors, shattered windows and wrecked a number of cars parked nearby; but mercifully, nobody was killed. For me, it was another lesson in the wisdom of listening to security advice. Jim had decided against turning his home into a fortress and hadn't even withdrawn his address from the phone book or *Who's Who*. I suppose he just wasn't prepared to allow a bunch of sociopaths to disrupt his life, but his stand was a mistake which could easily have proved fatal. As the IRA said in a statement afterwards, the bomb was intended to show politicians 'that they cannot sit in London in comfort and safety while nationalists suffer because of their policies'.

Evidently we couldn't count on sitting safe in Barnsley either. In 1993, the Irish Gardai arrested a Provo suspect in Limerick and found documents in his possession which showed that a thorough surveillance operation had been conducted against me. The material unearthed even included the fact that Madge and I were fans of Barnsley Football Club and gave the precise location and numbers of the seats we regularly occupied. That meant an immediate change in the security arrangements. From that moment on, sniffer dogs have been sent into the Oakwell Stadium before every home game. Special Branch officers arrive long before each match and occupy our seats until we turn up.

There have been other incidents since. In 1994, a paper picked up in the street not far from where I live showed a sketch of the approaches to my house. The following year, while we were staying at our cottage on the coast, a stranger to the area was arrested only 300 yd away in possession of a Kalashnikov rifle. In 1995, in the avenue next to ours, police found a binocular case containing a battery and wiring.

Evidence of a continued IRA interest? It's impossible to say for sure. There might be an innocent explanation for the sketch, though I can't think of one. The man with the Kalashnikov may have had no terrorist connections. We weren't told about him until long after the incident, presumably to spare our feelings, and I never did discover what happened to him. As for the binocular case, that remains a mystery. Since no explosives were recovered, I can't be certain that it had the makings of a bomb. On the other hand, what were the battery and wires doing there?

Speculation is pointless anyway. I prefer to confine myself to the official assessment of the risk; and that hasn't changed. From time to time, I see Mr Smith from the Home Office and he tells me – in general terms – the extent to which I'm still a target. His news is seldom encouraging. In January 1996, for example, I learned that the Joint Intelligence Services Committee wanted my protection to stay at the present 'threat level' for at least another six months – exactly the same message I had been getting so regularly for more than twenty years. It meant that I would continue to be guarded by a full squad of armed officers and be driven everywhere in an armoured car, followed by a back-up vehicle. What was different this time though was that the IRA had called its first ceasefire. There was a high degree of optimism in the media that perhaps this was the breakthrough for which everybody had been praying. Clearly, neither Mr Smith nor the JIC believed a word of it. Nor, in spite of my personal circumstances, did I. In a speech to the House of Lords that month I warned: 'All of us must be seriously concerned that the Provisional IRA still recruit, train, carry out dummy bomb runs to keep the militant element busy and kill and beat up their own kinfolk to control and dominate their territories.' In fact the 'ceasefire' was shattered by a devastating bomb in the City a couple of weeks later.

Of course the outlook seems much brighter today. The Good Friday Agreement has been ratified by voters on both sides of the Irish border. That in itself makes it more difficult for the terrorists to return to the savagery of the gun and the bomb. The tragedy at Omagh provoked such revulsion that even the lunatics in the 'Real IRA' felt obliged to announce an end to violence. And the coalition formed by David Trimble of the Ulster Unionists and Seamus Mallon of the SDLP suggests that at last the moderate centre has discovered its strength. It remains the case however that I'm still considered to be under threat. Until there is a change in that assessment by the intelligence professionals, I must suspend judgement on whether the peace can hold.

For Madge, my family and me it means a strange existence, halfway between freedom and imprisonment. Even when we're at home watching television or having a meal, the reminders are everywhere. There are panic buttons in every room in the house, blast curtains on all windows, floodlights in the garden and a battery of closed-circuit cameras monitoring the whole area. All the ground-floor windows have been sprayed with a special preparation making it difficult to peer inside. The rear garden wall has been heightened and strengthened. Electronic devices of various kinds have been tucked in every available nook and cranny. A TV telephone had been fitted inside the front door, so that my wife and I can talk to police and visitors without emerging.

Just outside, there's a bulletproof hut, occupied twenty-four hours a day by armed officers and linked by radio to police headquarters. It has become an essential feature of our lives. We do nothing and go nowhere without informing the protection team first. I list all my engagements for at least a month ahead, since every one of them has to be 'sussed out', as my protectors say. Whether I'm going to some official function or just having a bite in a restaurant, a proper surveillance has to be carried out in advance, sometimes using sniffer dogs. It's important too that the members of my team wear the right clothes for the right occasion. If I'm going fishing it's obviously inadvisable for them to turn up on a muddy riverbank in their city suits; and similar considerations apply when I'm golfing or sitting in the stands at Oakwell or attending a test match in summer. So it's necessary to give plenty of warning about whether it will be a 'welly day', a 'black tie day' or whatever.

That's only the beginning. I can no longer travel anywhere, not even to the local fish and chip shop, under my own steam. Instead I must be ferried in what looks like an ordinary car, but is in fact an armoured, bulletproof, blastproof vehicle very nearly as robust as a main battle tank but much faster if the need arises. There's no longer any such thing as a favourite route anywhere; my protectors and I decide what roads we'll take. They and the people in the back-up car are in constant communication with divisional police forces as we move through their territory. I always imagine chief constables heaving heartfelt sighs of relief when we're safely off their patch.

Sometimes it can be a little more complicated. At the 1996 Labour conference in Blackpool, for example, I stayed at Lytham St Anne's, well away from the daily bustle. We had been escorted in with heavier protection than usual, a force comprising seven men in three cars. At the hotel a police dog-van and patrol cars were very much in evidence, with a uniformed officer on the door. Our room had been thoroughly searched and now awaited us, with unbroken seals on the door. The adjoining room had also been searched and sealed. Three Special Branch officers patrolled the corridor outside, guarding our room day and night. Altogether, I counted no fewer than fourteen security guards in those few days. Because of the disruption, it's understandable that hoteliers are sometimes less than enthusiastic for my custom – though on the other hand it can be very profitable. When Madge and I come to stay it invariably means booking no fewer than six rooms – four for my protection team, one for the local Special Branch officer and a double for my wife and me.

Even then, my protectors aren't always satisfied. We once arrived at a hotel to discover a group of Irish builders working on the premises. Somehow they hadn't been picked up in the initial surveillance, or maybe the management had decided to have the work done on the spur of the moment. At any event, my team was obviously concerned. There was a quick, muttered consultation – and for all I know a check with the Criminal Records Office too – before Madge and I found ourselves being hurried off elsewhere. Over the years we've become accustomed to doing the occasional quick flit.

Party conferences remain a problem for my security team. My minders are always alert to the possibility that a delegate or visitor with Republican sympathies might seize the opportunity to cut up rough; so even when I'm inside the hall or the headquarters hotel, they hover protectively nearby. In fact we've devised a discreet signal so that I can summon instant help if an encounter looks like turning nasty. I've only used it once or twice and the 'rescue' has been so swift, discreet and efficient that I doubt if the other party has grasped what was happening. (Not that it's always like that. At one Blackpool conference, my old friend, the journalist Michael Toner spotted me in a corridor, called out 'Roy!' and made to slap me on the shoulder. Before his hand came anywhere near landing, he'd been grabbed in a throat-hold by a Special Branch man, pushed against the wall and before I had a chance to intervene, thoroughly frisked. The incident was all over in a few seconds, but it cost me a very large whisky to soothe the offended throat.

Sometimes the dedication of my teams takes even me by surprise. In 1987, just before my peerage was announced, I had to go into St Thomas's Hospital in London for an operation. Throughout my stay, an armed guard sat outside my ward round the clock. A few years later, when I was having a minor op done in Barnsley, one of my protectors actually gowned-up and accompanied me into the theatre.

Travel abroad can be troublesome too. It's impossible just to pack and go. The leader of the protection team has to make an assessment of the risks, liaising with overseas intelligence services and anti-terrorist squads to see what level of cover is required. In one or two countries, Madge and I can live almost normally, with a police presence that's barely visible. Elsewhere, it can be a very different story. Travel anywhere in America, with its large Irish population, requires the closest contact with the FBI. In much of Western Europe too, caution is necessary. At every annual conference or Ard Feis of Sinn Fein, a careful note is kept of overseas visitors. Their country of origin is logged and their home addresses too; such information helps determine what security arrangements should be made when I'm travelling. Even a tourist destination like Tenerife might be considered a risk, because it has Irish clubs and direct flights from Dublin.

The same meticulous precautions apply when Madge and I are in London. For more than twenty-three years, we've lived in safe-houses in the capital.

To begin with, the accommodation was quite grand. As Defence Secretary and Northern Ireland Secretary, I was put up most handsomely at Admiralty House and then in a flat at the top of Admiralty Arch, with a splendid view of the Mall and Buckingham Palace. Such are the perks of office, but they never last. After Labour's defeat in 1979, we were moved to a flat in Old Scotland Yard, just above the cells. Not quite the same.

With another spate of IRA bombs in London, we were moved yet again, this time to a military barracks – the cheapest and probably the safest place for us. I had been told that the key to our new home would be waiting for us in the guardhouse. When we picked it up, I checked the list to see who our new neighbours would be. It was immediately obvious that we wouldn't be getting an officer's flat; not likely. There were the names: Trooper This, Lance Corporal That, Warrant Officer The Other. I came at the end: Private Mason. There's something to be said for knowing your place – down from Secretary of State for Defence to private in one fell swoop. Fortunately we both saw the funny side of it.

The trouble is that privates tend to get shouted at, as I discovered when I was greeted (if that's the word) by the officer in charge. He was not only arrogant, overbearing and unwelcoming, but chose to deliver a short lecture on terrorism. At first I was tempted to laugh, but he was in deadly earnest; and as he went on my temper began to rise, the more so since I'd forgotten more about the subject than he would ever know. But something held me in check. I guess it was the memory of the soldiers and horses slaughtered by the IRA Hyde Park bomb. He didn't deserve to be glowered at. So for once I tried to behave meekly, just standing there until his outburst finished. It wasn't a happy beginning and in fact in those years we never settled in. We have since moved on to another safe house.

The cost and effort involved in this level of protection is incalculable. Of course the price has to be paid, since no nation can afford to leave its politicians or officials vulnerable to attack by enemies of the State; but it's unsettling nevertheless to try to compute that price in terms of pounds, shillings and pence. I've now been guarded by more than 120 protection officers from Scotland Yard over the years – so many, in fact, that as long ago as 1986 I designed a tie for them, presenting it at a secret ceremony in a London military barracks. Some secret; I handed out no fewer than fifty ties that day. Given the number I've presented since, I sometimes think I should have followed Marks & Spencer's example and given an order for mass production.

Generally, I get on well with my protectors. It isn't difficult. They tend to be diplomatic, well-mannered, friendly and discreet; in fact over the years I've called upon their commander to withdraw only two operatives who couldn't fit in with the Northern way of life or my country pursuits. That said, I don't develop a close social relationship with them or know much about their families or private lives. Partly, that's because they pass like ships in the night and seldom stay long enough for us to become personally involved. But more important is the question of privacy. It's undeniably a strain to be surrounded all the time by strangers, however affable they may be.

It can be especially difficult when we're visiting the homes of friends. The natural reaction of hosts when they see we're accompanied is to invite the protectors in. 'Put them in the lounge,' they'll say. 'We'll make them a cup of tea.' But I always resist. It would be unbearable if every one of my private social gatherings had a police witness; and besides, the officers themselves aren't keen. Understandably so. Whenever I'm on a visit, the local police are always informed. More often than not, a beat bobby or a patrol car is told to keep an eye on the premises; and it wouldn't reflect well on my team's alertness if unmarked official vehicles were spotted with nobody inside.

There can be a similar awkwardness when friends come to visit us. It's something of an ordeal to approach our house past uniformed officers with sub-machine guns. And it's even worse to be stopped and questioned while TV cameras monitor the scene. There's no question of simply ringing our doorbell. A message has to be got to us through our TV phone system, so that we can see and talk to our callers and all this before we've opened the door. To visit the Masons nowadays demands a certain determination.

Fortunately, most people are very mature and understanding of it all. Our neighbours, for example, have never really complained about the heavy police presence in our avenue and I've always been grateful for that. It may be some consolation that they're at less risk than most people of suffering a burglary, but they still have to put up with more than their fair share of inconvenience.

In August 1995, for example, the security squad rang me on the TV telephone. 'Are you expecting a package?' It seemed a routine enquiry. All our mail is electronically screened. 'No,' I said. 'Can't think of anything.'

The officer's voice took on a new urgency. 'We have a parcel in the hut,' he said. 'We're concerned because it has been tampered with and the contents are registering metal.' It was clear that he suspected the worst.

The squad inspector was sent for. He quite properly decided to err on the side of caution and ordered the house evacuated. We had a painter and decorator in at the time and my sister Edna was there too, helping Madge with the cleaning. I told them all that we had a suspect bomb outside and had to leave immediately. The painter was up his ladder, clearly flabbergasted and not knowing what to do. Edna, dusting under the dining-room table, was unenthusiastic about moving. 'I'll just stay here,' she said.

But Madge understood. When you've lived under threat for so long, you don't mess about. 'All out!' she ordered.

Along the avenue, meanwhile, police were evacuating other houses. Most of our neighbours were at work, but one boy was still in bed – at midday – and had to be woken up. In another house a young girl wouldn't answer the door and one of her parents had to be fetched from the workplace to get her out. The bomb disposal squad arrived from Catterick and began examining the package in minute detail. Eventually it was judged safe to open it. Inside was a silver medallion in a metal presentation box. The firm concerned had sent it without any order from me – a bit of misjudgement on its part, made worse by the fact that the outer covering of the parcel had been split, suggesting tampering. Though there was certainly relief all round, my security team was not best pleased. The operation had taken two tense hours. There were some grim threats to charge the company the full cost – some £1,500 – but I don't think they were ever carried out.

On another occasion, we had a scare which could have ended in tragedy. Police spotted a man with a rifle on top of the offices which overlook the back of my house. There was an immediate response. The offices were surrounded, picked marksmen deployed. Had they been less disciplined, the intruder might have been shot there and then. Fortunately, they were much too well-trained to be trigger happy. The 'rifleman' turned out to be a council employee, sent up to the roof with his gun to kill pigeons. Nobody had thought to inform the police or my protection team.

But then, however efficient a security operation may be, it is always prone to human error. Mistakes can so easily happen. One day, when Madge and I were in our seaside cottage we were awakened at 11 p.m. by one of our protectors. Somebody had managed to reach the front door unobserved and leave what looked like a bouquet of flowers. Were we expecting any such delivery? No, we weren't; and in any case it seemed the strangest of times to leave flowers. So once again the bomb squad was sent for. The package was carefully removed and destroyed. In turned out later that one of our neighbours had just bought a new car. The flowers were a gift from the local garage, but had been left at the wrong address. But that innocent explanation was no comfort to the members of my protection team. I could see from their expressions that there would be hell to pay for allowing a suspect package to be left on my doorstep. (I never learned what the consequences were for the unfortunate officer who let it happen.)

Other lapses have their humorous side. Madge and I were playing bowls at Bridlington one day, surrounded by a throng of holidaymakers, when one of my protection officers somehow managed to drop his gun. There it lay on the green, in full view, while bystanders pointed, oohing and aahing. I've never seen a man blush so scarlet – or move so swiftly to snatch his weapon and tuck it out of sight. That was another occasion when it seemed best to beat a hasty retreat. But it could have been worse. While we were at Walton Hall lake near Wakefield, one member of my team dropped his firearm as we were crossing a metal footbridge. It clanged and bounced, sliding towards the edge. We stopped, frozen to the spot. Fortunately it stopped just short of falling into the water.

But in truth there's seldom much to smile at in the constant presence of armed men. I at least have some escape as a working member of the House of Lords. Once inside the Palace of Westminster, I'm free; free to take part in debates, free to write in my office, to use the library, the restaurants and the bars. For a good part of most days during the parliamentary session I can be like any other politician, with ordinary political interests and concerns. It's an essential respite from the threat outside.

For Madge it's different. She accompanies me down to London every week, sharing the journey in my bombproof car and experiencing the occasional alerts when – for reasons we're never told – we suddenly start racing in the fast lane or pull off the motorway to drive along unfamiliar back-roads. These are reminders, every time, of our strange circumstances; but unlike me, she has no ready escape. When I go off to the Lords in the morning, she stays behind in our safe-house, perhaps to do a little shopping or go for a swim. But it can be a lonely existence cut off from family and friends and the everyday pleasures of life. I can't meet her for a casual drink or take her to a cinema on the spur of the moment. We rarely eat out in London, but occasionally enjoy the theatres or museums. But when every step must be planned and prepared in advance, even the most attractive outing loses some of its appeal.

But we have blessings too, far outweighing these disadvantages. The IRA hasn't come close to spoiling our lives. We meet every day for afternoon tea. We'll eat together in the Lords most evenings. Madge is an active member of the Parliamentary Christian Wives' Club, which with the voluntary work on cancer research and the charities she's always supported gives her another outlet. And fortunately she shares my passion for outdoor pursuits (with the exception of fishing). At weekends we'll hike through the countryside, shout ourselves hoarse for Barnsley FC, play a little golf, watch the cricket, meet friends. We regularly meet the former Test umpire Dickie Bird and have lunch with him at a local restaurant in Barnsley. Then we have our family. Our daughters Susan and Jill married and moved away long ago; but we see them as often as we can, with our grandchildren, Steven, Caroline and Andrew. These are the things which matter and make a difference. This is why we won't feel sorry for ourselves.

There's work to be done too, which may come as a surprise to those who think of the House of Lords as a retirement home for superannuated politicians, or perhaps an impossibly grand club where little of use is ever accomplished.

In fact I very nearly missed out on entering Their Lordship's House. I was coming round from an operation at St Thomas's Hospital in London and still groggy from the anaesthetic when I remembered that I hadn't replied to Margaret Thatcher's invitation to join the Lords. Worse still, there were only two days to go before my acceptance had to be in. In something of a rush, I scribbled my reply. One of my protection officers delivered it to Downing Street by hand.

I was still recuperating when the peerage was announced, sitting in my dressing-gown with other patients and watching the news on TV. As my face flashed up on the screen, they began looking at me as though I had just landed a huge win on the pools and would henceforth spend my days in the lap of unimaginable luxury. Peers of the Realm do that kind of thing, don't they?

The reality, unfortunately, is somewhat less exciting. After my introduction – sponsored by my old colleagues, Harold Wilson and Cledwyn Hughes, in a ceremony rather more complicated than the one which attended my entrance to the Commons – I discovered than a new peer comes very low on the pecking order indeed. It was well over a year before I got my own desk and telephone; and when I finally did find a billet, it was with five others in a tiny, overcrowded room. In the event, I didn't stay long. The office overlooked the Lords' car park and my protection team swiftly determined that it wasn't safe for me. So I was moved to another location, much deeper inside the building. I must say it was a considerable improvement. It's one of the very few occasions when being a target has actually worked in my favour.

When I first came into the Lords, I observed to my new colleagues (perhaps rather tactlessly) that compared with life in the Commons it was rather like stepping off a fast-moving escalator and dropping onto a li-lo. But I soon learned that the upper chamber is very much what you make of it. If you work hard, focus your energies and respect the conventions it's surprising what you can accomplish – even in a place so often derided by the brash, bleeper-carrying youngsters in today's Labour Party.

A peerage certainly helps if you're involved in voluntary work. For eleven years now, I've chaired Prince Charles's Youth Business Trust in South Yorkshire, a great if largely unsung royal initiative which aims to take young people off the dole and launch them in their own businesses. So far the Trust has helped 1,750 young men and women to start up on their own in businesses which are now providing employment and pumping millions into the local economy. Besides that, I've been closely associated for the past ten years with a joint venture between British Coal, Barnsley Council and private industry to develop high-tech products and a new technology culture in a town which has suffered more than most from the demise of the old industries. Having a title is a useful advantage in promoting such activity.

It works in other areas too, helping to promote the various charities in which I'm interested. One example: I formed the Lords and Commons Fly Fishing Club years ago and ever since we've obtained commercial sponsors for an annual competition which raises thousands of pounds to support disabled anglers. In fact one of the lesser-known advantages of the House of Lords is that its members can and do help a whole range of good causes in a similar way.

One other advantage of a peerage is that it provides a wonderful platform to promote one's own cherished opinions. I've been a devoted pipe smoker all my adult life and it has always seemed to me that the world would be a happier and more tolerant place if more people adopted the habit instead of resorting to acrid and unhealthy cigarettes. So in pursuit of this desirable end I formed the Lords and Commons Pipe and Cigar Club, a group of like-minded folk who meet for smoking dinners, visits to pipe-makers and the like. It's a bit of fun really, though there can be a sense of purpose too. On National Non Smoking Day we pipemen make a point of assembling in public with the largest and most outrageous briars and meerschaums we can find to puff away in defiance of the politically-correct who would deny us the pleasure, if they could. More often than not, we'll see a photograph of the occasion published in one or more of the newspapers the next day, a welcome sign that the anti-tobacco brigade aren't having eveything their own way. After all, the Labour veteran Manny Shinwell was seldom without a pipe in his hand, and he lived to be a hundred. Most pipemen in the Lords are well over 70. The message is clear: if you want to live to a ripe old age throw away those fags and smoke a pipe.

Of course not all my colleagues agree. We had a crisis in the Lords Reading and Writing Room, one of the most popular retreats in the building where peers who don't have an office of their own tend to do most of their work. One day the very fashionable New Labour peer Tessa Blackstone walked through and immediately began sniffing in disgust. Somebody had been smoking and she didn't like it in the least. In fact she was so appalled that she immediately stalked off to the House of Lords Officers' Committee to lodge a complaint. Smoking was unacceptable, she complained. It had to be banned.

I heard of this display of intolerance shortly afterwards and was determined to put a stop to it. Apart from anything else, the noble Baroness had an office of her own and didn't need to be in the Reading and Writing Room anyway. So I started a petition among my fellow peers urging the committee to leave well enough alone.

Then I discovered that some sneaky tactics were being employed. The Committee Clerk had been ordered to check the ashtrays in the Reading and Writing Room every day, to see if they were being used. The danger was obvious. Clean ashtrays would mean that smokers were in a minority and could therefore be ignored. So I made sure they were used. From that day on, a procession of smokers made their way to the disputed territory with pipes and cigars in hand. Even cigarette smokers were welcome for the purposes of this exercise. Of course the Clerk reported that the ashtrays in the room were in regular use. That was the end of Lady Blackstone's campaign.

But the real point of membership of the Lords, of course, is to be found in the chamber itself. It's the one forum in Britain where genuine, hands-on experience can make itself heard. The quality of debate is usually far higher than anything I knew in the Commons. Party discipline is weaker, for one thing; and for another, the Lords offers a deep pool of expertise, common sense and historical memory. Sometimes it matters.

The Labour government's attempt to reduce the age of homosexual consent to sixteen is a classic example. It wasn't a manifesto commitment. It has only minority support among the electorate. It has no resonance whatever in the Labour tradition or with the great majority of Labour voters. The measure passed through the Commons largely because the new intake of Labour MPs contains too many candyfloss politicians with no roots in the movement and no understanding of anything other than fashionable metropolitan opinion.

Members of the Lords are more independent and promptly threw the measure out. I was one of those who voted against my own party, along with other old stalwarts like Stan Orme, Don Dixon, Joe Dean, Jack Dormand, Jock Stallard, Geoff Lofthouse and a whole platoon of people who cut their political teeth under Attlee, Wilson and Callaghan. We were condemned, of course, as prejudiced, homophobic and all the rest of it; but the truth is, we were reflecting the instincts of our party far more accurately than its present leaders. We'll be defeated in the end, I suppose; that's a fact of parliamentary government. But perhaps our stand may serve as a reminder that Labour in the Lords isn't such a pushover. Not yet, anyway.

And sometimes our memories and instincts can make a difference. Early in 1997, I was approached by Philip Wood, Chairman of the Bevin Boys' Association, who wanted my help in getting official recognition for his members, lads who had been called up during the war to dig coal in the pits. His hope was that after years of being ignored by officialdom, they would at last be allowed to join in the annual Remembrance Day march past the Cenotaph.

To some, especially those born in more recent and happier times, it may seem a relatively minor issue, hardly worth a political campaign. But to those who were there, it's very different. The 'Boys' – of course they're all old men now – served their country as surely as anybody in the armed forces. They were conscripts, called up just as the overwhelming majority of our soldiers, sailors and airmen were called up. They had no choice in the matter. There was no court of appeal. They were sent down the pits because the country needed coal as desperately as it needed men to man the guns; and it was anything but a soft option. No fewer than 5,400 miners died in underground accidents. Thousands more were injured. I worked with them and knew the conditions they endured. Why should they be made to stand on the sidelines on Remembrance Day, as though their contribution was of no account? Why shouldn't they publicly honour their own dead and pay tribute to their old comrades?

After all, Winston Churchill had no doubt about their value. In a speech in October 1942 which was kept secret at the time, he told 3,000 representatives from the coal industry that they could be proud of the contribution they were making to the war effort. When the fighting was over, he declared:

> ... one will say 'I was a fighter pilot'; another will say 'I was in the submarine service'; another: 'I marched with the Eighth Army'; a fourth

will say: 'None of you could have lived without the convoys and the merchant seamen'; and you, in your turn, will say with equal pride and with equal right: 'We cut the coal'.

I wasn't alone in my dismay at the shabby way these men were now being treated. Admiral of the Fleet Lord Lewin was equally determined that something had to be done and between us we began to set the wheels in motion. I wrote first to George Robertson at the Ministry of Defence, who in turn passed me on to Home Secretary Jack Straw. Terry Lewin was busy too with his own contacts. At first it didn't do a scrap of good. We were met with a wall of bureaucratic resistance. Far from wielding a new broom, Labour ministers seemed to me to be swallowing the line fed to them by their officials. In October 1997 I was becoming so frustrated at the lack of movement that I wrote again to Jack Straw accusing his department of repeating 'false arguments' against the need for change and suggesting that he was being misled by the civil servants.

In fact I was being unfair to Jack. He replied at once saying that he had a good deal of sympathy for the views of Terry Lewin and myself, and intended to raise the issue with the Royal British Legion. Meantime, I arranged for the Bevin Boys to march in Barnsley with banners flying on Remembrance Day. From then on, all the old objections seemed to evaporate. A few months later Jack Straw wrote again, confirming that the way was now clear. On Remembrance Day 1998, more than half a century after Victory in Europe, the Bevin Boys received their recognition at last. Anyone who watched their faces as they marched as proudly as guardsmen past the Cenotaph, and along Whitehall will know that the fight was worthwhile.

The world has changed beyond recognition since first I went down the pit. The poverty of those days has been largely forgotten, except in the pages of history textbooks. The great campaigns have long ago been fought and won. Only a few of us remember how hard it once was and now uncertain the outcome of the battle. But for a few years yet, the parade of the Bevin Boys will show that there is still a legacy worth honouring and stories still worth the telling.

Enoch Powell once said that all political lives end in failure, but I think he was too much the pessimist. Whatever personal mistakes and disappointments any of us may acknowledge, we live today in a world that is indisputably safer and better in material terms than anything we knew when we were young. Pundits sometimes talk of technological advance or economic growth as though all human progress is produced by vast, impersonal forces. But if young men no longer expect to be conscripted for war, if the sick are offered the very best medical treatment as a matter of course, if bright teenagers now go off to university no matter now poor their family circumstances, it's not just a matter of historical inevitability. These things came about because people argued for them and fought for them. There should be some pride in that, not just for us politicians, but for the party members, trades unionists and ordinary voters who kept us up to the mark.

Some things of course I regret. I tried to give a new lease of life to the British shipbuilding industry, only to see it go to the wall in later years. As Minister of Power I defended the coal industry, only to see it all but destroyed by Margaret Thatcher and Arthur Scargill. I hoped to bring jobs and hope to West Belfast, only to see the DeLorean Company go bust. In each case, the collapse came long after I'd left the scene and was beyond my control; but when you've been the Minister in charge, it's hard to avoid feelings of anger and frustration when your legacy is thrown away.

Nevertheless, most of my life in politics has had a far happier outcome. It is tremendously satisfying to know that I've managed to make a difference in so many diverse areas, from helping to get rid of the muckstacks to promoting safer lifejackets for the Merchant Navy, from winning the fight for the maritime Harrier to getting a new hospital for Barnsley. In more general terms, the left-wing malignancy which came so close to destroying Labour has been cut out and Tony Blair leads a party which is not only in power but seemingly unbeatable. I think that those of us who spent a lifetime fighting our often unfashionable corner played some part in that transformation – even if it hasn't turned out quite as we expected. Meanwhile Communism has been swept away, and – almost – the threat of nuclear annihilation with it. Those of us who defended NATO and the deterrent when both were under such ferocious attack have every reason to feel vindicated.

Of course politics sometimes demands a price. I write these words with armed guards patrolling outside my front door, as they have patrolled every day for more than twenty-three years. As they will tomorrow. It's undeniably a strain, but bearable. I've been blessed with fifty-four years of marriage, a marvellous wife and a close, loving family. I've loved my life in politics. I know now lucky I am. No level of threat can change that.

On some future date, perhaps, the development of the peace process in Northern Ireland will make itself felt in my avenue and we'll again be able to live as normal human beings: no guards, no cameras or electronic sensors, no armoured vehicles or safe-houses. We'll be free, though we seldom talk of the possibility or allow ourselves to look forward to it. We'll go on together, whatever the disappointments, knowing that we did our best, knowing that we stayed true to our beliefs. That's something to hold on to, in marriage as in politics. It's enough.

I rose from pit boy to Minister of Power, from air cadet to Secretary of State for Defence, from a night school student to President of the Board of Trade. And I've managed to survive being thrust into a maelstrom of politics, religion and terrorism. I can't complain.

Index